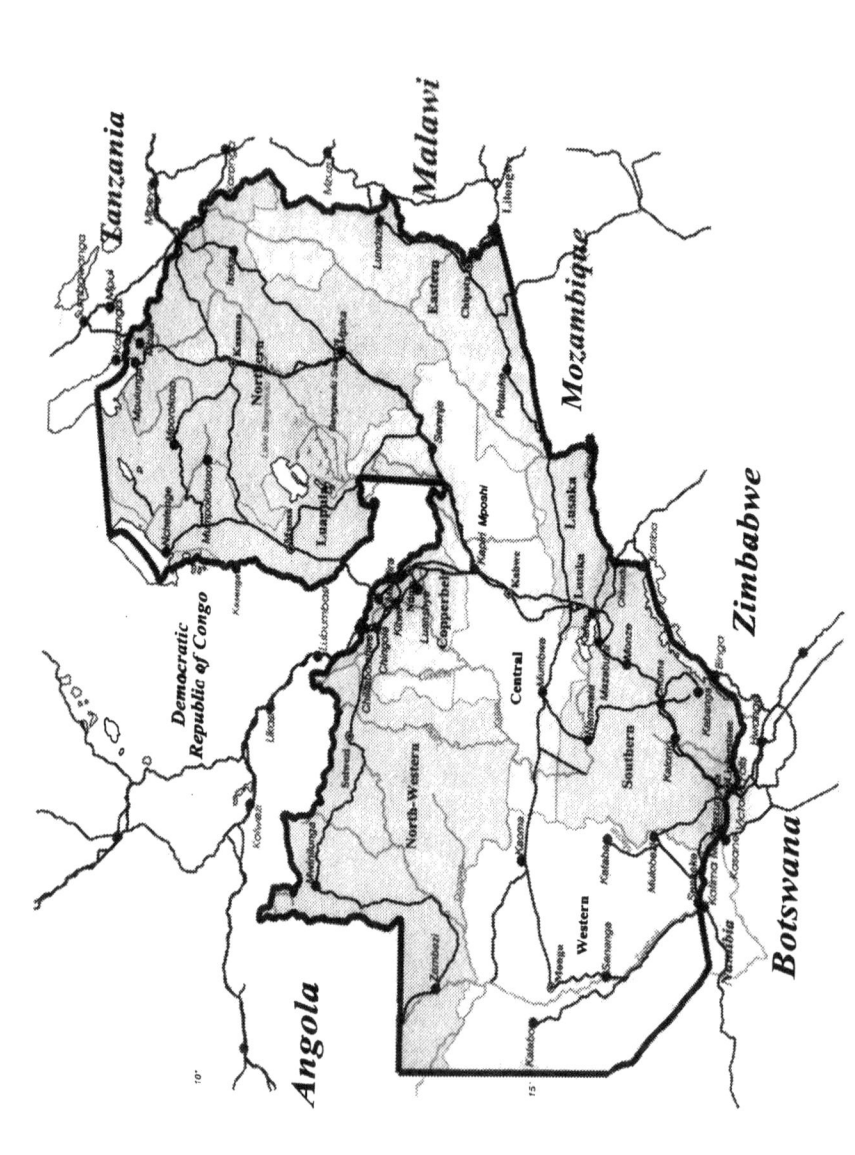

INTO EXILE AND BACK

SIMON ZUKAS

Published by Bookworld Publishers
PO Box 32581, Lusaka, Zambia.
2002

Copyright © Simon Zukas 2002

All rights reserved. No part of this publication may be reproduced, stored in a retrieval system, or transmitted, in any form or by any means electronic, mechanical, photocopying, recording or otherwise, without the prior permission of the publisher.

ISBN 9982-24-020-X

The author and publishers wish to thank The Wylie Agency for permission to publish an extract from Ariel Dorfman, *Heading South, Looking North* © Ariel Dorfman 1998

Typesetting by Fergan Limited, Lusaka, Zambia.

Printed by Printech Ltd, Lusaka, Zambia.

To our sons:

David and Alan

Cover photograph : Arrival in Ndola 1964 - Airport welcome

Errata
Page 2, line 1; 'thirty one' should read 'forty one'
Page 63, line 32; 1952 should read 1962
Page 137, line 12; 'ZAPU' should read 'ZANU'
Page 170, line 16 'level' should read 'lever'
Page 204, line 24 'that' should read 'than'

TABLE OF CONTENTS

Acknowledgements	vii
Chapter One: A Lithuanian Childhood; A Rhodesian Adolescence	1
Chapter Two: With British Empire Forces in East Africa	20
Chapter Three: Studying Engineering and Politics	32
Chapter Four: White Proposals for Central Africa	47
Chapter Five: Stiffening the Opposition to a White Federation	59
Chapter Six: Into Exile	81
Chapter Seven: A Life in Exile Cynthia's Postscript	93 107
Chapter Eight: The Rise and Fall of the Central African Federation	109
Chapter Nine: Going Home	119
Chapter Ten: One Zambia One Nation Sketch Map An Attempt to Force a Change of Course Cynthia's Postscript	128 133 149 155

Chapter Eleven:
   Working Part Time with State Institutions   157
      UNZA   157
      INDECO   164
      ZNBS   168
      NCSR   169
      EBZ   172
      Kariba North Bank   172
      Other Interests   174

Chapter Twelve:
   'The Hour' Came   176

Chapter Thirteen:
   Into Agriculture Food and Fisheries   190

Chapter Fourteen:
   Resignation   198

Chapter Fifteen:
   Epilogue   203
      Cynthia's Epilogue   206

Select Bibliography   207
Index   209

ACKNOWLEDGEMENTS

I want to record my thanks to Ray and the late Dr Jack Simons who urged me over the years to write my memoirs; to Ruth and the late Professor Yap van Velsen, who read an early draft and guided me into better directions; to Peter Fraenkel, who read a recent, uncompleted draft and offered many helpful comments and suggestions.

My special thanks go to Cynthia, my wife, for bearing with me while I was composing on my computer and neglecting her, for her encouragement to complete this memoir and for her critical comments from time to time.

22nd July 2002

CHAPTER ONE

A LITHUANIAN CHILDHOOD;

A RHODESIAN ADOLESCENCE

Have you ever watched poles being hammered into the ground to act as foundations for a structure such as a building or a bridge? The rhythmic thump of the heavy weight as it drops and repeatedly hammers the 'pile' into the ground somehow takes you over. You cannot move away until the piling hammer has done its job and its mast-frame or crane moves on to a new position. I have a memory of being mesmerised by such piling during my childhood in Ukmerge, Lithuania.

At the age of about eight or nine, during the summer months when we went swimming in the Sventoji river, I often went past a building site near the wooden bridge. My father and I would stop to watch men placing narrow steel cages in long coffins and later pouring concrete into them. These concrete posts, we were told, would be the piles for foundations to the new concrete bridge, which would replace the wooden one. In the following winter, when temperatures had dropped below zero, I watched the pre-cast concrete piles, looking like mammoth pencils, each being lifted off the ground by a crane and erected upright, with the pointed end resting on a mark in the ground on the line of the new bridge. A heavy weight, sliding down a mast and dropping on the top end of the pencil, would sink the pile deeper into the river-bed with every blow. I watched this from the wooden bridge while I could feel my toes aching from the cold inside my twenty-millimetre-thick felt, knee-high boots. I would only go home when I could no longer stand the pain in my toes, so fascinated was I by the construction process. I would keep coming back in the summer, to see the concrete piers and the bridge beams being constructed.

Then, on a brilliant summer day, in June 1997, a month before my 72nd birthday, I found myself at the same bridge site. It struck me, as I looked at the bridge from the river shore, that it might have been this childhood fascination with the bridge that led me to a career in civil engineering, with half a century in designing and constructing structures in Britain and Central

Africa. My thirty-one year old son, David, was with me at the bridge site. We were both there as tourists, he for the first time in Lithuania, I visiting a country that, fifty nine years earlier, I thought I has left never to return.

David and I had flown from London to Vilnius, the capital, and drove in a hired car to Ukmerge and from there to Jonava, where my mother's sister, her husband and her three children were killed by the Nazis during World War II. We continued to the old capital, Kaunas, where my mother's cousin and her family were also all killed in the Holocaust, except for her son, Shimson Schwartz, who survived a death camp and now lives in Israel as Shimson Sharir. We also drove to Klaipeda (Memel), Lithuania's only port, before returning to Vilnius. While in the former our interest was merely of a tourist nature, in the latter we planned to visit the killing fields, where Jews were killed by the occupying Germans, often assisted by Lithuanians. We also intended to visit the old Jewish cemetery, where my maternal grandfather was buried during the 1914-1918 War. He died of cancer, while the family was exiled there from Ukmerge. We also planned to see the Jewish Museum in Vilnius.

Ukmerge lies some sixty kilometres from Vilnius on the main highway which links Lithuania with its two northern traditional associates of Latvia and Estonia on the eastern side of the Baltic Sea. If Soviet occupation of over four decades has not resulted in much visible development, at least it has made an impact on the major roads. Even if the Soviet purpose was only strategic it provided a tarmacadam dual carriageway from Vilnius to Ukmerge which was still well maintained. As we were approaching Ukmerge I started looking out for two landmarks which had stuck in my memory. These were the pine forest of Pivonia, where, as a child, I had spent many happy summer holidays, and the Jewish cemetery which we used to pass on our way to Pivonia, with its incessant melancholy cawing of hundreds of resident crows. I had many fond memories of holidays spent in Pivonia. We used to go gathering wild strawberries on the pine forest floor, looking for birds' nests, and making walking sticks and whistles from pine saplings.

We could not find the cemetery and presumed that the road alignment now differed. But when we spotted a sign to a ceramic factory, which I recalled used to make wall tiles, we realised that during the Nazi occupation the cemetery had suffered the same fate as many other Jewish cemeteries in

Lithuania and Poland – destruction. (The next day we looked for a cemetery in Kaunas where my elder brother, Samuel, who died from pleurisy, was buried in 1934. All we found was a monument in an open meadow with the inscription that this once was a Jewish cemetery.)

We moved on to the Ukmerge town centre and I recognised the monument, an obelisk with a sculpture of a maiden in an alcove at its base which commemorated, according to my childhood memory, the event which gave the town its name: a wolf carrying off a maiden. From there David and I started to look for 'the house'. I had no recollection of street names and building facades did not trigger anything in my memory. Several times we turned off the main street into lanes where I thought the house had stood, only to find nothing familiar. We gave up and decided to explore the town. At the end of the main shopping street, the pavement of which I had remembered as being as wide as the Champs Elysées in Paris, and which now turned out to be pretty modest in width, I recognised the cathedral. (Shopping street was a misnomer: gone were the large shop windows with their displays. Shopkeeping as an economic activity had not survived the destruction of the Jewish community and the Soviet occupation). David now asked me for the sketch I had made from memory of the central part of town before we started out on our trip. We decided to follow from it a route that would take us to what used to be my parents' shop. On the sketch I had indicated a lane opposite the shop, which we used to use as a short-cut between house and shop. With no shops remaining, it was difficult to locate the lane, but we did, and ambled along it.

The lane did look familiar, at least in topography: it ran along the contour on the side of an incline, with the ground on our right sloping up to the monument and the ground on our left falling to a small tributary stream of the main river. 'Didn't Jacob, my brother, skate down the hill from our house and fall at the tributary when he could not stop himself? Was the resulting swelling near his ear not brought down by applying leeches to suck out the blood?' It all came back to me. When I next looked up to the right 'the house' was unmistakably there! (See Plate 1)

The double storey house still stood, although it was boarded up and in a dilapidated state, with glazing left in the upstairs windows only. It had been built by my maternal great-grandparents. I was born in it in 1925 and spent my childhood in it. The roof shingles had been partly covered over with asbestos sheeting, but the part of the roof which my maternal grandfather had arranged to be tiltable, so that one upstairs room could be converted annually to a *succo* for use during the Jewish festival of Succoth, was clearly visible. In this festival religious Jews take their meals under greenery. Although I remember my father using this facility only once or twice, I was told that my grandfather used it annually.

As David and I were peering through spaces between the boards that were nailed across the doors and windows, a couple from the house opposite approached us and wondered whether we wanted to buy the property. The query took me some time to understand as I can no longer speak Lithuanian and we had to communicate in broken German. When I explained that our interest was nostalgic, Mr Grinevicius offered to open up the house. He brought a crowbar and claw hammer and set to work. We were soon able to look inside: the ground floor had collapsed over the cellar, and the first floor, which we were able to enter from a side entrance up the hill appeared unsafe to walk on. Clearly, the building had been unoccupied for many years and I asked Mr Grinevicius, 'Why?'

Mr Grinevicius looked at me gravely and wanted to know whether my parents had stayed on in the house after I left in 1938 and, if not, whether it was left to relatives. I said that it was sold on our departure. Only then did he answer my question: 'The family that occupied this house and the house adjoining it were taken during the Nazi occupation to the forest in Pivonia and shot'. He must have noticed my mouth drop and expressed his sorrow. His remarks brought no surprise to David and me as it is well-known that all but five thousand of Lithuania's 220,000 Jews perished during the Nazi occupation. His answer brought home to me vividly how the same fate would have befallen the Zukas family had we not emigrated in 1938. Yet the reason behind my parents' emigration was *economic* rather than seeing the writing on the wall!

In emigrating, my parents were following an established process, common not only to Lithuanian Jews but also to Lithuanian Christians. When the economic going got too tough, anyone worth his salt would try his luck overseas, especially in the USA. In the case of Jews, South Africa was also a favoured destination. Thus, on my mother's side, three of her brothers and three sisters had already settled in South Africa at the turn of the century and had even had my maternal grandfather visit them there in 1902. Oddly enough, while his surname was Davidowitz, the emigrant children all went under the surname of Stern, because they had been sent immigration papers by a relative whose surname was Stern, who presumably pretended that he was bringing them over as *his* children. (My great grandfather on my mother's side was a Galvanski and he dealt in tarred ropes).

On my father's side, there is a similar history of migration of siblings and discrepancy in surnames. Before the First World War one of his sisters migrated to the Ukraine, then part of Russia, (I still have cousins there) and one to the USA; one brother went to the USA and one to South Africa. All siblings of my father went under the name of Segel (Seg*a*l, in South Africa). The explanation of the discrepancy in surnames between my father and his siblings, however, is quite different from that pertaining to that of my mother's family. My father was once a Segel, as were my paternal grandparents. Grandmother Miriam Segel, who lived with my parents until our departure from Lithuania, virtually brought-up my brothers and myself while mother was working in the shop or staying in Kaunas, where my elder brother was for a lengthy period in hospital. Why then did my father change his surname to Zukas?

Firstly, he did not change to Zukas but to Zuk, the suffix '*as*' being added in the Lithuanian language in the case of males. Secondly, the change of name became a necessity when, a short while after being conscripted into the army of the Russian Czarist regime, which he despised both on political grounds and for its anti-Semitism, he deserted. He then had to find a new name and somehow managed to obtain an identity card with the name of Zuk. As a result of this, I was destined to forfeit seven places and be last in every normal alphabetical queue. After Lithuania got its independence in 1918, my father's surname automatically became Zukas.

My maternal grandfather was part of the Ukmerge Jewish parish hierarchy, its treasurer. My mother was very orthodox: my father less so, but he was still quite religious. His birthplace was Vevios (Kurshik). In worldliness there was a similar distinction: my mother was intolerant of women smoking or playing cards and very judgemental: my father was a man of the world. Both followed a strict ethical code in their personal lives. When I reached the age of twelve and my father was already in Africa, my mother arranged for me to be tutored for my *bar-mitzvah*, the Jewish coming-of-age ceremony. Yet, for some reason, I had never been sent for religious studies to *cheyder*. Before my *bar-mitzvah* studies were completed I had turned freethinker and decided not to continue. This caused my mother much distress, but with my father away in South Africa, I managed to stand by my decision.

I became a freethinker after I had joined the Zionist-Socialist youth movement, Hachalutz-Hazoir-Dror. Before that, I had a short spell in Beitar, the right-wing Zionist movement, more appropriate to my middle-class background. In Beitar it was drilled into me that our programme was to achieve a Jewish state on both sides of the River Jordan. A relative of my father, who came to stay with us on Father's departure to Africa, influenced me to change parties. He came from a poor family and was already in his late twenties. In the Zionist youth movement, in addition to Boy Scout activities, we were taught that in Palestine, where we would one day migrate to help establish a Jewish national home, the ideal life would be in socialist kibbutzim tilling the land. We would not be a nation of shopkeepers and traders, occupations forced on Jews by their history in Europe. We were also taught about capitalist and imperialist exploitation: that in Africa whites were rich and Africans were toiling without shoes or shirts to their backs. We followed very closely the fortunes of the Republican forces in the Spanish Civil War and Stalin's show trials in Moscow. In the latter we were questioning the confessions of Bukharin and his colleagues and disbelieved the Stalinist propaganda that Trotsky was in league with the Fascists. This sowed in me a strong anti-Stalinist seed, but left me still with faith in Marxism.

My parents could afford a resident house-help. She was a Polish woman of peasant stock and I grew up able to speak more Polish than Lithuanian. My mother tongue was, of course, Yiddish. Maritke shocked me one Easter Sunday when she told me that this was a time when Christian children were in danger of being snatched and killed by Jewish rabbis who used their blood for Passover rituals. I disputed this, but she replied that I would not know about it because it was a secret rite. She had only learnt of it that morning, from the Catholic Priest at church. Maritke had helped my parents and grandmother to bring me up and I reflected that if she could believe such nonsense, then one should not be surprised that there was a good deal of anti-Semitism about in

Lithuania and Poland, where the Roman Catholic Church was very strong and very anti-Semitic. On consulting my parents, I became aware that what Maritke referred to was known in Yiddish as a *Bilbul* and was frequently used in Eastern Europe to instigate pogroms, killings of Jews by Christians. (The accusation became common in Central Europe as early as the Black Death (Plague) of the fourteenth century, when a scapegoat was sought to explain the mass deaths, but there is a record of it from the twelfth century in Norwich, England.)

At our Jewish school we were taught in Yiddish, with Lithuanian as a second language and the state inspector of schools would come once a year to examine each class. The most important subject appeared to be the question of Vilnius, the city Lithuania claimed to be its rightful capital, but which had become part of Poland following Polish occupation of the city soon after Lithuania and Poland obtained their independence from Russia in 1918. Since then Lithuania refused to have diplomatic relations with its southern neighbour. The question that the inspector would pose and the class would be well-drilled for was 'What do we want to do about Vilnius?' There were several possible answers, all involving the word take, but only one would be deemed the correct one: *atimtu* - to take back, not *paimtu* - to take away.

In 1935, my elder brother, Samuel, died at the age of eleven, after many months in a hospital in Kaunas suffering from pleurisy. My mother never recovered from this loss and nor did my parents' fortunes from the heavy expenses involved. They were small shopkeepers, trading in household goods like crockery, hardware and paints. With the world economic crisis not abating, a decision was made by my parents to follow in the footsteps of other siblings and to migrate to South Africa. Since immigration papers could not be obtained because of the quota system then in force for the immigration of Jews, my father took advantage of the 1936 International Exhibition in Johannesburg, travelling on a tourist visa, but with every intention of staying on. After staying for six months he applied and got an extension for a further six months, but then had to leave. Instead of returning to Lithuania, however, he was advised by leaders of the South African Jewish community to go to Northern Rhodesia, a British colony to the north where white immigrants seemed to be welcome if they had sufficient English. He qualified, having taken lessons privately while in South Africa, and was allowed to enter and stay in Northern Rhodesia.

With an area of 850,000 square kilometres, an African population of less than one and a half million and a white population of only a few thousands, Northern Rhodesia was, in 1937, still welcoming white settlers and people from the British Empire in India. An increase in the non-indigenous population was seen as essential to the development of the country. Attraction of settlers had been an uphill battle. The British South Africa Company, which ruled the territory until 1923, before handing over to the British Colonial Office, had offered vast tracts of land to would-be settlers for nominal sums, as this extract from an article by R. Murray-Hughes, in the *Northern Rhodesian Journal* of 1958 and 1960, shows.

> Mr Savage, as the Company's representative, told Duke [a would-be settler] that he could have 6,000 acres wherever he liked…. for 8d. [eight pence] an acre under the title of "Permit of Occupation" but that there was no need to pay the 8d. down. He told us that the Company would also pay a subsidy of £1 an acre for each and every acre that was turned over and planted; and, finally it would give all his dependents [sic] a 0.303 rifle and fifty rounds of ammunition…...

All this was offered in order to attract Duke to Northern Rhodesia to grow oranges and although the orange orchard failed, for lack of adequate water resources, the result was the development of Demo Estates near Choma for cattle ranching.

Having settled in Northern Rhodesia and having managed to establish himself as a mobile trader between Livingstone and the Copperbelt, my father thought it time for us to follow. So in May 1938 we sold up and arranged for Grandmother (Mire) to go into the Jewish old age home, much to my grief. We, my mother, myself and my two younger brothers, Jacob and Abraham, travelled to Kaunas and from there by sealed train, under travel-agents Thomas Cooke's guidance to Berlin.

At Berlin station, while waiting to change trains, I started strolling around only to be told by our Thomas Cooke guide that it was dangerous to break away from the group, as Jews were unsafe in Nazi Germany. We travelled to Antwerp and after a night there in some hostel we boarded a boat for Dover. During the crossing of the Channel I was dismayed to discover that my lessons in English before leaving Lithuania helped me to understand the language only when spoken by old people!

When we reached London we were taken to a hostel in the East End run by Shelter and stayed there for several days before travelling to Southampton to board the Balmoral Castle for Cape Town. While we were in London Louis Matz, my South African cousin who was studying at Jews College, took Jacob and me shopping to equip us for our new life. The grey flannel shorts that we changed into were later laughed at in South Africa and Rhodesia as being too long and I learnt that there were differences in white fashion between Britain and her colonies! When we arrived in Cape Town our aunt, Alice Miller, insisted on adding ties to our necks! At Cape Town I saw black and brown people, almost for the first time. I had seen only one black man before, an American negro on a visit to Lithuania, and that was such a novelty that we kids ran after him in the street. In Johannesburg we were met by several aunts and uncles at the railway station and stayed for a month in order to attend my cousin Minnie Fram's wedding.

One uncle, Morris, came up from Colesberg, Northern Cape, to attend the wedding and also to receive the library of religious tomes that we had crated and brought with us, the tomes that had stood in a glass-fronted bookcase in our lounge and that I often used to leaf through without comprehension. My father's brother, Joshua Segal [sic], also lived in Johannesburg. He operated a pavement fruit stall in the city centre. He was a member of the Jewish Workers' Club in Johannesburg and, I was pleased to learn, had *left-wing views*. Seeing his humble mode of earning a living, I understood why he did not contribute to the upkeep of my grandmother which my mother had frequently complained of. After the wedding, we travelled on by train to the north, stopping for a few hours in Bulawayo, where we were met by a Mr and Mrs Max Baron, with whom my father had stayed for a while on his way to Northern Rhodesia. We travelled on to Livingstone for immigration formalities and then another eight hundred kilometres to Ndola, where Father was waiting for us on the station platform. After an emotional reunion and happy tears all round, he drove us in his old Ford truck to our new abode, a rented house a few kilometres north of the town centre. The date was 26 July 1938, five days to my 13th birthday.

Ndola, I discovered, prided itself on being the 'gateway to the Copperbelt' and one could get a paper sticker advertising this to stick on envelopes next to the Northern Rhodesia stamp. The shopping centre consisted of one long street, which started at the railway station and led, after several kilometres, to a second shopping area, the second class trading area, where shops were owned by Asian traders and where Africans did their shopping.

While I recall the journey from Johannesburg to Ndola as lasting many days and nights, and while I recall the excitement of seeing the Victoria Falls, I have no memory of passing through Lusaka, the capital. It could not have been of any special significance then, certainly not as seen from its railway station. In any case, it had been the capital only since 1936. Before then the capital was Livingstone.

It was just over two years since Father had left us in Lithuania. After arriving in Livingstone on 10 July 1937 he stayed for a short while with a 'landsman', Mr Furmanovski, who advised my father to invest some of his money in a second-hand truck and some 'piece goods', obtain a hawker's licence and become a mobile trader along the road between Livingstone and Ndola. It seemed good advice for someone whose only skill was as a trader, but the venture, my father soon discovered, was not without its hazards. It all seemed to go well on the first trip and my father visited many outlying farm homesteads and sold dress lengths of cloth to the white farmers' wives.

On his second round, some months later, after arriving with new material which he had carefully chosen in Livingstone of different design from the first lot, and expecting his customers' approval, he found to his surprise that some of the wives near Choma were very antagonistic. Having worked hard to sew her new dress for the next big local event, more than one farmer's wife found herself matched by neighbours with the identical material! 'How could you have sold the same dress material to my neighbours?' one woman demanded. From then on he would hide away a roll after selling a dress length from it, until he was in another district.

My brother Jacob and I were enrolled in the all-white government school and soon made friends and joined separate gangs. Many of the other children were of Afrikaner families who had come up with the Rhodesia Railways and they would tell me how their grandparents had suffered in British concentration camps during the Boer War. We would together walk several kilometres to school and thought nothing of it. My only contact with Africans, at that stage, was with our African house servant and I was made responsible by my parents for writing passes to enable him to go, after our evening meal, to the municipal compound. He needed the pass to avoid being arrested for loitering after 21:00 hours, when the night curfew for Africans would start. (I do not recall reflecting at the time on this odd state of affairs, where a grown up African man could not walk home through the town during the night without permission from a European. I think I accepted this as normality.)

Our teachers, who were all from England, made no attempt to discuss with us our relations with Africans. We were, of course, an all-white school! There were no mixed schools. Our Scout group was also all-white. Later I would learn that Africans who were in a similar movement, were not Scouts but 'Pathfinders'! Yet, there was some feeling amongst my white schoolboy friends that the Government was one-sided: in favour of Africans. This was bitterly resented.

When an opportunity occurred to take over a shop in town from Mr Moss Dobkins, who was moving on to greener pastures in the mining town of Chingola, my parents decided to take it in order to put an end to my father's trips southwards. But he would still continue hawking, if only on the Copperbelt. There were living quarters at the back of the new shop for African trade at the eastern end of Cecil Avenue, Ndola's main street, and so we moved there. There was a convenient door between shop and house and my brother and I would be called to assist in 'watching' if the number of customers became more than my parents could keep under scrutiny. My father soon had built a new vehicle for his hawking: it consisted of a 3-ton chassis on which he had constructed an elaborate box so that it looked not unlike a remover's van. Not only did it have doors at the rear, however, but also on one side. These were like flaps, hinged at the bottom and when opened they became counters and revealed shelves stacked with shirts, blankets, etc. The travelling shop could be operative within minutes of parking.

From the shop in Ndola my parents graduated to a shop in the second class trading area of Luanshya, a township next to the Roan Antelope Copper Mine. My father's business as a hawker eventually ended when the shop in Luanshya proved capable of providing a living, but not before he had faced several summonses and fines for trading 'within less than one mile from a shop'. He always tried to respect this law but, at the same time, to be close enough to the mine or township to attract customers. On one occasion he was really convinced that the police were in the wrong and acting on the side of the shopkeepers. He had carefully measured a mile from a shop in Kitwe on his speedometer and allowed a further two tenths of a mile for safety before stopping and opening the sides of his van for business. Before long the police arrived and he was charged with contravening the mile rule. To his utter consternation, the police explained that he was less than a mile away from the nearest shop.

When the day to appear in court arrived he asked me to come to Kitwe/Nkana to check whether, in fact, the police were not wrong. I equipped myself with the front fork of a bicycle and attached a cyclometer on the wheel. My father was due to appear in court at 10 a.m. on a Monday morning and since it should not take us more than an hour to pace the mile and return, we planned and duly arrived at the scene of the crime at 8 a.m.

The licensed shop was not visible from our location but we guessed its direction by allowing for the curve in the road. We set out through thick bush. After thirty minutes we saw no sign of the shop, so we changed direction slightly. By 9 a.m. we realised we were lost. My father and I then became anxious lest he be late for his court appearance so we decided to turn back, but which way was back? When at 9.30 we had not reached the car I managed to climb a tree and got a glimpse of the road. It was well after 10 when we reached the car and my father got to court at about 11 a.m., an hour late. He was duly fined £10 and reprimanded for appearing late in court. It was too much for him to try to explain the reason why.

Luanshya was a more lively place than Ndola. It had an Olympic-size swimming pool, a mine club, well-maintained roads and parks and an integrated European community. But our living quarters were smaller and less roomy than those we had in Ndola. Once again, we were to live at the back of the shop, but this time in only three rooms, all in a line with no passage, only inter-connecting doors. One room was given to Jake and me, the next was occupied by my parents and my youngest brother, Abe, and the third was the dining room with access to the shop. Each room was three metres square. The kitchen, the shower and lavatory were outside, near the sanitary lane at the end of the small yard.

We were in the second class trading area and on each side of us we had Gujarati Indian neighbours, who lived similarly behind their shops. The shops would open at seven in the morning. Around six-thirty there would be a stream of men in pyjamas dashing across the yards from the rooms behind the shops to the toilets at the sanitary lane. There were low wire fences to separate the plots. I knew the precise morning ablution routines of Mr Vashee on the one side and Mr Desai on the other. (After independence Desai became a UNIP member of Parliament until his death in 1965) One of them would always clear his throat on the way to the lavatory and the other would brush his teeth on his way. I think the women managed to wait until the men had opened the shops.

Our furniture consisted of basic essentials: small wardrobes made from packing cases, iron bedsteads with suspended mosquito nets, a dining table with six chairs, but no easy chairs; there was nothing more, except a chiming pendulum wall clock which we had brought from Lithuania. I never brought friends home for a meal. In this house and with this furniture the family lived until 1947, when my parents had a house built in the first-class residential and shopping area.

My brothers and I spent much time in friends' houses, white miners' houses. These were simple bungalows, built of burnt brick with corrugated iron roofs, usually painted red. My days at school in Luanshya were very happy. I had now mustered sufficient proficiency in English to find little difficulty in being top of my class in most subjects. History consisted of 'Britain and her Neighbours'. Evidently, it was thought that this needed balancing with some African history, so we also read from a South African history book, which informed us of the Great Trek and of brave Volte Maade, who swam out repeatedly on his horse to save people from a shipwreck in Table Bay, until he and his horse were overcome by fatigue and drowned. No doubt, we were supposed to model ourselves on this brave Afrikaner.

We were taught no history of Northern Rhodesia, not even in the form of an extension to British Imperial history. Neither were we taught any geography of Northern Rhodesia. Clearly, we were being prepared for high schools in Britain or the Union of South Africa. No African language was taught at government white schools. Not until after the country gained its independence were white children who attended government schools, which were then multi-racial, taught African languages.

Our English and Latin teacher, Mrs Kynoch, came from a liberal Cape

Dutch family, had travelled in Europe and was married to an official on the mine. She was a strict disciplinarian and a very inspiring teacher. She must have been in her early fifties, teetotal, slim and with a back that could challenge any British guardsman for straightness. She would constantly admonish us to sit up straight and walk straight and tirelessly try to shape not only our spines, but also our characters. 'Are you treating your African servants like grown-up human beings, or like boys?' She would ask. She 'could murder' those drivers who had no sympathy for African pedestrians. 'There is so much human ugliness on the mine', she would complain. She made me feel less guilty about my own non-racial attitudes with which I had come from Europe. She also made me feel that socialism was not really a dirty word. I think she had just joined the Friends of the Soviet Union, a branch of which had been established in Luanshya by Bob Robertson and others, and she occasionally lectured our class on socialism. "Stand up anyone who believes in socialism", she urged one day. I jumped up and she made me explain what I meant by socialism. The rest of the class was not very taken with this preaching of socialism, even if Russia was on our side. After all, 'it would mean sharing everything with the blacks'.

Until Mrs Kynoch's challenge I had learnt to hide my socialist ideas and adopt the views of my white schoolmates. Many years later I was to reflect on this early transformation, when I saw new arrivals from Britain try so hard to fit in so as to be accepted by their fellow whites that they became, in the process, apparently even more prejudiced on race than the older settlers. The immigrant, generally, tries to adapt as quickly as possible to the established order and become accepted by those he seeks as his friends. Since the society was already segregated on racial lines, the white immigrant did not get much chance of really getting to know Africans before he was bombarded with the established prejudices of his fellow whites. You soon learnt that certain tasks, like carrying a shopping basket, were not the done thing for a European male. Above all, you should not shake hands with an African.

Another teacher, the wife of a mining engineer, taught us science. Mrs Sinclair was a Cambridge-trained botanist, and she was bored stiff with her life in Luanshya. She took an interest in me, encouraged my interest in science and, when she heard that at the end of my form II, I had resigned myself to looking for a job in the mine survey department, she set about dissuading me from such a course. 'Think of Disraeli and of Barney Barnato, of Beit.... You have more to offer the world than to serve this mine'. 'But', I replied, 'Mrs Sinclair, my parents are just not in a financial position to send me to Southern Rhodesia to do the Cambridge when I leave Form II'. Well, she would see that I got a grant from the Department of Education and so she did. Her interest in me continued throughout my days in secondary school and university.

At my parents' shop African miners, wearing protective helmets and copper identity bracelets, were the main customers, but I did not play with African children. My friends were all white, mainly English, but some, like the Van Rensburgs, Afrikaners. English usually meant English-speaking from South Africa. Now and then we would have a fight with some group of African boys but, generally, we knew how to keep up the white man's position: by not fraternizing with Africans, except with our servants, of course.

Scouting was a popular activity and I became Northern Rhodesia's first 'King Scout'! It was through scouting that I came to know Bob Robertson, a progressive white miner. He was the Assistant Scout Master and the concentrator superintendent on the mine. An Australian, he had first come to work on the copper mines in Katanga, then moved to Bwana Mkubwa near Ndola and, in the early thirties, to Luanshya or the Roan. His son, Peter, was in my scout patrol and Bob would not only teach us knots and first-aid, but would also talk to us about politics. He spoke Cibemba himself and would try to encourage us to learn this, instead of Cilapalapa or kitchen kaffir.

We became friends. Bob had been a Roman Catholic, but was now an atheist and Marxist. During the war he helped to form a Northern Rhodesia branch of the Friends of the Soviet Union and, at the end of the war, he founded the Luanshya Co-operative Store. He was a man of great energy. Bob, like Mrs Kynoch, revived the socialist ideas that I had formed in the Zionist-Socialist Youth Movement in Lithuania. He gave me reading material and we would often sit at his house at night until he had to go on night shift at midnight, debating various aspects of Marxism. I got to know from him that Northern Rhodesia was not a free society. I learned that Frank Maybank, the secretary of the white Mineworkers Union, had been deported to Britain because, taking advantage of the miners' contribution to the war effort, he had campaigned to improve pay and conditions for the white mineworkers with strike action.

My friends and I would cycle out to camp at Kafubu, build grass huts there and swim in the river. As the older boys left school and became apprenticed on the mine, we would visit them in their workshops and see them caught in typical journeymen-apprentice pranks, like being sent on errands with instructions to go and get a long weight from some other workshop. When they would report at their destination and announce their errand, they would be told to sit down. After an hour or so they would go back to remind the journeyman, only to be told 'I thought you asked for a long *wait*'! To see what life was really like on the mine, I spent one night at the mill bins, where one of the boys who had just left school was working the night shift. Here, the crushed rock comes up a conveyor belt and, after passing under a magnet to remove bits of steel, gets distributed in bins for storage before going to the ball mills for grinding. This lad was already in charge of several African workers, although he had just left school!

Since the war was on and the Defence Force in Luanshya needed a band, I became a part-time bugler. I soon mastered the five notes of the bugle and, although being hardly at all musical, I somehow managed to blow some of the calls. However, Jack Purvis, who later became leader of the European Mineworkers, thought I should progress to the trumpet. His father, a white trade unionist and an Australian, was bandmaster. My poor ear was now getting confused and Purvis the elder soon found that I was the culprit blowing flats and told Purvis the younger to 'take the trumpet away from him'. My military musical career ended soon as a result of Mrs Sinclair's efforts to get me to continue with my education and not waste myself on the mine.

Having been informed, towards the end of 1941, that the Department of European Education would pay for my boarding school fees in Southern Rhodesia, I was relieved not to have to go down the mine and set about applying for a place in a Southern Rhodesian School. There was considerable choice; Plumtree, Milton, St. George's, Chaplain. Some of my friends were already at Plumtree, so I was keen on applying there, only to be advised by Jack Purvis against it. He had been there and thought that there had been no Jewish students and I would meet with anti-Semitism. St. George's in

Salisbury was probably too religious for me and Chaplain School was stuck away in Gwelo, a small and not very interesting town. Milton in Bulawayo seemed the best choice: it had many Jewish *oppidans* from the large Bulawayo Jewish community and they had left their mark on the school. Anti-Semitism should not be a factor there.

Boarding school meant not only special uniforms, but also a long list of items of clothing which I did not possess and which my parents could not afford to buy. Mother thought that if I wrote to my rich bachelor uncle in Boksburg, South Africa, he might help me. He did, with £25. So, with this in my pocket to spend at the appropriate shop in Bulawayo, I boarded the school train in Ndola early in 1942 with two other boys from Luanshya, whose fathers worked on the Roan Mine. One, an American boy, lasted only one term before his parents took him away, because the other kids had bullied him. The other, a rather fat English chap, was teased mercilessly, but had been prepared by his parents for public school life and was, therefore, able to stand up to it.

One certainly had to be made of fairly tough material to put up with the pranks of kids from farming folk. Having your bed apple-pied so that you tore a sheet on getting into bed was a favourite. One had to be equally tough mentally to put up with corporal punishment both from house masters and prefects for minor misdemeanours, to fag for your prefect and, above all, to go through the initiation ceremony which included running the gauntlet and other physical punishments. This was no place for sissies or for sensitive boys. This was the training ground for Rhodesia's white ruling class. The Cadet Corps, to which all boys had to belong, had frequent target shooting practice and its annual camp in Gwelo attended by the Cadet Corps of all Southern Rhodesia's public schools was no Boy Scout affair. It was run by the Rhodesian Army and we were left in no doubt as to why we had to take cadet training seriously. A black uprising could occur at any time and Rhodesia had to be ready to deal with such an eventuality. The army was small and needed a large reserve, which would include us.

At school, I was assigned to Pioneer House. There was also Charter House, both names with deep roots in Rhodesian white history. Peter Fraenkel (whose career in broadcasting later took him to the headship of the European Programmes of the BBC) and my brother, Jake, were also in

Pioneer House. Before I left Milton I was made a prefect there. Our headmaster, 'Foxy' Morgan, had come to Milton from Chaplin School, where he had taught Ian Smith and 'was later very surprised to hear that "this dull boy" had risen to become "prime minister" of Rhodesia,' his daughter, Mrs Anne Lewis, told me after the end of UDI in Zimbabwe. It was Foxy who called me in after my first term in Form III to tell me that he thought I could skip a form and do the Cambridge School Certificate examination in that year instead of the next. So I was moved up to Form IV and, at the price of dropping Latin, I obtained at the end of the year sufficient credits to give me a university entrance qualification.

This qualification alone did not, however, enable one to go to university, one had also to have the means and from my parents the means were not available. They were still struggling to make ends meet. There were, however, various scholarship possibilities and so I stayed on for another year under a fairly liberal curriculum and wrote a general scholarship examination. This earned me a Junior Beit Engineering Scholarship and a place for my name on one of the shiny wooden panels lining the assembly hall. The scholarship could take me to a South African university for four years to study engineering. Also on a panel listing scholarship winners are the names of Vervoerd and later Stanley Fischer. (Stanley Fischer was born in Mazabuka in Zambia. He became deputy manager of the International Monetary Fund (IMF) and is well-known as 'the economists' economist'.)

At Milton I made many friends amongst the boarders as well as the *Oppidans* and we kept in touch long after leaving school. In particular, I became very close to Bernard (Bunny) Krikler from Salisbury, a friendship that was to last for many years. Bernard Krikler went on to become deputy director of the Wiener Library in London. I was also friendly with the two Bergman brothers, whose parents were missionaries of Swedish origin near Bulawayo. I only really got to know Peter Fraenkel, who was several years behind me, after we both left school. The Bergmans were sympathetic to Africans and we would often discuss the position of the African in Southern Rhodesia. Bunny Krikler and I already considered ourselves left-wing at Milton.

I had spent two years in a Southern Rhodesian school and was immersed in the Rhodesian culture: its attitude to race, the war-time thrust towards creating secondary industry with protection against competition from South African imports, its very pro-British position and support for the British war effort. Frequently old boys would come to address us on their war experience in Abyssinia and the Middle-East. Some of my friends had joined the Rhodesian African Rifles, others the Rhodesian Air Force. Most of the boys joined up when they were eighteen. There was conscription in Southern Rhodesia and the atmosphere created at school was such that one could hardly wait to do one's patriotic duty as part of the British Empire's war effort.

Although I was swept along with the Rhodesian mood and wanted to do what my friends were about to do, I was also determined to play my part against fascism and Hitler. I do not think that I saw joining up as a means of looking for adventure, as did some of my Rhodesian schoolboy friends. If I had, I would soon have been put right by some British Royal Air Force staff who were at the training base near our school. I met one training officer at a house where I used to go and stay for long weekends and he made sure I knew that war was *no* adventure!

Chapter Two

WITH BRITISH EMPIRE FORCES IN EAST AFRICA

After sitting for my Beit scholarship examination I decided to join up. My parents tried to dissuade me and, on failing to do so, sent me on a holiday to Johannesburg for a fortnight to be worked on by our extended family. But the only argument they could offer was: 'You do not have to. After all, there is no conscription in Northern Rhodesia!' This was insufficient to change my mind. In Northern Rhodesia there was direction of manpower and to join up you had to obtain permission from government. In December 1942, I went to see the Luanshya district commissioner, who got in touch with Lusaka and, after an anxious wait of a week or two, I received a telegram instructing me to appear before the director of manpower, who would soon be visiting Luanshya. The Directorate of Manpower was formed with the purpose of keeping European mineworkers working on the mines as essential workers. I do not think there was a rush of miners wanting to join the armed forces, but the Directorate probably did prevent a few key men from doing so.

When I presented myself at the district commissioner's office I was confronted by a rather large, fat man whom I recognised as Mr Roy Welensky, leader of the Northern Rhodesian Labour Party. He had been made director of manpower because the governor thought he had the confidence of the white miners and railway workers. I was aware that Mr Welensky was regarded as spokesman for the Northern Rhodesian settlers, and that his father was a Jew from Vilnius, Lithuania, who, like my father, had emigrated to Africa. I knew that Roy was born in Salisbury, Southern Rhodesia, and that he had come up to Northern Rhodesia as a fireman on the Rhodesia Railways and had settled in Broken Hill (now Kabwe), which was then a key railway depot on the single track from Livingstone to the Copperbelt. He had got himself elected to the Northern Rhodesia Legislative Council as far back as 1938 and started the Northern Rhodesia Labour party in 1941. He also had a reputation as a past heavyweight boxer.

Welensky was then a man of thirty-five and already exuded power.

Although I was destined not to meet him again, our paths would intertwine in the post-war years. As far as I can recall, the Jewish community did not regard him at the time as one of their own, because his mother was an Afrikaner and so was his wife. Yet, as he gained power in politics this attitude changed and many Jewish businessmen contributed financially to his political campaigns and sought his support when they found themselves up against a district commissioner or other official who might, as sometimes happened, be discriminating against them. I, however, came to see him for no favour, only to get his formal approval for my application to join the British Armed Forces and I could see no reason why he should refuse this.

I told him that I had a scholarship to go to study civil engineering at the University of Cape Town, but that I wanted to defer this until after the war and, in the meantime, join up. He argued that after the war the country would need engineers more than ever and that I would be doing my duty by preparing myself now for this need. After some fencing he gave way, no doubt because he could hardly insist that I was an essential worker.

A telegram soon came from Lusaka, telling me to report there. I duly arrived by train after being seen off at Ndola by weeping parents. When I went to sign up the major officiating told me that I was a bloody fool to volunteer. I could hardly believe my ears and spent a good few minutes trying to persuade him that I was not. He appeared unconvinced.

In deference to my engineering preference, I was signed up into the East African Engineers and given the number EB7073. Within a week or so, I was on my way to Kenya. It was February, 1944. The Great North Road route, which South African troops had earlier in the war used to go to East Africa via Tanganyika, had since been replaced by a route through the Belgian Congo. So we went by train to Ndola and then to Elizabethville (now Lubumbashi), Jadotville and Bukama. From Bukama we travelled by road to Kamina; then across the Lualaba (upper Congo) by paddle steamer to Kabalo and from there by train to Albertville (Kalemie) on Lake Tanganyika.

At Albertville I saw prisoners being led through the streets with steel hoops around their necks and chains joining the hoops, reminiscent of pictures of the slave trade. This seemed a more severe treatment of Africans than in Northern Rhodesia, but, on the other hand, the train drivers both on the Elizabethville-Bukama stretch, as well as the Kabalo-Albertville stretch, were Africans. Driving a train was a task deemed in Northern Rhodesia as too skilled for Africans. Some years later I was to discover that the management of Rhodesia Railways had their own reasons for not employing Africans in skilled work on the railways, reasons that had nothing to do with ability. But at the time it all seemed very puzzling.

From Albertville we crossed the lake to Kigoma and then travelled by train to Tabora and on to Mwanza, on Lake Victoria. From Mwanza we took a steamer to Kisumu; then a train again to Nairobi. It all took two weeks. I was later to travel the identical route several times, forwards and backwards, when going on leave or on transfer. I found the route well organised despite the involvement of four countries with different administrative systems and, in the case of the Belgian Congo, a different language. Key to all this were liaison officers stationed along the route at points where trans-shipment was necessary.

From Nairobi I was sent by train to Nanyuki, where the East African Engineers had their depot. Despite my lack of military training (except in the Southern Rhodesia Cadets), I was attached to some European NCOs who were drilling African recruits and I helped to shout drill instructions and learnt some rudimentary military engineering and general army routine. I would accompany the medical officer on the weekly short arm inspection, when the African troops would be inspected for any signs of venereal disease. This was an undignified event: the troops would stand on the parade ground naked, except for their greatcoats. For inspection, the soldier would drop his greatcoat and then start to masturbate lightly to achieve an erection. If a sore was spotted on his penis, the soldier would be marched off to the surgery and, apart from treatment, he would be penalized for not having made proper use of his ET (early treatment) kit, after having sex. This procedure seemed to keep to a low level the incidence of VD amongst the troops.

Only after some months was I to join other Northern Rhodesian and East African Europeans on a six month recruits' course in Nakuru and, at the end of that course, we were all upgraded to the rank of sergeant, the lowest rank for a European in the East African forces. Our training involved physical fitness, being put through assault courses, live fire practice and, above all, mental indoctrination.

On the wall of our lecture room was this slogan: 'A coward is *not* one that is afraid, but one that cannot conquer his fear'. This was meant to help you in battle and it was to prove of immense help to me when it came to risky political activity after the war. I would often repeat this to myself when I was confronted with taking steps that I knew would get me into trouble with the government in Northern Rhodesia. Much later, also, I remembered these words when I spoke at the Garden House Hotel Conference in Lusaka, where the Movement for Multi-Party Democracy (MMD) was being launched under the eyes of the security police of Kaunda's one party participatory democracy. Even later still, in 2001, I repeated them to myself when I came to participate in the movement to block President Chiluba's attempt at a third term.

From the recruits' course I was posted to the infantry, the 4th NRR, a battalion of the Northern Rhodesia Regiment. I spent some time first in trying unsuccessfully to reach it in Somaliland and then in moving with it from Kenya to Lusaka. In Lusaka I was often a guest at the Gore-Brownes and got to know Lady Lorna and their two daughters, Lorna and Angela. Sir Stewart was rather remote, being busy with his estate at Shiwa N'gandu and his work as a member of the Legislative Council.

It was not long before I was sent back to Kenya on a PT instructor's course. I had never excelled in gymnastics or in competitive sports at school and have no idea why the adjutant of the 4th NRR thought that I could be of any use in such a role. The course was run by a Major Geoff Dyson, a well-known British hurdle champion prominent in training British athletes before the war. I completed the course, but did not go back to the 4th NRR.

Instead, I was sent to join the 3rd KAR, a battalion of the Kings African Rifles stationed in Nanyuki, which was training on the slopes of Mount Kenya in readiness for being shipped to Burma to join the campaign against the Japanese. The white farmers in the area were very hospitable and I learnt to horse-ride on their farms. But I found myself bored with what we were doing in Nanyuki and applied to go on a course in military intelligence at Moshi, Tanganyika. During the course we were given a few days leave at the Mount Kibo Hotel at the foot of Mount Kilimanjaro, a welcome relief from learning to count in Japanese (only up to 10) and learning how to interrogate the odd Japanese POW that my unit might capture. Why the 3rd (Kenya) King's African Rifles should have more success in this respect than other East African (or, for that matter, other British or Commonwealth) units in the

Burmese Campaign was a question one did not dare pose openly. We all knew that the Japanese fought to the death and that our own chances of coming out alive from an encounter with them were pretty small. Those few days up the slopes of Kilimanjaro were also a relief from days of eye-strain from staring through stereoscopes in the search for camouflaged gun emplacements on aerial photographs.

We had hardly got out of our truck on returning to camp, when we were greeted with the breathtaking news that some immense bombs had been dropped on Japan and the Japanese were seeking peace. It was mid-August 1945 and I had been in the army for some one and a half years. For me, I thought, the war was over and I should soon be back home and a civilian.

But this was not to be. I rejoined my battalion, now as a trained intelligence sergeant, and found the 3rd (Kenya) KAR still busy north of Nanyuki playing at war, a trifle unrealistically perhaps, and in readiness for embarkation for Burma. 'Were we still going to be sent, at this late stage, to Burma as scheduled?' I wondered. The anxiety was soon dispelled by orders to march some eighty miles back to camp at Nanyuki and prepare to travel to Uganda where a disturbed situation had developed following the murder of the Katikiro (prime minister) of Buganda, a province in the Protectorate of Uganda.

I had volunteered to fight fascism, but now I was to be part of an action in aid of the civil power, an action in a country that I knew little about and on an issue of which I knew nothing. I was very uncomfortable. To my surprise, other white NCOs and even officers were just as uncomfortable, although some of them were from Kenya's white settler families. I soon discovered that these officers and NCOs would have been quite ready to act in aid of the civil power in Kenya, but to act in the Protectorate of Uganda was another matter! 'After we have done the dirty work, Uganda will still be far from being a whiteman's country', several complained openly.

A process of induction then began. Brigade Headquarters sent a legal officer to explain to us our duties in this new role. He agreed, when questioned, that the military were regrettably the potential scapegoats in such situations, since they could be withdrawn without loss of face, whereas the district commissioner or other civil officer would usually have to carry on in the country. 'Still, not to worry. Shoot only on the DC's orders' was the guideline. A few weeks later, when we were settled in our camp in Jinja, the process of induction was taken a stage further with an address to officers and European NCOs only, by the provincial commissioner of the Province of Busoga, in which Jinja was situated.

'Why are you here?' asked the provincial commissioner rhetorically, while adjusting a map of Africa slung over an easel. 'Because we were bloody-well sent here, you clot', muttered an old sweat beside me under his breath. Firstly, it seemed, we were there because the 4th (Uganda) KAR, which had restored order after some riots, were under strain and had to be replaced by an outside battalion! (No need to explain: everyone knew the policy in the East African Command of stationing Nyasa KAR in Northern Rhodesia, Kenya KAR in Tanganyika etc).

We were evidently there, also, because Uganda was vital to the control of Egypt. The PC went on to explain: 'Egypt means the Nile and the Nile rises *here*, at Owen Falls in Jinja. The recent outbreaks (following the murder of the Prime Minister of Buganda) have been dealt with; the underage Kabaka (king) flown out to study at Cambridge; stability has been restored; intelligence is now improving rapidly; but you might be called to aid the civil power if the rascals have another go. If they do, we shall put an end to Buganda's protectorate status by occupation'. Buganda was evidently the problem. The province of Toro was secure: 'We have installed in Soroti, Regimental Sergeant Major John, from the Jinja Depot, excellent man, as chief and he will stand no nonsense. Busoga, on the other hand, had to be watched!', the P.C. warned us. The troubles seemed to have arisen because 'these Bataka rascals went around fooling people to part with their savings. People were told to put their money into the ground outside their villages and there it would increase, only to find later that it had increased to vanishing point! No government could allow this to go on'. Presumably not, I thought, but was this really the whole story? Why was the Katikiro murdered and why was there rioting and why might it recur? These questions puzzled me.

'Protectorate status', the provincial commissioner explained, 'was a complication and might have to be done away with. Senior officials had made it known to the Colonial Office that if the new Labour colonial secretary, Creech Jones, would try to interfere in Uganda, they would resign en bloc. Labour ministers' statements about self-government for colonial people had been one of the causes of the current troubles!'

Ambitious Baganda, the PC told us, were saying that the British government wanted them to have self-government, whereas the local officials did not. 'Of course, we *are* preparing them for self-government, but *we* shall decide the pace', said the PC. At this point there was some uneasiness in our ranks and, when it came to questions, I stood up and asked: 'You say you are preparing them for self-government. How long will it be before they are self-governing?' The provincial commissioner reassured us: 'One, two hundred years', throwing up his arms above his shoulders with each century count.

Our induction was complete. Having been thus reassured, most European colonials would now do their duty willingly. I left the meeting in an uneasy mood. I was not in sympathy with the provincial commissioner's outlook. These officials were not carrying out Labour government policy, but following their own. The PC even gave the impression that he and his colleagues could create a situation to justify the annexation of Buganda and termination of its special protectorate status within the Uganda Protectorate!

As intelligence sergeant, I later read the report of the official commission set up to inquire into the disturbances. The commissioners had little to recommend except increases in intelligence-gathering services. I also came across an official publication for limited circulation, *An African Speaks*. This gave me an insight into why our battalion was really in Uganda. Some Africans had, apparently, taken seriously the sentiments of the Atlantic Charter and other pronouncements from the Allies. Although the war was now over, not only could Africans see no changes in East Africa but, on the contrary, they could see moves to keep things as they were. The document was quoting a senior African official or soldier. These observations were not that surprising. I had noted that our East African Armoured Car Units were being dissolved and their vehicles transferred to the Kenya Police: trouble was now expected on the civilian front. At the Victory Parade in London, African members of the East African contingent, I was told, had to be kept under tight rein by their European NCOs so that they would not get 'spoilt' by contact with Britons who might not respect colour-bar practices and some of the men complained of these restrictions.

In Burma, Ceylon and India, African troops had got a taste of relaxation of the colour bar in their units, only to find it reimposed, step by step, as their boat was approaching Mombasa on their way home. Unlike my fellow colonials, I was not worried as to whether Africans would fit back willingly into 'their place' on returning home. I was ready for the new world and looking forward to playing a role in it, as soon as I could get home.

Amongst the white colonials I served with, John Connell from Dar es Salaam was a notable exception. His father had been a surgeon there and John had graduated from Grahamstown University in South Africa. He spoke very good Kiswahili and had been brought up in Dar es Salaam without colour prejudice. We would often lament together on the raw deal the African soldier was getting and the little he had to look forward to after the war. John helped to rekindle my own earlier socialist values of fair play.

In linking Uganda with Egypt, the provincial commissioner was only repeating the old Foreign Office line dating back to the late nineteenth century: keeping Uganda in order to save Egypt. He can be forgiven for not reflecting that, if it ever had any validity, it held only for great power rivalry and would not hold for dealing with strong national movements such as would later arise in Egypt. But the PC cannot be forgiven for being a traitor at heart *viz-à-viz* the British Labour government's post-war policies for Uganda. His views on how long it would take for Africans to be ready for self-government were also commonly held in the Rhodesias and were later articulated by Sir Godfrey Huggins (later Lord Malvern), long-time prime minister of Southern Rhodesia and later of the Central African Federation.

The lecture by the PC, which I recorded in my diary, was given on 6 October 1945. Fortunately, my battalion was never called upon to shoot at civilians. In fact, we had a pleasant stay in Jinja which lasted for many months. On taking a tour in the countryside I met a local government administrative officer, an African educated at Makerere College in Kampala, and I taxed him to explain to me the cause of the disturbances. He thought that it was a matter of intra-tribal rivalry within the Kingdom of Buganda. 'One set of powerful chiefs agitated amongst the "commoners" against the treasurer of the Kingdom, labelling him a British stooge. Feelings were inflamed to such an extent that the treasurer had to be moved, but the efforts of this group to seize power through the disturbances failed and they were exiled'.

According to Mahmoud Mamdani, author of *Politics and Class Formation in Uganda*, the Bataka Association dates back to the early nineteen-twenties and was formed to articulate the grievances of the Baganda tenant peasantry. He goes on to describe the Bataka Party in 1946 as 'firmly a kulak party'. Presumably that is what it was at the end of 1945 during the disturbances. At the time that my battalion was there we must have been buttressing the regent in the Buganda Kingdom and the large landowner chiefs, allies of the British Raj, against the small farmers and landowners.

Some seven years later I would meet one of the Bataka leaders in London, campaigning for Uganda's self-government and quoting the Atlantic Charter as a basis for it. Doubtless, the disturbances of 1945 were the early beginnings of Uganda nationalism, resulting from the African awakening brought about by the 1939-45 War.

The situation in Buganda had stabilized by January 1946. When I heard that our battalion would soon be withdrawn, I went for an interview with the Northern Rhodesian liaison officer in Nairobi to seek my immediate release, so that I could take up my scholarship at the University of Cape Town in March. He explained that he could do nothing since the armed forces were working strictly on the principle of first in first out. However, he undertook to apply for a Class B Release (education grounds) on completion of three years service. If this was successful I would get out in time to start at university in March 1947. My disappointment at losing another year was tempered by my recalling what the major said in Lusaka when signing me on: 'you are a bloody fool to volunteer'.

We were soon on our way back to Nanyuki and from there through the Northern Frontier District of Kenya and Mogadishu to British Somaliland. We passed through Wajir where I had spent two weeks in 1944 in an abortive attempt to reach my Northern Rhodesian battalion in Somaliland. Our convoy was marooned there by freak rains which had made the desert tracks impassable and we had eventually to return to Nairobi. Our route now took us through the Ogaden scrubland to Hargeisa and from there to Jigjiga in Ethiopia. The Ogaden, including Jigjiga, came under OETA (Occupied Enemy Territories Administration). It was, since Italy's defeat in this sector and despite Haile Selassie's reinstatement on his throne in Addis Ababa, being excluded from his domain until a peace treaty was signed. It was, in fact, being treated by the British forces as part of Somaliland. Because of this, my battalion remained there for the next few years.

The Ogaden would later be the subject of a heated dispute between Ernie Bevin, the British foreign secretary and Molotov of the Soviet Union. Britain tried to get the Ogaden ceded to Somaliland in the Peace Treaty with Italy, on the basis that the Somalis traditionally grazed their sheep and goats there and that in that respect it was part of the Somali economy. Also the majority of the people there were ethnic Somalis. In later years Somaliland fought a war with Ethiopia in a failed attempt to annex it and once again the Soviet Union were on the Ethiopian side, after a considerable period when they had sided with the Somalis. This time they provided Ethiopia with heavy armour.

We were stationed some miles from Jigjiga, along the foothills of the mountain range that contains the Marda Pass, through which the road from Hargeisa led to Harar in Ethiopia proper. The pre-war international border between Ethiopia and British Somaliland was some seventy kilometres east of Jigjiga and the nomadic Somalis would, while we were there, graze their flocks right up to these hills, usually without interference from the Habash. The British Somali Camel Corps patrolled the Ogaden to the south east of us. In Jigjiga, however, there was an Ethiopian Office with a royal representative who sold postage stamps and performed minor administrative duties.

Our battalion seemed to have no duties except that of a presence and officers and NCOs had to find tasks to keep the men busy. As a result, my year of waiting to be released took a long time to pass. On one occasion when my Kipsigi batman, Kimengich, grumbled that he had had enough of this empty place and wanted to get home, I jokingly reminded him that he had volunteered for the army and now had no option but to stick it out. 'Volunteered?' he countered 'the authorities came and told the chief how many men he must provide and he sent his messengers to round up that number. There was no volunteering!'

In 1946, Britain decided to pull its small garrison of Sudanese troops out of Addis Ababa, where it had been guarding not only the British Embassy, but also some Italian prisoners of war who somehow got stuck there and now would have to be evacuated. This proved to be a very delicate operation which involved some of our battalion moving to Diredawa to provide protection to the evacuees who would arrive there by guarded train from Addis and would travel on by convoy up the escarpment road to Harar and Jigjiga. The delicacy arose because among the evacuees was an Italian pilot whom Abyssinian patriots regarded as having been responsible for dropping bombs filled with mustard gas on Abyssinians in the aggression of 1936. Intelligence reports coming in told of a planned ambush to get this pilot and hold him for trial as a war criminal or perhaps to mete out instant justice. We brought him out safely together with some Greek civilians who felt it unsafe to stay on in Ethiopia without the presence of British troops. On our arrival in Jigjiga, the white officers and NCOs celebrated the success of the operation with a party where we danced with the Greek girls, the first white women we had seen for many months.

In February 1947, almost three years after I joined up, I was informed by telegram that my Class B release had been granted and that I was to proceed immediately to Hargeisa Airport from where I would be flown to Nairobi. At Hargeisa I boarded an RAF Wellington bomber and was flown to Mogadishu and from there to Nairobi. From Nairobi I was flown to Ndola in a Dakota and after a day with my family in Luanshya I travelled to Lusaka to be demobbed. I then went on to Cape Town to enrol for the course in civil engineering, for which I had obtained a scholarship three years before.

There was hardly any time for reflection on my period in the forces as I had to adjust quickly to a new life of study and decision-making. Army life had its routines and major decisions were usually made for one by people higher up. Looking back now, I can see that one result of my three years wandering about in British East Africa with both men from the UK and its colonies was that I had come to understand the nature of the British colonial system in East and Central Africa, its relationship with the white settler communities and the indigenous African populations.

The post-war task for the officials on the spot was to get back as quickly as possible to the situation that had existed before the war: to contain the disturbance resulting from it. The settlers had a similar purpose. Both were apprehensive about the Labour government in Britain, with their Fabian ideas for Africans. Both wondered whether the returning askari would settle down in his 'old place'. In Northern Rhodesia the Rhodes Livingstone Institute did some research on this and one author concluded that the demobbed askari went back to his village and settled down in the same way as the migrant labourer returning from a spell on the mine. Few of my fellow white colonials were inclined to abandon the colour bar at home. For many of the officials, the days of 'paramountcy of African interests' were gone and, with Britain weakened and in the wrong hands (Labour), they felt that the settlers should now play a wider role in governing the colonies and even the protectorates.

In contrast to the above, I had formed the view that the African deserved a new dispensation. He had participated in a war, which was fought for human freedom and he deserved some dividends for his sacrifices. I knew that though the askari might settle back now, the day would come when he would, as a result of his experiences outside, question the status quo. I remember a major in Nanyuki during a kit inspection expressing satisfaction with my askaris' turn-out and saying: 'if they can lay their kit as well as this, they can fight', and my thinking that perhaps this could also apply to fighting for their rights in civvy street. (Unbeknown to the major, I had shown my askaris how to achieve a neat looking bedroll without much effort, by using two small pieces of cardboard concealed at each side of the roll to stiffen the sides).

I had been inspired by our wartime propaganda that we were fighting for a new world order and was very encouraged by the election of the Labour government in Britain. I was looking forward to playing my part in building a new order in Northern Rhodesia, but first I had to prepare myself by qualifying as an engineer. There would be the four year course at university and then a period of training for a year or two with a civil engineering firm in Britain before coming home to help develop the country. There were new roads to be built, dams, buildings and bridges.

Above is my political transformation. I did, of course, change from boyhood to manhood and learn to command men and to discipline myself. I had resisted alcohol and the trail to brothels and I was physically very fit and self-confident. I was looking forward to the new world, free from Nazism and fascism. I felt I must play my part to make it also free from racism.

Chapter Three
STUDYING ENGINEERING AND POLITICS

After three years of holiday from intensive study, I found it difficult to get into a study routine at university and this soon showed up in tests at the end of the first term. Fortunately, there were many ex-servicemen at the university and the authorities seemed well-aware of our difficulties. Their response consisted, at least in the case of science and engineering students, of numerous tutorials and frequent tests. These got us back on the study track. Once I felt I could cope with my studies I started taking an interest in student politics.

The Student Socialist Party (SSP) attracted me as it seemed to embrace socialists of all kinds: communists (both Stalinist and Trotskyist), social democrats and, even Zionist-socialists. The SSP focused on university life and had campaigned against the colour bar in the School of Medicine, where non-white medical students were prevented from handling white cadavers. It would later organize a demonstration against the introduction of a colour bar at the Labia Theatre. The SSP was not one of the societies recognized by the Students' Representative Council (because it was political) so it operated behind one of the approved societies, the Modern World Society. I later became chairman of this society and we organized meetings on the campus with progressive speakers like Dr HJ Simons, lecturer in Native Law and Administration, and a member of the Central Committee of the Communist Party.

In my final year, when the SSP ceased to meet in order to escape repression by the Nationalist government, I was part of a small group of students who formed the Students Liberal Association. The SSP leadership had in mind a front organization, but at the inaugural meeting, which included Zach de Beer, who later became a director of the Anglo American Corporation and headed it for a while in Zambia, the Liberals gained the upper hand.

In addition to campus politics, the SSP discussed political topics affecting the country as a whole and there would often be clashes of opinion between the various socialist tendencies. A major focus of interest was the National Union of South African Students (NUSAS) and we would urge our members to attend its annual conference so as to push for progressive resolutions on education in South Africa. I attended its annual conference in Grahamstown in 1950 and played a part of some prominence in nominating Lionel Forman, a Communist, to its executive.

I started in the SSP as a Zionist - Socialist, but on the formation of the State of Israel in 1947, I felt that Zionism had fulfilled its aim and that I should devote myself to working for socialism in the country where I lived: in Northern Rhodesia. Through my close friend Bernard Krikler, I had become friendly with several sociology students, including Myra Baskin and Lionel Forman. The four of us spent much time together. Lionel was already a prominent Communist and often spoke at public meetings on the Parade in Cape Town. He influenced me to work closely first with the Communist Party faction in the SSP and later with the CPSA itself. In 1949 Lionel and I shared a flat in Mowbray, Cape Town.

In 1948 a general election took place in South Africa. Smuts' United Party lost and Dr Malan and the Nationalist Party came to power. Despite their anti-British record, I was soon to discover that the Nationalist government was cooperating with the Northern Rhodesian government on security matters. I discovered this because I was the subject of their cooperation. Lionel Forman had moved to Johannesburg and under the new government his letters were being opened. A minister in the Nationalist government quoted in Parliament from an intercepted letter Lionel had received in Johannesburg from another Communist student, Percy Denton, on some matter pertaining to South African politics. Earlier, I had written to Lionel enclosing five pounds for him to purchase and send to Northern Rhodesia a Roneo duplicator - a simple hand-roller type, which I had undertaken to obtain and donate to the Northern Rhodesian African Congress. This letter to Lionel was also opened and resealed with a sticker by the South African police. When I next went home for vacation work at the Ndola Municipal Council, I discovered that the Special Branch of the Northern Rhodesia police had been making discreet enquiries about me from one of my colleagues at work. Clearly, the two police forces were collaborating and, indeed, Sir Percy Silitoe, head of M15, was out in South Africa organizing this collaboration.

This collaboration was, no doubt, a response by the British to the threat they saw in Soviet Communism in the early days of the Cold War. However, I would later take with a pinch of salt the argument, advanced by British advocates of the Federation of Central Africa, that one of its purposes would be to act as a bulwark against South African influence spreading in the region! (Perhaps not relevant, but of some historical interest, is the fact that Sir Percy was once a policeman in Northern Rhodesia).

While at Cape Town University, my interests ranged widely. I attended some lectures on politics given by the right-wing Professor Murray; on philosophy by the Catholic Dr Martin Versfeld; and on politics and sociology by the Communist Dr HJ Simons. Extramurally, I also attended Marxist study-classes conducted by the latter and I had the privilege of discussing with him the likely consequences of the amalgamation or federation of the two Rhodesia's. What impressed me was his historical approach to many of the issues being debated at the time in South Africa, such as the industrial colour bar and whether there was an identity of interests between white and black workers. On the latter, I found myself in disagreement with Marxist orthodoxy, which held that there was such an identity in South Africa.

My experience in Northern Rhodesia went against this concept and when I returned home I did not apply it in my political approach. Similarly, on the question of African nationalism, the official Communist view at the time was to see it as secondary to the struggle of the working class against capitalism; whereas, in my view, it was primary. I heard much criticism of the Communist Party from friends I had in the Unity Movement. This was a small group of mainly coloured Marxist-Trotskyist intellectuals. I chose to work as closely as I could with the Communist Party and with its newspaper, *The Guardian*, which I collected donations for from the Copperbelt Indian community during my trips home.

I worked closely with the Communist Party, despite my misgivings about Stalin and the Soviet Union, misgivings which began in my days in the Zionist-Socialist youth movement in Lithuania. I took the view that South African Communists were primarily concerned with Southern Africa and that the international issues were secondary. Later I was to discover that this did not apply to most of the leadership for whom the fate of the Soviet Union and international Communism were of equal importance to the South African situation. I admired the Communist Party members for their policies in South Africa and I was only sorry that I could not participate openly in their activities because of my visitor status. I felt I should avoid giving the South African authorities any cause to send me back to Northern Rhodesia before I completed my university course. I had, however, promised myself that once I finished my studies and returned home I would emulate the South African Communists in fighting for an end to racial discrimination and for the emancipation of the African masses.

The Nationalist government introduced apartheid on the suburban trains in Cape Town and I watched an abortive attempt at collaboration between the Communist Party and the Unity Movement to organize resistance through the Train Apartheid Resistance Committee (TARC). There was no love lost between the two movements, yet the Unity Movement had a following of Cape Coloured intellectuals and these could have played an important part in mobilizing the Coloured community into resistance to extensions of apartheid. In the event, TARC was a flop and apartheid was soon in force not only on the suburban trains but also on the municipal bus services.

I came to know Brian Bunting, editor of *The Guardian*; HA Naidoo, also of *The Guardian* and his wife Pauline, both leading trade unionists; Fred Carneson, the Cape provincial secretary of the Communist Party and Ike Horvitch, its national chairman. I also got to know Sam Kahn, the Communist member of Parliament and Jack Cope, the Communist writer. He was a lover of art and he showed me round the Beit Art Collection, then on loan to the Cape Town Art Gallery, and thus introduced me to the world of painting. I was introduced by my close Rhodesian friends, Harry and Marjorie Chimowitz, to Gregoire Boonzaier, the Afrikaner painter who was either a member of the Communist Party or close to it. I got to know the Reverend Johnson Ngwewela, a Communist leader in Langa and member of the Party's Central Committee, during the campaign for Sam Kahn's election to Parliament. Before leaving for home in 1950, I spent one evening visiting Bill Andrews, the retired chairman of the Communist Party, and he gave me a pipe as a parting gift. I learnt from him that he was against the decision of the Party to dissolve itself in the face of the government threat to ban it. These were all leading figures in the Communist Party, some of whom I would meet again in later years. One Communist whom I used to meet who was not in the leadership but was to haunt me for a long time was Wulfie Kodesh.

Wulfie was an activist, later mentioned by Mandela in his auto-biography. He was a prominent participator in the Johannesburg City Hall steps' battles against Afrikaner Nationalist supporters. He would often challenge us students to action, when we were reluctant to rise to the challenge while our studies were not completed. I promised myself that I would one day respond to his challenge. What impressed me most about the Communists I got to know in Cape Town was their fearless determination to fight for the common man and their strict non-racism and spirit of self-sacrifice for their causes.

On returning to Cape Town from a vacation in Luanshya in mid '48, I got together with some other Rhodesians to form the Rhodesia Study Club. Among its members were Robert Chikerema, later to become prominent in the struggle against white rule in Southern Rhodesia, Cyril John Shoniwa, who became a Senator in Zimbabwe and Harry and Marjorie Chimowitz. Harry was born and educated in Southern Rhodesia and, after serving with the South African Engineers in Italy during the Second World War, had taken a job as a civil engineer in the Roads and Sewerage department of the Cape Town City Council. His wife, also born and bred in Southern Rhodesia, was working on *The Guardian* newspaper, making regular appeals for donations under her maiden name of Marjorie Till. Chikerema was the organizing secretary of the club and he managed to rope in many Southern Rhodesians who were working in Cape Town.

Robert Chikerema, who was my age, was born in Salisbury. He had received his secondary education at Marianhill in South Africa and had then come to Cape Town. His parents wanted him to continue with his education but could not afford to support him, so he started work as a despatch clerk at a pharmaceutical firm, while becoming a part-time student at the university. In an interview with a Northern Rhodesian paper in 1964, he described his membership of the Rhodesia Study Club in 1948 as the 'first rung on the ladder of political struggle'. (*Northern Star*, Lusaka, 10/9/64). He proved a reliable and hard-working member of the club.

The Rhodesia Study Club met periodically to discuss the situation in the Rhodesias and on several occasions Dr Simons from the University of Cape Town was invited to attend. Dr Meyer Fortes, visiting from the UK, was also once invited to participate, as was Mr Hugh Waterfield, a journalist and a former editor of a South African provincial paper. (Hugh would later attend, as a journalist, a crucial conference on Federation at the Victoria Falls and give publicity to a telegram from our Copperbelt Committee opposing the scheme.) With the practical and editorial efforts of Marjorie and Harry Chimowitz respectively, the Study Club began publishing a monthly newsletter. The first issue came out in October 1948 and thereafter was published regularly until February 1950.

In the first issue we introduced ourselves and directed ourselves to the workers, students and teachers of the Rhodesias. Each issue was wrapped in 'respectable' newspapers and sent off to friends in Salisbury, Bulawayo, Ndola and Luanshya for redistribution. My brother Jake, then working in Lusaka, received bundles for distribution.

It was not long before the newsletter was referred to in the Northern Rhodesia Legislative Council by Roy Welensky, leader of the unofficial members. The August 1949 issue had been passed on to him by a European employer, whose workers used to receive mail through the employer's post box. Mr Welensky read to the House several articles from it. One dealt with the devaluation of the currency and one commented on an agreement whereby the Northern Rhodesian government and the employers agreed on a *maximum* wage for African labourers in Lusaka of forty-five shillings per month, with the starting wage not to exceed 22/6d per month. Our article condemned the government for trying to interfere with the African workers' bargaining power. In the same issue there is a critique and condemnation of Welensky's agreement with the British South African Company to limit the tax on their mining royalties to as low as twenty per cent, after he had previously campaigned and moved a motion in the Northern Rhodesian Legislative Council to tax them at fifty per cent. Mr Welensky, however, made no reference in Legco to this article in the newsletter!. He, nevertheless, urged the Northern Rhodesian government not 'to sit back and to view this type of literature with equanimity'. (See *Northern Rhodesia Legislative Council Debates* No. 66, 1949). It became clear later on that Welensky, by easing his pressure on the BSA Company, was paving the way for the mining companies' support for Federation.

Apart from the regular monthly issues of the newsletter, the study group published in mid 1949 a pamphlet entitled *What will Federation Mean?* I wrote this after several club discussions at which Jack Simons was present. He was of great assistance to us in analysing what the results of Federation of the Rhodesia and Nyasaland would be (See Zukas Papers at National Archives, Lusaka). Roy Welensky also quoted a paragraph from *this* pamphlet in his speech in Legco, the pamphlet having been sent out with the August issue of the newsletter.

Although I did not leave Cape Town until the end of my degree studies in December 1950, we ceased publication of the newsletter in February 1950, when Cyril Shoniwa reported that the Southern Rhodesian authorities were suspecting his participation and making life difficult for him. Chikerema, in an interview in 1964 recalled: 'the newsletter... came to the attention of the Southern Rhodesia government and it contacted the South African government to outlaw the club' (*Northern Star* 10/9/64) In fact, the club was not outlawed. The interview claims that Chikerema hid from the South African police for three months before fleeing home. I do not recall this, but it might have happened after my departure in 1950.

The anti-Federation pamphlet was published immediately after a conference on Federation which took place at the Victoria Falls with Sir Stewart Gore-Browne attending, together with Sir Godfrey Huggins and Mr Roy Welensky. Sir Stewart's participation and support for Federation soon led to his resignation from Legco as government-appointed representative for African interests. This resignation came about in response to African criticism which came from Luanshya, Livingstone, Mufulira and Lusaka. Sir Stewart, in an article in the *Northern News*, said 'I am getting out before the bricks start flying'.

Sir Stewart allowed himself to be enticed by Welensky to support Federation, but decided to pull out only when he saw the strength of the African reaction in Northern Rhodesia to his position. I, however, became convinced that I should oppose Federation, not only because I knew that it was generally opposed by Africans in Northern Rhodesia, but also because I saw it as a retrogressive step, which would create in Central Africa a powerful white-dominated dominion, similar to South Africa, where African advancement would be delayed for many decades. Like Sir Stewart, I did not oppose Federation *in principle*, (in fact, I could see the logic of the economic arguments for it). But unlike Sir Stewart, at that stage, I knew well why

Europeans were generally for it and I had no doubts that, to obtain their acceptance, the constitutional basis for it was going to be far from democratic. Nor did I doubt that once Europeans had a majority of seats in its Parliament, the clock would inevitably be put back. Things may not have been all that bright and fair at home on the racial front, but at least the door was open to change while we could press for it through members of Parliament in Britain. This was no longer effective in the case of Southern Rhodesia, where Europeans had had self-government since 1923. We spelt out these points in our pamphlet and these convictions would later spur me on to fight tooth and nail against the threatened imposition of Federation.

At the end of 1950, with a B.Sc. degree in civil engineering, I left Cape Town for Johannesburg from whence I would travel home to Luanshya. I stopped over in Johannesburg in order to say goodbye to Harold Wolpe and Lionel Forman, both student activist colleagues of mine. While doing so I discovered that there was some dissatisfaction there with the self-dissolution of the Communist Party by its Central Committee in the face of its being banned by the Nationalist government and that steps to revive it were being contemplated by Lionel Forman, Ruth First and others.

Lionel Forman asked me to accompany him to see Dannie Duplessis, the Transvaal Provincial Secretary of the Party at its dissolution, and to tell him what Bill Andrews' views were on the voluntary dissolution of the Communist Party. Lionel's urging on Dannie to restart the Party underground fell on deaf ears. Indeed, the leadership had good reason not to make plans for a revival at that time, as the police were in possession of the Party's membership lists and many would have been arrested on the banning law coming into force. Revival would have to wait for new developments.

*****

When I first got involved in political activity in Cape Town I felt I should make contact, also, with Northern Rhodesian *African* political activists and, on the suggestion of Miss Lorna Gore-Browne, I contacted some students at Marianhill College. Emanuel Chalabesa, who later became Head of the Citizenship College at Mulungushi, Kabwe, responded and I also addressed senior boys at the government school in Luanshya. We discussed the formation of a Northern Rhodesia Student Association. Nothing came of this and I transferred my efforts to adult politics.

There was a branch of the newly-formed African Shop Assistants Trade Union in Luanshya. During a holiday from university in mid 1948, I met the branch secretary who introduced me to a Mr Best Kofie in Ndola who, in turn, arranged a meeting in Kitwe with the union's president, Mr Henry Malenga. The union had been formed with the assistance of Mr W Comrie, who had recently come out to Northern Rhodesia, under the auspices of the British TUC and with the approval of the British Labour government, to encourage the formation of trade unions amongst African workers.

Until Comrie's arrival and the passing of the necessary legislation, only European trade unions were legal. Both the white mineworkers and white railway workers had been legally organized and active since well before the Second World War. African workers' trade unions, in contrast, had no legal recognition and their formation and even advocacy were regarded by the authorities as subversive (See the Elwell Affair, p42). With Labour in power in Britain, the situation started to change. A district officer, RE Luyt, attended a course on unionism at Oxford in 1948 and, on his return, published a pamphlet, *Trade Unionism in African Colonies*, in which he urged the wisdom of recognising African trade unions. Luyt later saw Northern Rhodesia into independence as chief secretary in the colonial administration, before going on to become vice-chancellor of the University of Cape Town.

My meeting with Henry Malenga was arranged to take place in the bush, off a minor road outside Kitwe and he brought along with him a tall, grey-haired man, Mr Godwin Mbikusita Lewanika, the president of the newly-formed Northern Rhodesia Congress. The meeting had a clandestine air and I was questioned with suspicion by both Malenga and Lewanika, who reminded me, since I was white and expressing myself in sympathy with the cause of African emancipation, that 'blood is thicker than water'! I met their suspicions by explaining that my experience in South Africa had convinced me that Africans here would also have to stop begging for concessions and become militant and that we should not take for granted that the declared Colonial Office policy of paramountcy of African interests would last. I added that I was surprised to see the colour bar enforced so rigorously in shops and post offices in Northern Rhodesia when it was absent in Cape Town. Both Malenga and Lewanika expressed their faith in Protectorate Status and thought the South African ANC's slogan of votes for all was 'too far-fetched, votes should be for educated people'. I was cautioned that a gradual approach was necessary in order not to fall foul of the authorities. 'It is most important not to lose one's good name', said Lewanika, 'one's name is everything'!

Loss of good name had, I later learned, occurred at least twice in Mr Lewanika's long life. However, until then, it had been with the Lozi hierarchy and the Northern Rhodesian government. The test was still to come with the people of Northern Rhodesia, whom he was now going to lead as president of the only national political body that they had, Congress. This body had come about by the coming together in 1946 of various local welfare societies to form the Federation of Welfare Societies (See Plate 3) and in 1948 this turned itself into the Northern Rhodesia Congress. The welfare societies had been the cradle of African politics and they were often in rivalry with the urban advisory councils, bodies hand-picked, until 1951, by district commissioners and favoured by them in preference to the welfare societies. The latter were political groupings operating under the cover of welfare and some dated back to before 1933 when a conference of native welfare associations took place.

Mr Godwin Mbikusita Lewanika had established a good relationship with the Indian High Commissioner in Nairobi, Aba Pant, and obtained several scholarships for Northern Rhodesian Africans to study in India. Simon Kapwepwe and Munu Sipalo had already been sent there. While Lawrence Katilungu was the undisputed leader of the African mineworkers, Lewanika spoke as the undisputed leader of African *political* opinion. I visited Lewanika again, with my friend Bob Robertson from Luanshya and we undertook to obtain a cyclostyling machine for Congress. We were both impressed with Lewanika, but somewhat disturbed that he insisted on writing down what we said. He justified this on the basis of his having a faulty memory!

Mbikusita Lewanika had come to the Copperbelt after coming into disfavour with the Lozi royal establishment in Barotseland. At the time of our visit he was employed on the Nkana Mine as a member of staff. He had been part of the Lozi royal establishment and regarded himself as a son of King Lewanika and, in fact, grew up within the Lealui Palace. But his mother was not an officially recognised royal wife. King Yeta III, who succeeded Lewanika, refused to recognise Godwin Mbikusita as a royal son, but saw that he received a good education. Yeta then employed him as secretary and took him to the UK when he, Yeta, was invited to the Coronation of George VI in

1938. During Yeta's absence, a plot against him was discovered by the colonial administration in Mongu whose members ensured that it did not succeed while Yeta was in Britain. In the investigations that followed Yeta's return to Mongu, Godwin Mbikusita, despite his absence overseas at the material time, was implicated in the plot. One of the decisions of the Barotse authority, confirmed by the governor, was the provision that Godwin Mbikusita 'was not again to hold a post in the Barotse government'. Thomas Fox-Pitt, who had served in Mongu as an acting provincial commissioner, related all this to me when we met in 1951 (See also Caplan, *The Elites of Barotseland*).

Mbikusita's loss of good name with the Lozi hierarchy was followed by a loss of good name with the Northern Rhodesian authorities in Kitwe in what became known as the Elwell Affair. African political stirrings in Kitwe in 1945, centred on the Kitwe African Society (KAS), whose declared aim was 'to work for and promote the welfare of the African people'. Its secretary in 1945 was Mr Jason Achiume, a Nyasalander. Mr Elwell was welfare officer with the Kitwe Municipal Council. Mr Best Kofie was a member of the KAS at the time.

At a KAS meeting, which Mr Elwell attended as a guest speaker, he was asked: 'How can we Africans get more money?' 'By forming trade unions' was his reply. Kofie, who attended the meeting, later explained to me: 'Of course, we knew this already, but it was nice to get an honest answer from a European'. With a Labour government installed in Britain, this honest answer should have been pretty safe: not, however, in Northern Rhodesia. The district commissioner soon learnt of these 'seditious' remarks through one of his informers who attended the meeting and called for the minute book from the KAS Chairman, Godwin Mbikusita Lewanika.

Mbikusita, after consulting Elwell, declined to hand over the minute book. Elwell advised him that the district commissioner had no right to the minutes of the society. News of this consultation *also* reached the ears of the DC. If Elwell's earlier remarks, as reported to the DC, merely raised suspicions, his subsequent behaviour confirmed beyond doubt that a seditious character had penetrated the Copperbelt citadel. Elwell was soon suspended from his post and sent to the less sensitive area of Livingstone before being returned to the United Kingdom. (Facts related to me by Fox-Pitt and Kofie)

In protest and, no doubt, out of fear lest the government also act against the listeners to Elwell's seditious remarks, the Kitwe African Society shut up shop. This was more than the authorities had bargained for. Tolerance towards the various welfare societies had developed because they were seen as safety valves. So long as they were in the open, informers would bring in useful information not only about African thinking, but also about individuals with dangerous political views. With Elwell out of the way, government did not want Africans to be driven into underground discussion groups. So Commander Fox-Pitt, one of the most liberal officers in the Northern Rhodesian native administration was brought in to revive the Kitwe African Society.

In the company of Rob Moffat, another liberal member of the native administration, Fox-Pitt, having managed to revive the Kitwe African Society, gave an address to its members on trade unionism. Fox-Pitt records: 'The mining company spies lost no time; next day, Faine-Smith, the provincial commissioner, asked me if it was true; he said "I say, I think I would lay off that line. It's upsetting the mines, and one can't say where it will end" '. (See Fox-Pitt Note Books, SOAS London). Fox-Pitt came to realise that government would not easily stand up to the mining companies on the issue of African trade unions and, indeed, it was not long before he was transferred from Kitwe. However, his concern that Africans should get a square deal was not diminished by this event.

Kitwe also lost their next welfare officer, Major Lee-Tattersall. He had worked closely with Lewanika and I well-understood why Lewanika was then careful in his political contacts with Europeans and why he was so meticulous in keeping notes of our meetings. Clearly the government was determined to keep Kitwe, the hub of the Copperbelt, in a cocoon, free from any influences on the African mineworkers to form trade unions. This was, however, soon to change under Creech Jones, the colonial secretary in the post-war British Labour government.

I had a further meeting with Lewanika in January 1951, after I came home on completion of my university studies. On a Saturday afternoon Bob Robertson and I went to hand over the duplicating machine that we had undertaken to obtain for Congress. It was a simple Roneo machine, using a hand roller. Lewanika welcomed us at his house in Wusakili township in Kitwe and again took notes of our conversation.

While Lewanika wrote diligently in his notebook on his lap, I suggested to him that African opinion should be mobilized against Federation while the officials of the Rhodesias and Nyasaland were still meeting in London on the subject. However, he thought that it was wiser to wait until they had reported. I pointed out that Welensky and Huggins had pressed for a consortium of officials from the three territories to make recommendations on closer association and the Colonial Office, with Sir Andrew Cohen at its head, appeared to have given way. Welensky was taking no chances. Settler opinion was being mobilized at public meetings while the officials were still sitting in London. At a public meeting which I attended in Ndola, Welensky was confident that things were moving his way in London. Lewanika, however, was not moved by my argument for mobilization of African opinion.

I was disheartened by Lewanika's approach and confided this, on my return to Ndola, to my African friend and only other political contact at the time, Best Kofie. He suggested that I should come along to explain my views to a discussion group that met in the Welfare Hall in the location once a month on Saturday afternoons. Kofie explained that there was a Northern Rhodesia African Congress branch in Ndola with Amonson Mugala, a council housing officer, as chairman, but that it was inactive. A shadow branch met behind the scenes, under the leadership of Bridger Katenga, the African welfare officer. This group included Jonathan Chivunga, Reuben Kamanga, Justin Chimba and Alick Kafunda.

Kofie was a customs clearing agent's clerk with fair English, but with a pronunciation that I could follow only with difficulty. He had reached Form II and, by 1951 standards, Kofie was an experienced politician. He had been a member of the Kitwe African Society and attended the famous Elwell meeting. Was his name adopted from contacts in Ghana? I cannot recall an answer to that. Kofie was also a competition ballroom dancer, as well as a member of the Ndola Urban African Advisory Council. When he later moved into his small newly-constructed two-bedroom council house at the Chifubu Location Extension, he had a car-parking bay laid out. I immediately became suspicious lest some Europeans were trying to bribe him by offering him a car, but Kofie explained that it was only for the occasional taxi to draw into!

The next discussion group was scheduled to be addressed by Dr Clyde Mitchell, a sociologist, on the impending sample census. Before his arrival,

Kofie introduced me to a suspicious audience of about twenty, which included a policeman, Mr Mwanza! There was not much interest in the census and when Dr Mitchell left a political discussion took place amongst us. I suggested that we touch on Federation. While Alick Kafunda, a solicitor's clerk, appeared politically the most advanced among the group, Justin Chimba, a lay preacher and employee in the government Mines Department, appeared the most determined to stand up for African rights. 'We must have our own newspaper', he pronounced and later he would work hard with me to bring into existence the first attempt at this, the *Freedom Newsletter*.

It was agreed that at the next monthly discussion I should speak at length on Federation. However, before this took place, there was a quickening in the pace of events which would replace such leisurely and non-directional discussions with meetings that would no longer be confined to the few Africans who could speak some English. These meetings would draw in hundreds of people: they would become not only meetings of men, but also open the doors, for the first time I believe in Northern Rhodesian politics, to participation by women *together* with men.

As I moved into African political circles and made friends, I came to be haunted by the ghosts of my two European radical forerunners: Mr Elwell and Major Lee-Tattersall. Both, I was repeatedly told, had been deported by government for showing 'real sympathy for Africans. Africans could not afford to lose another European friend: there were so few around.' I was asked to take care not to reveal myself as a man who was helping Africans politically or I too would suffer the same fate as had befallen Elwell and Lee-Tattersall. No one seemed to think, however, that a similar fate might befall liberals like Sir Stewart Gore-Browne or John Moffat. They were seen to be in a different category. 'They worked very closely with government', Africans would explain. Prudence, let alone historical or political curiosity, dictated that I should find out all I could about the events surrounding the deportation of the two Europeans who tried to help Africans.

Major Lee-Tattersall had followed Mr Elwell as welfare officer in Kitwe. He used to be very friendly with Godwin Mbikusita Lewanika, president of the Northern Rhodesia African Congress, and even addressed meetings of Africans from the same platform. He often attended African funerals. There were rumours that some informers had written letters to the authorities revealing how strongly sympathetic he was with African aspirations. He was dismissed from his job in 1947 and forced to leave the country. He went to Durban and later to the United Kingdom. (When I met him in London for the first time in 1960, I saw the deep scars that these events had left on him.) The public explanation for the dismissal and expulsion of Lee-Tattersall was a statement in Legco that he was suspected to have associations with the British Fascist Movement. Few could believe, in the light of his local associations, this to be anything but a cover story issued by government. The Elwell case seemed to me the more significant politically, as it was linked with African efforts to form trade unions on the Copperbelt, long before these had Colonial Office blessing.

What lesson was I to learn from these events? That a European who wanted to take sides with the African masses had to do so discreetly, in order to avoid the wrath of the government? Some Africans thought so. I rejected this on several grounds. Firstly, the authorities used too many African spies and informers for one to escape detection for long. Secondly, my stand was not as an African *sympathiser*, but as a radical for a just cause which was in the interests of the Africans as well as Europeans wanting a future in the country. Elwell, I thought, should have made his views known quickly enough to the mass of Africans, who could have stood up to defend him much more effectively than the small group in the Kitwe African Society could. No! *I would speak openly to the African people and trust in their solidarity.* If I was to be put out of the way by the colonial authorities, I would first make sure that I left behind something that would kindle the spirit of struggle against not only amalgamation (or Federation) with Southern Rhodesia, but also against colonialism and *for* self-government on the basis of votes for all. I would show Africans that begging for concessions needed to be replaced with militancy and mass action, if results were to be achieved.

Chapter Four

WHITE PROPOSALS FOR CENTRAL AFRICA

After listening to Welensky at a public meeting in Ndola, in early 1951, I was left in no doubt that he and Sir Godfrey Huggins, prime minister of Southern Rhodesia, had recently managed to persuade the Colonial Office, if not the British government, to support amalgamation or something close to it. All one could now expect from the conference of officials still meeting in London, I concluded, was sugar-coating for the bitter pill. 'Make haste slowly' was Welensky's prescription for dealing with African aspirations for improvement in their status. Few of the audience present at that meeting could have not understood the cynicism contained in that coded prescription: it had the same flavour as Sir Godfrey Huggins' 'equal rights-one day, but not in our lifetime'. Only Europeans were at the meeting and there were about one hundred of them. Welensky was the only speaker. The only question came from me.

Welensky had argued that Africans were privileged in not paying income tax, only poll tax. So I asked if the poll tax were abolished and Africans made to pay income tax 'at the same rates as ourselves' how much more would this bring in? He did not know, but I knew that there was probably not a single African, at the time, who would have been earning enough to be liable for income tax. A resolution proposed from the floor included Welensky's advice to make haste slowly. Welensky then got an ovation from the floor and the meeting ended.

Unlike Sir Stewart Gore-Browne, I had never been fooled by Welensky's pretended liberalism. Seeing him in action for the first time with an all-white audience was, however, an education for me. He was skilful in exploiting white prejudices and made no attempt to guide or educate whites in a liberal direction. He urged increased white immigration, including 'those that would not shirk unskilled manual labour'. Was there a shortage of unskilled manpower in the country, I wondered. 'Look at me', he went on, striking his hands on his rather large chest, 'I shovelled coal and it has done me no harm'.

At this meeting Welensky dated his success against the officials in Legco politics to 'when they appointed Geoff Beckett and he swung to my side'. Geoffrey Bernard Beckett had been nominated by the governor as an additional member of the Legislative Council in 1945, when the unofficial members were given majority status. Was the governor expecting Beckett, a white commercial farmer from the Southern Province, to play a neutral role on matters of racial politics, as Welensky implied? Perhaps.

Around the time Welensky was touring the Copperbelt, the announcement of plans to transfer their head offices from London to Salisbury was made by the copper-mining companies. The political centre of gravity had been shifting from Britain to the Europeans in Central Africa since the end of the Second World War and this move would contribute to making this shift even faster. Only imminent amalgamation of the Rhodesias could be the reason for this move, we realised.

'How could we in Northern Rhodesia stave off this coming transfer of power to the white minority? Were the African people strong enough to resist the imposition of amalgamation of the Rhodesias through their Congress, trade unions and the African Representative Council?' These were some of the general questions that exercised me, but there was also the local and immediate one: on the publication of the officials' proposals, what should we do in Ndola?

At several meetings Best Kofie and I discussed this problem and worked out the following plan. We should first form a study group, which would study the proposals. Once sufficient people understood them, we should publicise our reaction. In order to ensure that the study group did not finish up as a mere debating society, I would be proposed as secretary; the chairman could probably be a man like Justin Chimba, who could be relied upon to be firm in the conduct of the meetings.

When the white paper on *Closer Association of the Rhodesias and Nyasaland* was published on 13 June 1951, I lost no time in studying it. True, what was being proposed was not amalgamation of the Rhodesias and Nyasaland, but their closer association into a federation and so there might still be opportunities for democratic development in Northern Rhodesia and Nyasaland. However, the proposed federal power structure left me with little doubt that even in these northern territories emancipation would be slowed under the white-dominated federal umbrella.

Meeting Bridger Katenga on the day after publication, I proposed that some of us hold a small private meeting to discuss our course of action. By the next Saturday afternoon, the study group idea was accepted and its first meeting was held in a classroom at the primary school alongside the Ndola-Lusaka Road, on the edge of the Ndola African Location. I was elected secretary and Justin Musonda Chimba chairman.

Most Africans with a knowledge of English in Ndola attended these discussions. Mr A Kazunga, a small trader and member of the Urban Advisory Council and of the African Provincial Council, always attended and contributed, as did Mr Israel Kasomo, a garage attendant and tribal elder, representing Chief Tafuna from Mbala.

The group met nightly for two weeks. The classroom chosen as a meeting place was convenient for everyone except myself. It was within the location so that Africans would not have trouble with passes after curfew, as they would have had were the meeting to be held within the town. But I had to cycle some five miles from home in Northrise to get there. My colleagues would see me clear of the location after the meetings, as they thought that such protection was needed, but I was never molested. Meetings would start at seven and end at midnight.

Every paragraph of the white paper would be read out and then dissected from the floor. I would offer explanations here and there to show how Africans could be affected by the proposal. More discussion would follow. Eventually, Chimba would close the discussion and I would read my summary on that point from the notes I had taken. If my summary was not generally acceptable, more discussion would follow.

A parable or apt example from rural life would usually be made to illustrate or clinch a point. Discussing the difficulty that would arise in sharing of wealth between the three territories and between the two racial communities, when there was already such disparity in their state of development, a speaker would conclude: 'when many people eat out of the same dish, he who eats fastest is going to eat most'. Few could dispute that and we could move to the next point. (Ten years of Federation would later prove the aptness of this beyond any doubt: Southern Rhodesia took the lion's share).

By the time we had finished discussing the white paper, we had a group of several dozen people in Ndola whom the government would find difficult to hoodwink. Not only could this group handle the arguments against Federation with conviction, it would, I was sure, also be able to mobilise the people of Ndola to stand firm against its imposition. Wittington Sikalumbi in his booklet *Before UNIP* refers to us as 'one of the most active Congress branches'. We were, in fact, not a branch, but included the Ndola branch, which had not been active as such.

Towards the end of our two weeks of sessions the school was denied to us as a result of pressure from above on the headmaster. In August, we published a cyclostyled pamphlet *The Case Against Federation,* giving the conclusions of the study group. In the circumstances prevailing at the time this was no mean achievement. We had no typewriter and no duplicator, nor any previous experience in producing a leaflet, let alone a ten thousand-word pamphlet (See National Archives, Zukas Papers for copies).

Typing of stencils was done by our members during lunch-breaks at the offices at which they worked, which included government offices. Gestetner took on our stencils without regard to politics - somewhat unusual in the atmosphere that prevailed - providing we paid in advance. The Indian community in Ndola came to our assistance with donations of cash.

After the twenty-three pages of each set were stapled together, one of our committee members would colour in the red stripe of our logo, the black having been produced already on the duplicator and the set would be ready for despatch to Lusaka or to some address outside the country. We sent copies to Nehru in India, Nkrumah in Ghana, Jack Simons in Cape Town, Julius Lewin in Johannesburg, Tom Driberg, MP at Westminster, etc. Local (Copperbelt) distribution would be taken care of by members travelling to the towns by bus. Sikalumbi writes that '*A Case Against Federation,* ... served as a guide at all Copperbelt meetings'. (*Before UNIP*).

This being the first political pamphlet produced within Northern Rhodesia by the nationalist movement, our members were not unconscious of the historical role they were playing. Every sentence that I wrote had to have the approval of the committee and there were all sorts of dialectics involved. For instance, if we said 'Federation on a basis of truly democratic principles might merit consideration by the people, but the officials' proposals form no such bases', were we not leaving ourselves open to being put in a false position by the press? Would they have banner headlines 'Federation acceptable to

Africans'? I would then argue that it was important to show that we had a reasoned case and were not just closing our minds and that this was important enough to take risks. Others would argue that we should not even say 'we accept Federation in principle' even if, in fact, we did. Eventually, we agreed by consensus to an acceptable modification to the draft.

Our preface said the following:

> This pamphlet does not deal with the subject of federation in general. It is a detailed examination of the *Report of Conference on Closer Association* (Comd. 8233). The Conference was convened in London; only Officials took part; no Africans attended the Conference.
>
> The Report was issued in a highly dramatic manner on June 13, 1951, at 4.30 p.m. All channels of publicity available to the government were utilised. African Advisory and Tribal Councils were summoned by the Administration, given free copies of the Report and urged to study it. This publicity was in marked contrast with the original departure of the Officials for London. Although it had been announced that the Officials were going for a Conference on Closer Association, it was done in such a discreet manner as to leave the mass of the people and even members of various government-recognised African councils, ignorant of the fact.
>
> While the Conference was meeting in secret session, the settlers, well primed by Welensky, formed themselves into various bodies to act as pressure groups. The Africans under the paternal guidance of various 'Commissioners' and 'Officers' were lulled to sleep!
>
> Once the Conference had finished its secret deliberations and made its decisions, the African people were gradually awakened by the Officials and prepared for the issue of the Report.
>
> If the issue of the Report did not come as a surprise, the recommendations did. Federation had been the battle-cry of the Settlers for many years but the government had not taken it up. One expected the Officials to recommend, at most, an improved form of Central African Council; after all their terms of reference were based on *Closer Association* not Federation.
>
> Clear thinking Africans saw immediately that the years of courting between the government Officials and the Settlers had resulted in the birth of an illegitimate child. It had long ago become clear that the majority of Officials had become "settler-minded"; this Report was the final proof. This was more than a mere report; it was part of a conspiracy to bring about Federation by sacrificing the Africans on the altar of Imperialism and European Supremacy.

And we ended off with the following two exhortations:

> <u>TO THE GOVERNMENT WE SAY</u>:
> 'If what is desired by the Officials and the Settlers is a federation in the interests of ALL the people - black, white and brown; if it is desired NOT for the purpose of halting African advancement in the northern territories; if it is desired NOT for mere imperialistic reasons, then there is a way still open to

achieve it - the democratic way: let Universal Adult Suffrage be introduced in the three territories immediately; let all forms of colour discrimination be outlawed; let all restrictive laws be repealed. When you have done that, much suspicion will have been removed and general agreement on Federation will have become a possibility'

TO THE PEOPLE WE SAY:
'Study and understand the dangers in the proposals. Condemn the Proposals in strong terms; give a definite NO! But do not leave it at that. Back your answer with organization; organize opposition to the implementation of the proposals. Federation will be inevitable only if the African people do not rise to the occasion of self-preservation. The Africans of the Cape Province failed to oppose the Act of Union in 1910, hence their plight since. We must not repeat their mistake.'

We said that we were not against closer association in principle but we were against the closer association of the Rhodesias and Nyasaland as proposed by the government officials in Legco because the basis was undemocratic. We rejected their argument that the subjects to be handed over to the Federal Parliament were those that do not impinge on Africans. It requires little hindsight to see, today, how insincere or, at best, naïve that argument was and what racism was cloaked under it, and yet it came in the name of officers, who claimed to be guardians of African interests. We argued that *all* subjects will affect Africans and whether the results are adverse or favourable will depend on the distribution of political power.

We argued that the distribution of seats in the Federal Parliament, while balanced as between the three territories, ignored the fact that 'the real division in Central Africa is a racial one, based largely on the class relationship between the two main races.' The officials, we pointed out, gave no justification for their recommendation that in a racial balance of six million Africans against 169,000 Europeans, there should be, in the Federal Parliament, a mere four Africans out of a total of thirty five seats. 'Clearly, the African people', we stated, 'would have no POLITICAL POWER in the Federal sphere'. (See Zukas Papers at National Archives, Lusaka).

It is, perhaps, worth quoting our conclusions in full:

> Federation on a basis of truly democratic principles might merit consideration by the people, but the Officials' proposals form no such basis.
> Almost all the proposed federal functions would affect the African people to one degree or another, yet they are not to be given any constitutional means for self-protection. All but an insignificant amount of political power is to be

in the hands of the settlers, thus ensuring European domination; the protective measures are full of loopholes and could never protect the African people; they are completely undemocratic; they would be a mere constitutional cover for discriminatory legislation. Even if the proposed protective measures were perfect they would not form a substitute for universal adult suffrage; they could act only in addition to it, in order to protect minorities.

The proposed Federation would be in the interests of only a minority of the people of Central Africa; it would place the African workers at the 'tender' mercies of their employers; it would stifle the growth of the Northern Rhodesian trade union movement; it would result in the alienation of African trust land; it would result in a policy of segregation not integration of the races; it would extend Southern Rhodesia's Native policy to the northern territories; it would close the constitutional door to African political advancement in the northern territories; it would be a complete denial of democracy. We have no hesitation in completely rejecting such a federation. The proposals do not form a basis for discussion.

When the study group, or more precisely, the Ndola Federal Proposals Examination Group was being formed, some of my colleagues thought it was a waste of time. 'Was it not' they argued, 'enough to reject the proposals out of hand, since we are already against Federation?' I advised against this, on the basis that a full understanding of the dangers inherent in the proposals would strengthen our resolve to act and enable us to deal with the government and settler propaganda machinery - and so it turned out. At the conclusion of our period of study, there was strong support for forming an Anti-Federation Action Committee. However, in order to involve the public from the start, we decided to launch the idea at a public meeting before we published our findings in full. We called the meeting for 5 July 1951, in the Welfare Hall at the Ndola Location.

Although it was mid-week and in the evening, the small hall was packed with about one hundred people and the atmosphere was electric. Mr Mwanza, a well-known plain-clothes policeman, was seated a few rows from the front, without apparently disturbing anyone by his presence. 'Let him tell the district commissioner how strong we are now', Chimba remarked to me when I drew his attention to Mr Mwanza's presence.

Patiently, we explained to the meeting our findings and asked for support. My presence, although I was not yet widely known, was used by other platform speakers to show that the proposals were bad enough to be rejected even by some Europeans. To meet the point in the government propaganda that senior Northern Rhodesian officials, who 'had the trust of the African people', had taken part in producing the proposals and that the proposals, therefore, merited acceptance, the meeting passed resolutions declaring no confidence in these officials. (This, I was later told, went home in government circles even more than our resolution rejecting the proposals. Initial rejection was expected, but not a resolution of 'NO Confidence' in officials. That sort of stuff was not heard before!)

There was no shortage of speakers from the floor, and all opposed Federation, each giving his own reasons. A common factor amongst all these speakers was not so much an understanding of the proposals as a mistrust of local Europeans and, therefore, objection to their being given more power. The Colonial Office appointed officials were grouped with local Europeans! This I found rather interesting as it showed that through bitter experience, if not analysis, the people were coming to the same conclusion that I had come to: that the old triangle of political relationships: officials, settlers, Africans had been giving way since the war to a duality: Europeans (officials and settlers) on one side and Africans on the other.

Our study group's report to the meeting was as follows:

> These proposals were the latest and best-disguised, of many attempts to satisfy the ever- increasing demands of the Settler minority.
> All such attempts involved the sacrificing of the African people, and represented a cowardly escape from the fulfilment of the so-called solemn promises to the African people.
> The present proposals did not differ in any essential from earlier proposals. That they were made to originate from officials was an attempt to hoodwink Africans into accepting proposals that they have repeatedly rejected in the past.

Three resolutions were then passed at the meeting. The first condemned the proposals for Federation 'as going against the interest of the people of this Protectorate'. The second expressed no confidence in the chief secretary of the Protectorate 'for his part in making (the) Proposals'. The third resolution expressed no confidence in the secretary for native affairs 'for his part in these Proposals'.

From this meeting a committee of eleven was elected to be known as the Ndola Anti-Federation Action Committee. Justin Chimba was elected chairman and I was elected secretary. There were nine other members, namely Alick Kafunda, Reuben Kamanga, Jonathan Chivunga, Safeli Best Kofie, Abner Kazunga, Amoson Mugala, Bridger Katenga, Israel Kasoma and

Nephas Tembo.

Our next step was to try to get our resolutions into the press. *The Northern News* printed our circular as a letter. Its editor, David Cole, with whom I kept on friendly terms and who had worked on *The Yorkshire Post*, believed in 'stirring it up to increase the circulation'. *The Northern News* immediately benefited by a sharp rise in circulation and we benefited in the numbers that flocked to our meetings.

Unbeknown, I think, to the editor of *The Northern News*, I kept on even friendlier terms with his chief reporter, Ian Hess, and Ian contributed to our efforts by helping me draft the above resolutions. His particular contribution was the word 'hoodwink'. This word caught the imagination of many Africans.

Ian, who was born in Nyasaland where his father edited a newspaper, had been very radical during his student days at the University of Grahamstown in South Africa. He was leader of the Communist opposition in the university's mock parliament towards the end of the war. Ian and I were kindred spirits. We had both grown up in Central Africa and through our radicalisation in South African universities had freed ourselves of racism. We both wanted to work for genuine democracy in Central Africa by helping Africans to get off their knees and assert themselves.

As a journalist working closely only with Europeans, he soon found himself enmeshed in various contradictions which drove him to excessive drink. He later died in Salisbury when working with an agency that was doing public relations for Roy Welensky, prime minister of the Federation. I will always remain sympathetic to Ian's plight. He knew what was right, but could not pluck up sufficient strength from within himself to stand up to the system. (This was equally true of many Africans, who had far less to lose and far less to hold them back.) Ian helped us, not only with information from the Welensky camp and with suggestions and encouragement, but also with a second-hand typewriter. I relied a lot on my discussions with him and another European, Fred Butler.

Unlike Ian, Fred had no roots in Central Africa. He came from the United Kingdom on contract as a meteorologist and had worked at Lusaka Airport before coming to Ndola. In Britain, Fred had had a good political grounding in the then very left-wing Electrical Trade Union. As a proud member of the

British working class he saw it as his 'international duty to help African workers to resist the imperialist plot of Federation'. Ian had come to know Fred and then introduced him to me.

Although he was often inflexible, I found Fred's advice sound. We met frequently in clandestine fashion, for Fred had a civil service job and had to keep his political opinions hidden from the authorities. The one time that Fred abandoned his prudence was when Basil Davidson, then writing for *The New Statesman and Nation*, arrived by air at Ndola. Ian Hess informed us of this impending visit and Fred approached Davidson discreetly at the airport to whisper to him that there was a small group of Europeans in Ndola working with Africans in opposing Federation who would like to keep him informed of events here. (See letter, Davidson/Zukas at National Archives, Zukas papers). After Fred Butler finished his contract and left Northern Rhodesia at the end of 1951 I wrote to him in the UK about political developments. Despite his caution, it turned out that he had been under police surveillance and the Special Branch intercepted one of my letters at the Ndola Post Office which later figured in my trial.

In addition to Hess, Butler and Robertson, another European joined our ranks, Commander Thomas Fox-Pitt, who had recently retired. He explained that he, too, was against the officials' proposals and would help to organize opinion in Britain against them. He was sympathetic to African aspirations and even owed his life to an African. We 'should trust him', he pleaded in a letter to me.

'Commander', as he endearingly became known in our circles, was born in London in 1897, and was educated in the Royal Naval Colleges of Osborne and Dartmouth. He served in the British Navy both in the First and Second World Wars. In the latter he was involved in the operation to sink the German battleship, Bismarck. He was awarded the OBE for salvage operations off the Somali coast. In 1927 he came out to Northern Rhodesia to join the provincial administration as a cadet. He served in the Northern and Eastern Provinces and in Barotseland. Commander had a reputation in the administration for having rather liberal views and because of that he was posted to Kitwe as district commissioner in the aftermath of the Elwell Affair in 1946. However, government was now moving towards partnership with Welensky and his settler constituency and this required a different ilk of civil servant than Commander Fox-Pitt. He was acting provincial commissioner in Barotseland in 1947 and in Eastern Province from 1950-1951, when he was forced to take early retirement after he displeased governor Gilbert Rennie over the issue of allowing Africans to grow flue-cured Virginia tobacco. On that issue Commander had first displeased the Eastern Province white farmers when he would not accept their arguments that to allow Africans to grow Virginia tobacco, which needed flue-curing, would lower the general reputation of the Eastern Province crop. Fox-Pitt tried his best to convince them that this need not happen because the expatriate European, assisting the African co-operatives, would closely supervise the operation. Commander suspected that the white farmers' motives lay elsewhere and, indeed, at one meeting this came out when one of them complained that allowing Africans to grow this lucrative crop would 'reduce the availability of labour for commercial farmers'. These were, of course, all white!

Pressure from the white farmers' member of Legco on the governor succeeded in Commander being asked to take early retirement. But before doing so he wrote to the colonial secretary, Creech Jones, protesting against the process of discrimination against Africans when *proclaimed* Colonial Office policy had been the opposite.

How come Commander owed his life to an African? He was a keen horse rider and, true to his class background, he even used to organize an English traditional fox-hunt with a pack of beagles which he imported into Northern Rhodesia. An appropriate trumpet could be seen amongst the knick-knacks in his house. He was also an occasional hunter of big game. On one occasion he and an African servant went hunting buffalo. Commander took a shot at one at close range, but only wounded it and the beast turned on him. His faithful African servant came to his aid by shooting at the buffalo and thus saving Commander's life. Unfortunately this shot did not kill outright either and the wounded buffalo turned away from Fox-Pitt and went for the African instead and killed him. Fox-Pitt kept the buffalo's horns and they were later displayed at the entrance to his farm barn in Exeter, UK. He always remained grateful to his loyal African companion. However, the tendency by his white civil servant colleagues to ascribe his sympathy for African interests merely to this episode was mistaken. He was a man of high moral principles.

Fox-Pitt threw himself immediately into our campaign, but refrained from speaking publicly because he was technically still a civil servant, on leave pending retirement. He contributed a two page appendix to our pamphlet in which he analysed in great detail the 'Differences in Native Policy between Southern Rhodesia and Northern Rhodesia' in order to dismiss the argument in the officials' report that Africans had nothing to fear from Southern Rhodesian Native Policy.

With the help of these few European colleagues, Bob Robertson, Ian Hess, Fred Butler, Tommy Fox-Pitt, and my brother Jake, I thought we would be able to help stiffen African opposition to Federation to a point where Britain might hesitate to force it through.

CHAPTER FIVE
STIFFENING THE OPPOSITION TO A WHITE FEDERATION

Congress, under Mbikusita Lewanika's presidency, was to meet on July 21 and 22, 1951, in Lusaka, to decide on its attitude to the federal proposals. Our Ndola committee was a little anxious, for Mbikusita had not given a lead to the people to reject the proposals. We did not expect any leading Africans to accept them, but how many would *militantly* oppose them was still an open question. One of the reasons for keeping the Ndola Anti-Federation Action Committee distinct from the Congress local branch was to enable the Action Committee to carry on a campaign of militant opposition to the proposals, were Congress to reject them only passively.

About a week prior to the conference, Mbikusita invited me to come to his house in Kitwe at a specific time in the evening, to talk to Kitwe leaders in private. Chimba, Kafunda, Kamanga and I travelled in Jake's car on the specified evening and went straight to Mbikusita's house at Wusakili, Kitwe, where we expected the meeting to take place. To our surprise, Mbikusita took us to the house of Mr Katilungu, President of the African Mineworkers Union. It then turned out that the meeting was not to be held there either, but in the Wusakili Welfare Hall.

When we walked over to the Wusakili Welfare Hall, we were led to a room upstairs, next to the cinema projection room. For some reason not apparent at the time, the electric light bulb was missing and we had to meet in darkness. Katilungu chaired the meeting and he seemed a little sleepy. Simon Kaluwa, the secretary of the Mineworkers Union, was present and some six others. Katilungu asked me to give my views on the proposals and how to deal with them and I did so, frankly and at length, being careful not to say anything which, to my lay legal mind might be actionable, for I always suspected an informer at such meetings. I was left to speak without interruption and when I finished Mbikusita was the first to put a question: 'Were you not asking Africans to be disloyal by suggesting that they resist Federation by non-payment of taxes and passive resistance?' I explained that Federation was being pushed by some Colonial Office officials in league with Huggins and Welensky. There were many in the British Labour movement who would oppose it if they knew how determined Africans were against it: it was therefore important to show our determination to resist its imposition. 'It was not a question of being disloyal, for loyalty is owed to one's country, not to some officials or some undemocratic institutions', I said.

Kafunda and Chimba, who were sitting on a table near the window, thought they saw a police car moving off as our meeting was ending, but I was *not* concerned, for we were, after all, not an illegal meeting. It was not until after the Congress conference that I discovered that by attending this meeting, arranged by Mbikusita, I walked into a police *trap* and that all I had said had been recorded on a dictograph by the police in a room next door. Over the years since, I have wondered about the motivation behind this loyalty question from Mbikusita Lewanika. Was it intended to provoke me to reply in such a way that it would be useful to Special Branch? Or did it merely reflect his conservatism? I think, now, that the latter was the case.

Simon Kaluwa and Namitengo, secretary and treasurer, respectively of the African Mineworkers' Union, called on me in Ndola after the Lusaka conference and described how some of those who attended the Wusakili meeting had been called to the Kitwe Police Special Branch offices to hear a dictograph recording of the meeting, presumably to instil fear into them. Since official pretence was that the federal proposals were for free discussion, police snooping seemed out of place, so I sent the whole story to *The Guardian* of Cape Town who published it. Much later I learned from a policeman in Salisbury that a cutting from *The Guardian* was posted on the Salisbury Criminal Investigation Department notice-board.

At my trial in Livingstone, Mbikusita was brought to give evidence and he was examined on what I said at this meeting. The government did not reveal to the court that they had a recording of it all, but I urged my lawyer, Mr Grayling, to ask the Attorney-General for the record. Reluctantly, the head of Special Branch agreed to hand over dozens of closely-typed sheets of foolscap, giving every word that was said. Evidently, the authorities were shy of using the transcript of the recording and were relying on Mbikusita's verbal evidence in lieu! Later on police recording of what was said at political public meetings became routine and the practice was carried on under Dr Kaunda's presidency. However, there has never been a legal provision for bugging, although it has, no doubt been practised by the Special Branch before and after independence.

A follow-up on this meeting was a banner headline in *The Central African Post* some weeks later, to the effect that the police had evidence to charge me with sedition. The sensational story was obviously based on a police leak to the CAP's chief political reporter. This article was the first in a series in which *The Central African Post* and its sister paper, *The Livingstone Mail*, were to hound me and to libel me, on one occasion even criminally. On that occasion they were had up for criminal contempt and fined in the Livingstone Magistrate's Court (*Livingstone Mail*, 4/4/52).

After the meeting, when we returned to his house, Mbikusita showed his proposed presidential address to the forthcoming conference to Kafunda and me. It contained only mild criticisms of the federal proposals. What was worse, it included an offer to consider Federation, if Huggins would agree to have two Africans in the Rhodesia Territorial Parliament instead of the provision for only one in the federal proposals! This mildness was not altogether a surprise to *me*, for I had already sensed that Mbikusita was a rather conservative man and unlikely to do battle with the Northern Rhodesian or British Governments on the issue of Federation.

However, the problem before us then was not Mbikusita's views as such. The real problem was that, in the absence of a formal democratic mechanism through which the majority view could be, beyond doubt, established, the authorities would choose to identify as 'African opinion', the views of a few conservative men, if these views were to their liking. Although later discarded by the British Tory government as a criterion, when the proposals were published African acceptance was an implied requirement.

The coming conference promised to be interesting and I decided to attend by flying to Lusaka. In order to be back at work on the Monday, I could stay in Lusaka, unfortunately, only for the Saturday session. While waiting in the Ndola Airport departure lounge for the plane to take me to Lusaka, I overheard a European businessman from Kitwe (Mr Gersh, who later became Kitwe Mayor) tell some colleagues about the municipal reception held the previous night in Ndola in honour of a visiting team of British

Parliamentarians. They had come to ascertain Central African opinion on the federal proposals. The team included Stanley Evans, of the Labour Party, William Coldrick, a Co-operative Party member and Archie Baldwin and Julian Amery, both of the Conservative Party. Mr Gersh reported Julian Amery as saying: 'you ought to learn from our experience in India. This chap, Nkumbula, came back from Britain and asked for thirty pounds per month as a teacher. It was refused and he has now turned nationalist. If you had given him fifty pounds he would now be on your side'. Mr Nkumbula had been making strong statements against the federal proposals and was clearly seen as a threat to the federal scheme.

Although Amery was wrong, I think, in his assessment of the strength of Mr Nkumbula's convictions at the time, he was not wrong in thinking that there were leading Africans who could be bought off. Our purpose, in the Ndola AFAC, was to organise the people in such a way as to create, not so much counter *inducement*, (we had none to offer) but a strong counter *pressure*, which would make it difficult for the authorities to play on African poverty and buy off some educated Africans. We were able to utilise the period while Labour was in power in Britain to organize African opinion to such a point that when the Tories took over they could not impose the scheme *with any significant African support.*

The conference took place in Lusaka on Saturday and Sunday (July 21 and 22) in the Kabwata Welfare Hall, which was not very full. There were two Europeans present in addition to myself, John Moffat and Fox-Pitt. Mbikusita invited me to speak from the floor and said that many Africans were wondering about my sincerity since 'blood is thicker than water'! I took up this point and suggested that the federal proposals had to be opposed not only by Africans who would be the first to suffer, but also by Europeans living in Northern Rhodesia who would, in the long run, also suffer from Federation, because it would result in economic exploitation by Southern Rhodesia. I explained that I was neither a negrophile nor a wishy-washy white liberal, but I was determined to fight something that I thought bad for Northern Rhodesia as a whole.

Mbikusita's presidential address was as weak in its criticism of the federal proposals as the draft that he had shown me the week before. It gave only the pretence of opposition. Some fairly woolly discussion took place and I could sense that those attending were 'keeping their powder dry'. I suspected that this was either for fear of being recorded by the white Special Branch snoopers seen hiding in the projection room, or of being reported to the authorities by suspected informers present. There was, however, condemnation of the proposals and no support from the floor for Mbikusita's view that there was room for negotiation.

I had to leave early and learnt later that in the election for the presidency that took place on the Sunday, Mbikusita had been replaced by Harry Nkumbula. Safeli Chileshe, who also stood, got only one vote, not surprisingly since his intervention on the proposals was rather mild and ambiguous. The new, tougher Congress line was demonstrated by a ceremony at which the white paper was burnt to signify NO NEGOTIATION: 'Dogs show your teeth' was the call that went out from this conference, heralding a new militancy. Sikalumbi ascribes this slogan to a delegate from the Rand, who 'cried that as the Europeans angered the indigenes (sic), the delegates were gathered to show the white man their anger. One of his Swazi proverbial expressions was translated in the press as "Dogs show your teeth!" ' (See: *Before UNIP*, p.10).

Later, I was informed by the Mineworkers' delegates that it was not only Mbikusita's lukewarm criticism of the federal proposals that led to his replacement as president: it was also the story of our Wusakili meeting and the suspicion that Mbikusita had had something to do with helping the police to bug it. It had also become known by then why Mbikusita needed to write down what European visitors said to him. John Kalima, who was accommodated by Mbikusita for some time before coming to work for me in Ndola, revealed that following a meeting with European visitors, Mbikusita would send him to take these notes to an officer in the police whom Mbikusita described as a friend. Noah Sambona, a Lozi like Mbikusita who also stayed with him for a while, corroborated this. (Both John and Noah died within a few years of independence: John in a car crash while he was a member of Parliament and UNIP regional secretary at Namwala and Noah from illness while district secretary at Livingstone. In 1952 John was gaoled for seven months for political activity).

With Nkumbula's election and the burning of the federal proposals, the campaign against Federation was put into full swing. In Ndola, we called a public meeting for the following Saturday, 28 July. Government officials were also in action and their objective was clearly to give prominence to the few Africans who were prepared to speak favourably of the proposals and then to present them as African opinion. Our task was to show that such views were unrepresentative of the majority of African opinion. Government was able to exert pressure on small traders who feared losing their licences and, in some cases, on chiefs. From Fort Jameson (Chipata) the press carried reports that chiefs had approved of the proposals. Legco members Yamba and Sokota rushed there and had these so-called approvals reversed at public meetings.

At our post-conference meeting in Ndola, there was a lot of feeling against the Federation Working Committee set up by the Ndola Urban Advisory Council on the instructions of W Billing, the acting provincial commissioner. It was felt that the members of the Advisory Council were all government-appointees who could not be deemed to represent African opinion. A resolution was passed to this effect but, for good measure, it concluded 'Anyone who remains on the above committee be regarded as a traitor to the people of Ndola'.

This resolution effectively blocked the work of the Advisory Council's committee and, at a later date, when elections were called for the Urban Advisory Council, our candidates were successful and the working committee was abandoned by the council. But before the council elections, the members of the Ndola Anti-Federation Action Committee were summoned by Acting Provincial Commissioner Billing and warned that the government would act against us, unless we tempered our tactics! Present also at this meeting was Ndola district commissioner Kennedy Trevaskis, who had recently come to Northern Rhodesia from the Sudan. He had more experience of politics than Billing and was far more astute.

I had been informed that when officials were asked by the governor, Gilbert Rennie, whether they could 'sell the proposals', Trevaskis asserted that in Ndola this would be difficult, if not impossible. Billing, on the other hand, although long in the Northern Rhodesian provincial administration, thought he could sell the proposals! (Trevaskis later moved on in the colonial service and became the last British governor of Aden, where Yemeni nationalist forces made an attempt on his life by throwing a bomb at his motorcade).

A black and red stripe was adopted by the NAFAC as its emblem in

August, 1951, at one of our regular public meetings in the Ndola Welfare Lecture Hall. The dual stripe badge was easy enough to obtain, at no cost, from the pavement tailors who would make it up from dress offcuts. The wearing of it on a lapel or shirt pocket became popular in Ndola and then spread to the other Copperbelt towns. Later the colours would become the flag of Congress and, at independence, they were incorporated in the flag of Zambia.

When I proposed the colours to our committee I had in mind that they would represent the black working people and I explained that red was the colour adopted by the working-class movements throughout the world, including the British Labour movement. Both in the committee and at the subsequent public meeting, considerable elaboration was necessary to explain the red element. There was no problem with the black and, indeed, some thought that black would have been sufficient, were it not that it lacked impact on its own. I reflected at the time that this latter view could be applied not only to the emblem, but also to our movement. Black on its own lacked impact, it needed an injection of international revolutionary experience if it were to present a real challenge to colonialism. *I made it my task to achieve this.*

Red had no special local significance *yet,* at least, in the anti-Federation context. No blood had been spilt on that account, nor was there a wish to have any spilt. However, for me, then, anti-Federation was not an end in itself. I had in mind that the anti-Federation struggle should evolve into a militant campaign that would lead to votes for all, majority government, self-government and independence from colonial rule.

One could predict that whites in Northern Rhodesia would not approve of our choice of colours and, indeed, they did not. Defiantly, we withstood the press and other pressures that tried hard to make us abandon our chosen emblem or logo. It was, in fact, worn as an act of defiance of the established order, as well as a symbol of resistance to Federation. The emblem became a mobilising factor as we had hoped and, in the absence of street demonstrations, it became the outward visible sign of our protest. It has been suggested that the black and red colours were chosen on the basis of Marcus Garvey's writings: black for Africans and red for the blood spilt, but this was not so. None of us in Ndola had at the time read the West Indian educationist, Marcus Garvey, or even heard of him!

The NAFAC had won the battle for African opinion in Ndola and from there we spread our activities to the Copperbelt towns of Luanshya, Kitwe, Mufulira and Chingola. Harry Nkumbula, Dauti Yamba and Pascale Sokota (the latter two were the African members of Legco) were doing equally well in Lusaka and the provinces and Dixon Konkola, the leader of the African Railway Workers Union in Northern Rhodesia was active in Broken Hill. We heard reports that a Congress group was active against Federation in Chinsali, but the press carried no news from there.

It was becoming clear to government that African consent for Federation would not be forthcoming. So official propaganda tried to discredit African opposition by seeking to show that some of the views expressed by Africans were not their own, but those of left-wing Europeans. Africans, presumably, were not entitled to benefit from such views. The racism behind this sort of argument was palpable and we exposed it in our publications.

I had been so immersed in our anti-Federation work on the Copperbelt towns that I had found no time to visit the rural areas. However, my employment with the Ndola Municipal Council was terminated in October 1951, by a Council resolution. I then toyed with the idea of touring some rural areas, and said so in a press interview. The sacking decision was made in full Council and this was, of course, entirely white. No reasons were given to me, but as I was not on the permanent staff, none had to be given.

The necessity to tour rural areas occurred to me when we were being bullied by Provincial Commissioner Billing. He kept telling us that we had no knowledge of what people thought or wanted in the villages as, unlike the 'officials that you are so fond of condemning, Zukas had never visited a village'. He was almost right, and I decided to make good this omission now that I had all the time in the world.

I had no vehicle, so I had to do the next best thing, tour on a bicycle like district officers were doing. I chose a village south-east of Ndola, because a friend, Peter Nyeleti, with whom I once travelled to Chipata, came from this village. He agreed not only to go there to arrange the meeting, but also to cycle there with me a week later to show me the way. Peter was working for a transporter firm as a spanner-boy (a motor mechanic's assistant) and was an uneducated fellow, with whom I kept in touch to know feelings at grass-roots level.

We set out from Ndola one Sunday morning in the humid November heat, with me cycling behind Peter along a bush footpath. Whenever I asked Peter how far we still had to go, he answered 'not very far'. I soon learnt that this could mean many miles. As we were climbing a rise, with thick grass on either side of us and no village in sight, Peter suddenly stopped in front of me. 'Is the village here?' I asked hopefully as he turned to face me. 'No', he answered and his hand shot to his rear pocket in a premeditated manner, as if he had been planning this moment for a long time.

A chill ran down my spine and a thought went through my head that this could be a pre-arranged job. Peter might have been paid to do me in by his employer, who was a well-known Federationist. He had handed over to Welensky a copy of a Rhodesia Study Club pamphlet, which I had sent to Peter in 1949 through his employer's postal box. (The same employer, Mr Len Catchpole, was caught gun-running for Tshombe from the Federation to the Congo by United Nations forces and arrested there during the attempted separatism by Katanga after Congo's independence. He was doing it for money, but, no doubt, also out of sympathy for Katangese separatism.)

I stared apprehensively at Peter as he was withdrawing his hand from his back trouser pocket. I remembered occasions when fellow Europeans had warned each other never to trust an African and not to get too friendly with one. What Peter pulled out, however, was not a gun or knife, but something green and flat, a hard cover pocket notebook. 'Can you give me reference?', he begged rather diffidently. (Such books with employers' references were in common use for seeking work). An odd situation for seeking a reference, but we were *really* near the village this time and Peter must have felt that this was his last chance to ask me for it before politics infringed on our privacy. Fortunately, I knew from our joint trip to Fort Jamieson that he was a good spanner boy and I was, therefore, able to write so in his little notebook.

My arrival was expected at Chief Chiwala's village, which had an historical connection with the Arab slave trade. I addressed about fifty people in Kiswahili, in which I was fluent as a result of my service with the Kings African Rifles in East Africa. I found the response against Federation as strong there as in Ndola and other Copperbelt towns. Indeed, it was more vehement because I was told 'only we haven't guns, if we had guns we would stop Federation'. I replied that Federation could be defeated without guns, if we united and planned mass action, like civil disobedience, strikes and demonstrations.

As part of our campaign against Federation, our committee in Ndola encouraged our members to stand for election to the African Urban Advisory Council, which was being expanded. In the election our candidates were all successful and were able to influence the work of its hand-picked Working Committee on Federation. In a letter to Marjory Nicholson, secretary of the Fabian Society Colonial Bureau, Fox-Pitt commented on the success of our committee as follows.

> This committee scored a triumph by having its manifesto accepted by the African Urban Advisory Council, a government sponsored body, as their resolution on Federation. The Acting Provincial Commissioner is very angry. The official Federation Discussion Group keeps on trying to vote itself out of existence, or to co-opt the Anti-Federation Committee as members, but is not allowed to as it is feared that it will adopt the Action Committee's manifesto as its findings. (See letter No 22, Fox–Pitt papers at SOAS.)

Our campaign in Ndola against colour bar practices, which were widespread not only in the private sector but also in government institutions started with the latter. A glaring example was the post office counter. Unlike in South Africa during the apartheid period, where such counters were defined for 'Europeans Only' or for 'Non-Europeans Only', government in Northern Rhodesia achieved segregation at the postal counter in a more discreet way. There was at the post office one long counter with two server positions, far enough apart to avoid contact between the two queues. One position was unlabelled, while the other had a notice board above it, saying: 'African Counter: all types of business'. There might at times be a queue at the latter counter stretching to the post office entrance door, with no-one at the unlabelled position. The practice seemed to have been generally accepted and those who could not read English were assisted by the postmaster general providing an African to serve at the labelled position and a European (usually a woman) at the unlabelled position. There could be no mistaking as to what was required of a person requiring Her Majesty's Postal Services.

One of our committee, Nephas Tembo, required such services. So we suggested that he obtain them from the unlabelled position while some of us waited outside. Nephas duly ignored the notice meant for his guidance and approached the unlabelled position. Before he could indicate his requirements, in his good English, the European lady screamed at him to go to the other counter. We rushed in to witness this incident. Nephas was the son of a police officer in a special unit stationed near Ndola - Bwana Mkubwa. He was born in 1928 in Lundazi in the Eastern Province and had received some of his education in Southern Rhodesia. He was working as a book-keeper with a trading agency and I took a special interest in him. He would question me on the wisdom of advocating self-government 'since we have no African professionals like engineers, architects, etc.' I explained that if we advocated it now, it would take time to achieve and by then some professionals would be trained.

It so happened that we chose a day for this test when Mr David Wood, from *The Times* (of London) was in Ndola, covering the Federation issue. Not surprisingly, the notice above the labelled position disappeared the next day. Satisfied with our success in the conversion of the postmaster to non-racialism and to more efficient use of his services, we decided to show our achievement to Dauti Yamba when he arrived in Ndola to visit us. He, too, at our urging, proceeded to buy some stamps from the counter position served by the European lady, only to be told that the other position (though now unlabelled) was there to deal with him! Mr Yamba then proclaimed his status and promised the lady that she would hear more of this event. On his return to Lusaka, Dauti Yamba had a similar experience of colour bar practice at a bank there and made his embarrassments public.

Soon after the post office incidents, Jonathan Chivunga, who was working as a typist in the provincial administration offices, brought me a copy of a confidential circular from Acting Provincial Commissioner Billing to his senior (white) staff. Billing wrote of an incident in a butcher's shop where Tom Mtine, an African accountant, had been refused the purchase of meat unless he went to the rear window, the outlet serving Africans. Pigeon-hole shopping for Africans was widely practised in the first class shopping streets in all towns until a full-scale boycott campaign by Congress caused it to be abandoned some years later. Mr Billing's lament was that with incidents like this 'no wonder Zukas is developing such a following'. Clearly, he regretted these colour bar practices. While I appreciated his grudging recognition of my successes, I thought that with the help of his district commissioner, Kennedy Trevaskis, he could have urged the governor to introduce measures to eliminate colour bar practices. However, if he did so, he would not have been successful because the governor, Gilbert Rennie, was all for not upsetting the settlers as Fox-Pitt found in Fort Jamieson.

Fox-Pitt, in a letter to Marjorie Nicholson of the Colonial Bureau of the Fabian Society, gives this thumb-nail sketch of Billing and his relationship with me:

> he (Billing) has a visible sense of importance and takes the line of being a plain blunt man. No politician, loyal to a fault and all that, he has a clever wife.... Billing admitted the influence Zukas had with Africans. He couldn't get Zukas out of his head. It was pathetic, this strongly entrenched senior official having such fear of a twenty five year old stateless Lithuanian.... (See Letter No. 21 at SOAS).

The Ndola committee also discussed the future of the country without the proposed Federation. While I stood for self-government, other members of the Anti-Federation Action Committee thought we should demand continued, but genuine protectorate status, leading eventually to self-government. Commander Fox-Pitt was of this opinion. There was a general feeling even in our committee that the African people of the territory were not yet ready for self-government. Indeed, with so few people educated to advanced levels, they may not have been. However, I argued that by the time our slogan of votes for all took root, self-government would be possible and it was up to us to educate people towards it. I had a discussion on this topic with Nephas Tembo, one of our committee members who was about to be sent by his father for further education to Cape Town. I am not sure whether I convinced him then, but in 1964 he was appointed a deputy minister on the territory attaining independence, and must have by then been convinced by events!

Trade unions were now legal, not only for whites, but also for Africans. Although Mr W Comrie was officially the latter's advisor, I had frequent meetings with Lawrence Katilungu, Robinson Puta, Simon Kaluwa and Namitengo, the African Mineworkers' leaders, on trade union matters. The delegation that was travelling to Britain as guests of the British National Union of Mineworkers came to see me before boarding their plane in Ndola. However, apart from keeping in close touch with my old friend and mentor, Bob Robertson, I deliberately avoided any direct contact with European Mineworkers, including their progressive secretary, Frank Maybank. He was back in Northern Rhodesia after exile in Britain for the duration of the war. While in Britain Frank had got Lord Citrine, a member of the government, to look into his case. When Lord Citrine called for Maybank's file, he found an item mentioned in the index missing. It took some perseverance to get the Colonial Office to find and hand over the missing item. It was a Northern Rhodesian police report, which said: 'We are giving Maybank enough rope to hang himself'. He used to keep in touch with Fox-Pitt, but I avoided contacts with Frank, because I took the view that the European mineworkers were Welensky's constituency and pro-Federation. They were mistakenly opposed to African advancement in the industry, while hiding behind the slogan of equal pay for equal work. A South African Communist, Jack Hodgson, had worked on the Copperbelt before the war, but did not manage to convert the European union to non-racism.

As an integral part of our committee's campaign against the proposed Federation we were early fighters on the gender issue! Our study group and our public meetings had been attended only by men, so I proposed that we encourage women to attend also. The committee agreed without hesitation, but thought it advisable to discuss this, first, at a public meeting and to get approval for this risky step. At the subsequent public meeting in the Welfare Hall in the Ndola Location some thought this very risky indeed! 'Why?' I asked, surprised. 'Why', replied Mr Adam Frog, a middle-aged scrap dealer and a hand-picked member of the Urban Advisory Council, 'I will tell you why: we once had a problem with a district commissioner who was pushing us around and he addressed a gathering in the village where women were also present. When he demanded too much from us and we men just sat without uttering a word, some women suddenly shouted "are you all going to behave like men or not?" and then there was a riot and the kapasus (district commissioners' orderlies/messengers) had to intervene to protect the DC. Later we all got into trouble from this. I am against women at our meetings!' Despite Mr Frog's warning, we managed to persuade the meeting that women should be allowed to attend future meetings.

Giving women permission to enter was one thing: to get them to attend, the committee recognised, was quite another. For the next meeting Alick Kafunda undertook to encourage his wife to attend and break the ice. She duly did, and came in very shyly to sit at the rear of the hall. Once the meeting got underway without protest at this incursion, a few more women who were waiting outside also came in. At subsequent meetings women frequently attended, but I do not recall any of them speaking from the floor. (There would come a time when women would not only speak at public meetings, but lead in demonstrations, as when they confronted the colonial secretary, Ian McLeod, in Lusaka in 1962.)

I devoted my energies to opposing Federation, which I thought likely to be imposed on us unless the people were organised on the basis of mass action: demonstrations, strikes, mass meetings and non-co-operation with the colonial government. The proponents of Federation condemned this as Communism and, since the world was at a critical stage in the Cold War, anti-Communism would pay off, not only with British Tory opinion, but also with some Labour and Liberal opinion in the UK., and certainly with Europeans in Northern Rhodesia. I did have a good deal of support from *The Guardian* in South Africa, which was edited by Communists. I sent them several reports of events in Northern Rhodesia and I organized the sale of the paper on the streets of Ndola.

Although I was seen by the colonial administration and the Welensky camp as a trained and dangerous Communist, I could more accurately have been regarded as a Northern Rhodesian nationalist, as far as my *actual* activities were concerned. I certainly had no time to preach Communism, or socialism for that matter. I did regard myself as a Marxist, but in the absence of a Communist or socialist party, I did not need to make the choice of joining one. However, the cold war had led to fairly simplistic thinking amongst our British civil servants. Fox-Pitt gives us this little tale:

> When Comrie, the British T.U.C. advisor to the Northern Rhodesian government on trade unions, arrived Stubbs was sure that he was a Communist. He thought all trade unionists were Communist. He said to Comrie's wife "why isn't your husband wearing his red tie?".

Stubbs was then commissioner of labour. The description of me as a trained Communist is contained in a letter to Fox-Pitt from his close friend Roland Hudson, who had left Northern Rhodesia after a stretch as secretary for native affairs to take up a senior post in the Colonial Office in London. (See Fox Pitt papers at SOAS, London).

After being sacked by the Ndola Municipal Council, I started practising as a structural engineer on my own and was given work by some architects. Jake and I were busy building a house for our family as an investment and were living in the already-built servants quarters. We were also making our own slop-moulded burnt clay bricks and getting up in turn during the nights to ensure that the fires in the kilns did not die down. We produced several hundred thousand bricks, enough for two large houses.

When I visited my parents in Luanshya, they would beg me to abandon politics for the sake of the family. They were being shunned by fellow Europeans and there were complaints from the Jewish community that my activities were having negative effects on their members' welfare. While I sympathised with my parents and even the Jewish community, I had to tell them that for me African interests were paramount and that I could not compromise. Jake, on the other hand, was very supportive and assisted me wherever possible.

I lost many European friends on the Copperbelt as a result of my political activities, some because they thought seeing me would reflect badly on them in government eyes (including local government) and would affect the award of contracts. Unfortunately, this loss was *not* made good by intimate socialising with my African political colleagues: society was then too socially stratified on a racial basis for that. Fox-Pitt suffered a similar fate in Kitwe. Our African colleagues, on the other hand, had full support, not only from their extended families, but also from African society at large. *The Central African Mail*, edited by Dr Alexander Scott who was liberal on race issues but, at the time, supported Federation, introduced a little anti-semitism to muddy the waters, when it referred to me as a 'stateless Lithuanian Jew' in some of its articles.

There were some notable exceptions amongst the Europeans. I have already referred to Ian Hess. There was also Leon Mow, an Ndola businessman who served with me in the 3rd KAR in Ethiopia and Lorna Gore-Browne and Major John Harvey, who even sent me an invitation to their wedding at Shiwa Ngandu. Both Fox-Pitt and I declined our invitations to this wedding because we knew that the governor, a friend of Sir Stewart Gore-Browne, would attend and we did not want to cause embarrassment. Fox-Pitt had been a long-time friend of Sir Stewart while I had been friendly with Lorna since 1944 and with John Harvey since 1943, when we trained together in the East African forces. My work colleagues, who included a young English-speaking Afrikaner woman secretary at the Ndola Municipal Council and the town engineer, a South African, as well as the town architect, remained very friendly.

Being a gregarious person, I felt my social isolation, but this did not affect my political militancy. Militancy was also made easier by my being single and not having to worry about the effects on a wife and children of my activities. As for the welfare of parents and siblings, I must have known in my heart of hearts that whatever the authorities might do to me, they were sufficiently fair-minded not to molest them. It also helped to know that my family were not dependent on employers and that their shop in Luanshya relied on African rather than European patronage.

The above notwithstanding, there were many guilts, not least concerning Mrs Sinclair, the teacher in Luanshya who encouraged me to go for secondary education and not to seek employment on the mines after completing Form II. Mrs Sinclair had treated me almost as a son and had those high hopes of my following in the footsteps of Jewish immigrants in South Africa who made their fortunes on the Rand and then became philanthropists. I always wanted to explain myself to her but somehow never did.

On 30 January 1952, the first issue of *The Freedom Newsletter* was published. Its editorial board consisted of the following members of the Ndola Anti-Federation Action Committee: Nephas Tembo, Simon Zukas, and Justin Chimba. Seven closely-typed foolscap pages made up the newsletter. The first issue set out to show that we were not alone in opposing the federal proposals. It quoted from *The New Statesman and Nation* and from a pamphlet published in America by a Council of Christian Churches. It also quoted a statement by the Union of Democratic Control. This was probably the first attempt in Northern Rhodesia at a free non-settler and non-government press.

With the drive for Federation not abating from the Welensky camp nor from the officials, our committee intensified its efforts by holding meetings and conferences in the major Copperbelt centres. At Luanshya the meeting was chaired by Mr Musumburwa and despite the chairman's lukewarm opposition to the federal proposals, the meeting enthusiastically supported our committee's stand. (Mr Musumburwa later became a territorial minister for African Education in the short-lived Federation and was responsible for the expulsion of many students from Munali, the territory's elite secondary school, for their firm political stand against the Federation). I spoke at this meeting and what I said was duly recorded by the police and brought up later at my trial as evidence of my advocacy of mass action.

At Kitwe a meeting was organized for us by Mungoni Liso who later became the deputy president of Congress and a deputy minister under Kaunda after the creation of the one party Second Republic. Chingola became the venue for a major conference chaired by LM Lipalile. I publicly advocated for a general strike against the imposition of Federation, but Robinson Puta, vice-president of the African Mineworkers Union advised that such a strike should be prepared for, but secretly. This was a widely held view, that all would be prepared and one day, on a call from the president of Congress, the African workers from the towns and European farms would pack up and return to their villages. This was a naive view and much of my efforts were devoted to dispelling it. I emphasised the need for organization and a protest of short duration in the towns and on the commercial farms. A meeting in Mufulira came to life when Mathew Mwendapole rose to support our stand against Federation and spoke in favour of strike action. Mathew later became a prominent leader of the African Mineworkers Union.

Government was preparing for a visit from the British prime minister, Clement Attlee and a conference at Victoria Falls, so we called a conference in Kitwe to coincide with it. The Northern Rhodesia African Representative Council was represented at the Falls Conference by John Moffat, appointed by the governor to represent African interests, Dauti Yamba and Paskale Sokota. The conference made little progress and closed without conclusion on the announcement of a general election in Britain. During the conference there was a declaration by John Moffat that Africans in Northern Rhodesia would be prepared to consider Federation after the policy of partnership between the races had been defined and, as so defined, put into progressive operation. Yamba and Sikota later repudiated this declaration, as did the African Representative Council, by which Moffat was supposed to have been mandated. His good work for the Colonial Office was later rewarded with a knighthood, but the meeting of the ARC, where Moffat tried to get his partnership declaration endorsed, broke up in disorder and he 'had to make do with a disintegrating meeting' (See Fox-Pitt Notebook at SOAS).

Clearly, Moffat had given the ARC mandate a tilt of his own - towards

Federation. He, no doubt, regretted this later when he became so disenchanted with the Federation that he resigned from the African Affairs Board in 1960 in protest at Welensky's disregard of the Board's views. (The Ndola AFAC had warned that this Board would be of no value in protecting African interests). Partnership became a big issue as Federation was being imposed and during the Federation's short life. Sir Godfrey Huggins (later Lord Malvern), first Federal prime minister, defined it as the partnership between a rider and his horse. This may have satisfied most of his Rhodesian whites, but naturally annoyed all Africans and British liberal opinion.

Our *Freedom Newsletter* commented at length on the futility of this partnership definition as a basis for accepting the proposed federal scheme, but we did not reject partnership, as such. We proposed our own simple principles on which such a definition should be based:

1. Each adult person, whatever his or her race or economic status, should have an equal say in the governing of the country.
2. No citizen should be subjected to discrimination on account of his or her race.

We also warned that as far as Federation was concerned, 'the leopard was not dead; only wounded' and that we must not slacken our efforts. When the Victoria Falls Conference ended, it appeared as if the drive for Federation had reached stalemate and the campaign against Federation therefore sagged. However, after the British election of 1952, which brought the Tories into power, the new secretary of state for the colonies, Oliver Lyttelton (later Lord Chandos), lost no time in declaring the Tory government's support for Federation and its intention to bring it about.

In response to this declaration, we started preparing for a national conference in Lusaka, called by Congress, which had been under Nkumbula's leadership since August, 1951. Chimba and I were chosen as delegates from the Ndola Anti-Federation Action Committee, but we had difficulty in funding the trip. With only five pounds in our coffers, travel by air was out of the question and so was travel by road as we had no vehicle. The train was the only answer, but even for that our funds were insufficient unless one of us were to go by 4th class. I would, naturally, have to go by second-class as the lowest class available for a European. Could we accept that Chimba should go by 4th class?

All, except one committee member and myself, thought that this would involve such a loss of face for Ndola that Chimba had better not go at all, unless more money could be collected for him to go by third class. Best Kofie settled the argument about loss of face. 'By me, 4th class is quite all right. If I arrive in Lusaka, people will not say Kofie came by 4th class; they will say Kofie came by train!' (This simplicity of outlook on status, appearances, etc. alas, did not prevail after independence. When there was to be a meeting in Lusaka of the African Development Bank in the seventies, government imported dozens of Mercedes-Benz cars to ferry delegates. The economy was in shambles and people were starving, but on no account must we allow loss of face!)

At Lusaka, on the eve of the conference, a few of us met in Hiwa's Tearoom in Kabwata. Those present were Nkumbula, brothers Simon and George Kaluwa, Katilungu, Fox-Pitt, Chimba and myself. We agreed that the conference should adopt a tough line: the Ndola AFAC should move its resolution to set up a national body, which would prepare for a general strike to protest against the imposition of Federation.

The next day, I moved and Chimba seconded the following resolution:

> Realising that the British Tory government is about to force through Federation against the unanimous wishes of the African people, and in the absence of normal constitutional power to prevent such a move, Congress adopts the principle of mass protest action and resolves to begin a campaign to organise the people for such action. Further, Congress appoints a Supreme Action Council of nine, including five seats to be filled by the Trade Union Congress, to plan such action; this council to be empowered to issue orders for action in the name of Congress up to and including the serious step of calling for a national stoppage of work. The council shall have the power to call for mass action at any moment during the time of the federation crisis that they think tactically wise.

Various speakers supported this motion, including Lawrence Katilungu, president of the African Mineworkers Union, who supported it very vehemently. It was passed without any votes against, but Godwin Mbikusita Lewanika, former president of Congress, left the meeting after the resolution was moved. On his departure, a tall man with a white scarf around his neck jumped up and shouted: 'Long live Harry - death to the traitor'. This man, who had not spoken before, was Kenneth Kaunda from Chinsali and the Harry he was referring to was Harry Mwaanga Nkumbula, the then president of Congress; the traitor, no doubt, was Lewanika. We later learnt that, accompanied by a senior government official, Lewanika flew to Barotseland to persuade the Litunga to support Federation.

Fox-Pitt thought this visit might have needed some reinforcement, because

> the governor, Rennie, went to Barotseland and told the Paramount Chief that he must declare in favour of Federation or England would repudiate the Barotse treaty. The Paramount Chief told me this himself. He said that it was all done in a great hurry and no time to call together his 'Parliament' so that the declaration was not constitutional. He had been afraid to say no, as the governor was very insistant (See Fox-Pitt Papers at SOAS, notebook 1).

It is also recalled by one former European civil servant that the Litunga was promised a trip to the UK to attend the Coronation in 1953 as a reward for urging his people not to involve themselves in violent opposition.

Conference went on to elect members of the Supreme Action Council. The successful list included the president, the two African members of Legco, Katilungu, Kaunda and Simon Zukas. In the vote I beat Dixon Konkola, who was then leader of the Railway Workers Union. Very soon afterwards, the two members of Legco elected to the Supreme Action Council were summoned by Edgar Unsworth, the Attorney-General, who warned them that the contemplated action by Congress would lead them into trouble. This notwithstanding, the newly-elected council met on 27 February in the small house near the Legco, allocated as offices to the MLC's, and we decided to meet again on the Copperbelt. The mood was militant, but I had no illusions about the difficulties that lay ahead, nor had I any illusions about our ability to block the imposition of Federation with a one day strike, however successful.

When Colin Legum, the *Observer* correspondent, was visiting the Copperbelt he questioned me on this issue, and I replied that even if they were defeated, the African people would at least have gone down fighting and this would stand them in good stead in future struggles. Africans had their own built-in mechanism to fortify them after a likely defeat and imposition of Federation: 'We did not agree to it and no matter how they impose it we shall not be part of it in our hearts'. This was a widely-held view.

The British government was waging a war in Malaya and steps were being taken locally to send a Nyasa KAR battalion to fight there. We saw no reason why our askaris should be used as mercenaries for Britain when Britain was about to sell-out to white settlers on Federation. *Freedom Newsletter* therefore carried an article attacking the war being waged by General Templar in Malaya.

We had won the battle for the minds and the line was holding, apart from some softening of the resolution of many Copperbelt Lozi residents under pressure from Induna Kalonga who was sent by the Litunga to influence their stand. Yet I knew we could not relax. Harry Nkumbula arrived one night to tell me that he had information that the government had plans to deport us to the Seychelles if we called the general strike.

More seriously, I was worried by reports from Fox-Pitt that Comrie was working hard to persuade Katilungu to keep the African mineworkers out of a political strike as it would result in legal action by government against their union. Katilungu was obviously persuaded to this point of view. At the next provincial meeting of the Supreme Action Council in Kitwe, he did not argue for a switch in tactics, but we could not get him to focus on the issue. This was a major set-back for our campaign. It would also prove a major set-back for the whole trade union movement in the territory.

Comrie was too short-sighted. The opting out by the mineworkers' trade union leadership from the fight against the imposition of Federation gave the African miners some gains in wages, but lost the African trade unions their leading position in the territory's politics. The trade unions had been part and parcel of the nationalist political movement, indeed they had been in the forefront. They now took a road of pure unionism and this led them down a sterile alley. Later, in the run-up to independence, Katilungu would try to recapture this lead, but it was too late. Despite his links with the Bemba royal house and financial support from right-wing white sources, he failed to gain ground against UNIP in the late fifties and early sixties. Splits would follow in the trade union movement and the unions lost out when Zambia became independent. (It would take some twenty-seven years after independence for the trade unions to regain their leading position in Zambian politics as the backbone of the Movement for Multi-Party Democracy. By then the collapsing economy reduced their room for action. Their leaders, having used the strength of the unions to gain the top positions in government then distanced themselves from unionism to deal with the country's economy as a whole.)

By contrast, Welensky made full use of the support given to him by the European mineworkers and he often threatened Britain with a Boston Tea Party on the Copperbelt. His analogy with the American Revolution was faulty, not only because there was no harbour or sea on the Copperbelt, but also because the Europeans he spoke for already had fairly good representation. However, there could be little doubt that his threat entailed an illegal act, should Federation not be acceded to by the British government. The Tory government in Britain, far from taking action against Welensky, would soon be mobilizing the local colonial authority into action against *us*.

Chapter Six
INTO EXILE

Despite the foot-dragging by Lawrence Katilungu while he was still a member of the Supreme Action Council, preparation for a general strike was proceeding apace. I was working hard for this. Justin Chimba came up with the idea of organizing the compounds on the basis of lines of houses, with a leader appointed for each line: meetings would be held of such leaders and instructions issued for the big day. Edward Mungoni Liso reported that miners in Nkana were strongly in support of strike action against the imposition of Federation, even if Katilungu was not. Not surprisingly, the authorities were also intensifying their efforts against us.

One evening, on returning home from some meeting in the location, I found our Congress president, Harry Nkumbula, waiting for me in a taxi. We had a long review of the organizational situation in the country and it did not look unhopeful. However, Harry thought that we should rescind our resolution to call a work stoppage of two days. His spies in government had seen a document which said that in the event of our calling the strike the whole Supreme Action Council would be deported to the Seychelles.

The authorities, both in Northern and Southern Rhodesia, used this tactic of leaving documents lying around to be seen by African typists when they wanted the information to act as a deterrent to the nationalists. I was not sure whether this was done in this instance, but I did my best to reassure Harry that deportation to the Seychelles might not be the worst fate that could befall us. 'Why', I said, 'when I was in the forces in Nairobi, girls from the Seychelles were very popular'. In a more serious vein, I reasoned that there was bound to be a price to pay for our planned actions, and that we should brace ourselves and conquer our fears. 'After all', I said, 'we did pass a resolution in open Congress to organize such action'. Harry, however, thought that we must remain free in order to organize. We parted without agreement when I saw him off at the railway station.

Soon after this visit from Harry, Jonathan Chivunga noticed that one of the suspected police informers, Mr Foch Manda, who lived in Kitwe, was frequently visiting Ndola. Jonathan came to tell me that he and some colleagues were aware that Foch Manda had been detailed to watch me. This came as no surprise to me, but what did come as a surprise and even shock was a letter Jonathan showed me, which said that the Star Chamber, had decided to 'do away with Manda by putting crushed glass into his food'. Manda was a relative of Jonathan's and, as a frequent visitor from Kitwe, he was bound to call upon Jonathan's hospitality while in Ndola. I persuaded Jonathan against this planned move and pointed out that once we knew what Foch Manda was up to, we could watch him. I then sought out Jonathan's close friend, Reuben Kamanga, and asked him to make sure that their plan was abandoned. Assassination of enemies was not in my political book. Quite apart from the moral aspects, the ramifications on our movement of such an assassination could have been disastrous and the government could have used it to ban us.

It was not long after this report from Chivunga that I was paid a visit by Foch Manda, ostensibly to buy some back-copies of our newsletter. I sold him some and asked my clerk, John Kalima, to follow Manda discreetly after he left my office. John did - all the way to the police station! So Chivunga was right, but I was glad that he listened to my advice. (Reuben Kamanga became the country's vice-president at independence and Jonathan, after leading the nationalist wing of the trade union movement, became Zambia's ambassador to China).

On the morning of 29 March 1951, I was on the roof of the house Jake and I were building discussing the erection of roof trusses with our foreman carpenter, when I was called down to meet some visitors. The visitors turned out to be two Special Branch officers: one was Superintendent Hicks, later to become a Federal police commissioner and, on Zambian independence, the territory's chief of police. I was shown a document to the effect that the Attorney-General was proceeding to ask the Chief Justice for a recommendation to the governor for my deportation from Northern Rhodesia on the grounds that I was:

>.........a danger to peace and good order;
>.........inciting Africans against Europeans;
>.........acting against the lawfully constituted authority in the colony.

They proceeded to search my quarters, took away some papers and then asked me to follow them to my office in town for a similar process. I was told that I should travel by train to Livingstone, where there would be a hearing in the High Court. The police would make all travel and accommodation arrangements.

With the fate of Mr Elwell and Major Lee Tatersall always in mind, and particularly since the Tory government, which had declared its intention to proceed with the Federation, took over in Britain, I had been expecting some move against me - some action in the courts. I recall being particularly upset by the allegation that I was inciting Africans against Europeans. My association with the South African Communist Party had taught me not to indulge in such politics and to react against those of my colleagues who might. Non-racism was a cardinal point in my political philosophy. Fox-Pitt once told me that our use of the word 'settlers', when referring to the Europeans of Northern Rhodesia, was seen by the authorities as anti-European. I defended its use by saying that by the same token one could say that the use of the word 'natives' should be seen as anti-African. With hindsight, I can see that the use of the word 'settlers' could have been found offensive by those Northern Rhodesian whites who had made the country their permanent home, but to be accused of inciting Africans against Europeans was painful.

While the other two grounds might be used, with justification, to describe my activities, they were not, in my view, grounds for deportation. I therefore decided to instruct a lawyer and to be ready to go into the witness box to argue that my activities were not only not illegal, but were *justified* in view of what the government was doing and proposed to do against a people which had Protectorate status.

After informing my committee in Ndola of these developments, I travelled to Luanshya to tell my parents and Bob Robertson. From there I went to Kitwe to inform Fox-Pitt and Katilungu. My parents were shocked and I had to calm my mother from becoming hysterical. Back in Ndola in the evening, with the help of Ian Hess I phoned Johannesburg to speak to Bram Fischer, the South African Communist Queen's Counsel, who later would defend Mandela and would himself be sentenced to life imprisonment after leading the underground struggle for a year. I found that Sam Kahn, South African ex-MP and attorney, was with Bram. I told them of the pending court case and explained that I would brief Mr John Grayling, a solicitor in Livingstone, to appear for me. He had once been recommended to me as likely to be sympathetic. Grayling had come out to Southern Rhodesia with the RAF during the Second World War where he was known to be progressive. I had hoped that Bram would be able to act for me with Grayling. However, Bram explained that he was not accredited to the British Bar and suggested that I ask DN Pritt, QC to come out from Britain to act with Grayling if I could get a postponement of the hearing.

At the railway station in Ndola I was seen off by Jake and some political colleagues, including Bob Robertson, and I then travelled overnight to Livingstone to face the government in court. Before leaving Ndola I sent a telegram to Professor Julius Lewin in Johannesburg. He and I had been corresponding as he knew the Copperbelt situation, having been sent up by the South African Institute of Race Relations after the 1940 African miners' strike and the killing of 17 miners. In 1941 he had published a pamphlet entitled *The Colour Bar in the Copperbelt*.

This telegram and one I sent from Livingstone to colleagues in Ndola were to become the basis for a contempt of court charge against me, since they were taken to imply that I wanted *pressure* to be exerted on the court for a postponement of the hearing. The judge refused our application for a postponement and court proceedings lasted two days, with government calling several witnesses to outline my activities. Witnesses included Harry Nkumbula and Godwin Mbikusita Lewanika, president and past president of Congress respectively. The former was asked to confirm that he had received a letter from me urging him to get back to the line of rail from Namwala to organize the people, now that the Tory government had declared itself in favour of Federation. Nkumbula did so without allowing the Attorney-General, who was leading for the government, to twist his answers to suit the government's line that he was being given orders by me!

Lewanika was used by the government to reveal what I had said in the meeting of leaders in Wusakili, Kitwe, at the beginning of our anti-Federation campaign. This was the meeting that had been recorded by the police Special Branch with a hidden microphone. Lewanika's evidence was truthful and I did not deny it. government could have used the transcript that they had, but that would have revealed a police practice of which they were in those days somewhat ashamed. When I instructed my lawyer to ask the Attorney-General for the transcript of the recording, my lawyer could not believe that there was such a thing!

However, he followed my instructions and was told at first that there was no transcript and, on insisting, he was answered that 'in any case, we are not using it'. After insisting further he was asked to come back several hours later, when he was presented with a wad of newly-typed foolscap pages. On checking through this transcript we found that nothing in Mbikusita Lewanika's evidence was contrary to what was recorded, so we decided not to refer to the typed transcript in court. Unlike Nkumbula, Lewanika seemed to be a willing witness for the government, although he was a former president of Congress. Whether he was legally obliged to appear as a witness was in doubt as this was a hearing not a normal court case.

While I was in Livingstone, I met several times with Nkumbula to discuss my case and future tactics of Congress against Federation. After two days, Justice Lewey found that I *was* 'a danger to peace and good order' and recommended my deportation on that ground *only*. He rejected the other two grounds. Grayling gave notice of appeal.

During the hearing the Attorney-General referred to telegrams I had sent and said they would be subject to contempt of court proceedings. He also referred to comments that appeared in *The Livingstone Mail*, owned by Dr Alexander Scott. *The Mail* of 4 April thought that 'almost the whole of colonial Africa will be focused on Livingstone today. It promises to be one of the most interesting inquiries ever held in Northern Rhodesia'. It was not, however, to these remarks that the Attorney-General was referring, but with what followed under a column headed "IN PASSING" by Observer:

> So our friend Simon Zukas is being brought to trial at last. Most of us have wondered how much longer he would be permitted to pursue his nefarious practices without apprehension.
> A local solicitor to whom I spoke the other day expressed the opinion that the Crown must have built up a pretty solid case against him. An acquittal at this stage simply cannot be risked. It would strengthen his hand immeasurably and send him back to his Copperbelt stronghold a far bigger hero than he is already.
> Whether he will be deported or not will depend to a large extent on the evidence brought against him and the way in which it is handled in Court.
> I am inclined to think that it is a great pity we could not have hired a mobile

Gestapo unit to eliminate him without fuss one dark night. He would probably be forgotten inside six months. As it is now there is always the danger that constitutional action will make a martyr of him in the eyes of his many supporters.

The editor of *The Mail* appeared in the magistrate's court and was fined ten pounds. I, too, appeared in the same court for contempt of court for the telegrams I had sent to my friends and was fined fifty pounds. In Ndola, Reuben Kamanga and Noah Sambona were each fined ten pounds or two weeks in gaol for the telegrams they had sent to Justice Lewey, demanding a postponement of the hearing to allow my chosen Queen's Counsel to arrive. Being unable to find what for them were enormous sums of money, they both went to gaol for two weeks and became our nationalist movement's first PGs, (Prison Graduates). Nephas Tembo, protesting by telegram from his school in Cape Town, was beyond the reach of Northern Rhodesian prosecutors.

Immediately the court proceedings were over I was arrested by the police, taken to collect my suitcase from the railways hostel I had been staying in and driven to the Livingstone prison. There I was frisked, my pockets emptied out, a list made of all my chattels, fingerprinted and taken to a small courtyard, where there was one cell and a separate room with a bucket latrine and steel bathtub. It was late afternoon so I was given some tea and locked into the cell.

The cell was three metres long and two and a half wide with an iron bedstead and a small wooden table. What the cell lacked in width, it made up in height: the distance from the floor to the rafters was at least four metres. The generous room height made a ceiling unnecessary for security. Corrugated iron roofing was just discernible over the forty watt light bulb suspended close to the rafters. I spent the next eight months in this cell and I grew accustomed to all its details, especially the small window, which allowed in some light and air, but was located too far up to allow one to look out, even if one stood the only chair on the table and climbed up on top of it. The solid wooden door had a small peep-window in it, through which the guards shone their torches when checking during the night, which they did several times. Beneath the door, at floor level, there was a channel to allow the water to run out when the floor was swilled down - and allow in a large rat for frequent nocturnal visits. I suppose it could also serve another purpose if you got caught short.

That first night was the worst. As if it was not difficult enough to get used to these strange surroundings and get some sleep, the guards seemed to make this impossible by coming at hourly intervals and flashing their torches. It took a few days before the African guards accepted that I had no intention of escaping, but had every intention of fighting an appeal. After a while, our relations were so good that one of the sergeants even brought me a late-night snack of hard-boiled eggs with fried onions prepared by his wife, as a sign of sympathy and this strengthened my spirits no end.

My spirits were, in fact, growing stronger by the day, as news came through that the Copperbelt had reacted to my imprisonment. That, together with the reaction in Ndola, I found heartening. After all, it was not my personal situation that was of concern, but whether the people for whom I had been making sacrifices were standing by me and not allowing the government to hoodwink them into believing that justice had been dished out to a wrong-doer.

On the Copperbelt

> a spontaneous strike broke out at Nkana by miners in protest against this. Rhokana management declared a dispute and demanded the dismissal of the Union Chairman and Secretary, Jamieson Chapoloko and Comrade Chewe Another victim was Edward Liso who was a District Secretary of Congress but employed by the company as Medical Assistant at Wusakile. (See MR Mwendapole, *A History of the Trade Union Movement in Zambia*).

Fox-Pitt, who was in Nkana at the time, has recorded the events as follows:

> "When Simon Zukas was finally arrested there was very nearly a general strike, but Katilungu and Simon Kaluwa worked hard against it and stopped it. At the same time the police nearly mutinied, but the African sergeants held the force together. It would have shaken the government more than anything. It would be interesting to know if they knew how close a mutiny came." (Letter 20, Fox-Pitt. papers at SOAS).

Fox-Pitt was living near Nkana at the time and in close touch with officials of the African Mineworkers Union and Congress. As an ex-district commissioner of the area he also had his contacts amongst Africans in the police force. Katilungu and Kaluwa had by then disassociated themselves from the Supreme Action Council and were trying to keep the union out of politics in order to safeguard it from de-recognition.

My cell was normally used to house a prisoner condemned to death so, in order for me *not* to be in solitary confinement, a European railway pensioner was employed by the prison authorities to keep me company during the day. He would pace around with me in the twenty metre square courtyard, play draughts and talk with me. As time went on he was instructed to take me for a walk around a parade-ground, where African policemen were being drilled and trained for riot control. This was outside the prison grounds.

Since I was allowed to buy food from outside, I made arrangements with a Livingstone cafe to send me one main meal daily. The food was cold by the time it reached me, yet more palatable than the prison food. A doctor would come in for a weekly visit, but never found me needing his services. I was once visited by two Justices of the Peace, one of whom was Maurice Rabb, the newly installed mayor of Livingstone. Later in life I joined him in a large farming enterprise and we spent many days touring ranches together and often discussed this early encounter and touched on Maurice's relationship with Federal Prime Minister, Roy Welensky. Maurice said he had urged Welensky to lead the Federation on a liberal course, but Welensky thought that this would cause a revolt of the white Copperbelt mineworkers against him and his party. Fox-Pitt and I knew at the time that this would be the case and that is precisely why we had to fight the federal proposals: because their proposed franchise would give a veto to the white mine and railway workers against any liberal tendencies in the Federation.

Fred Chandler, my appointed companion, would tell me how he was recruited from London by Rhodesia Railways when he came out of the army after the First World War. He was shipped out to Rhodesia to be trained as a truck fitter, one of those nasty people who used to wake up the train passengers in the middle of the night by banging with an iron hammer on the carriage wheels while the train was in a station. Fred explained that the ring would tell them whether the axle had developed a 'hot box' and the carriage should be taken out of line to have the bearing replaced. On retirement, Fred had reached the post of leading truck fitter and would deal with carriage and wagon retrieval after accidents. He was trained on the job and had only a primary education. I became quite fond of Fred as time went on and saw him as typical of a large section of the European population of the Rhodesias.

When the African warders addressed me in English, Fred would get upset as he thought that they should use 'kitchen kaffir, their own language', yet Fred always tried to assure me that he was a liberal settler; as was his wife Annie. 'Why, Annie always cuts off the end crust from a new loaf of bread and gives it to our native servant'! I had to agree that this put her in the liberal camp. However, some weeks later I was surprised to hear from Fred another explanation for Annie's liberal generosity with bread crusts. Fred, seeing me about to eat the end crust (my favourite piece) of a loaf of bread which had arrived with my main meal, urged me to discard it, as it 'always gets dirty from handling by natives'!

One day Fred arrived at about five in the morning instead of eight, his usual time, and urged me to get dressed. 'Why, am I being released?' I asked. 'No, we are only going for a walk outside'. Once out of the prison grounds, I saw some cars near the prison gates and was then told that a hanging was about to take place. I was being spared the condemned man's cries, since the place of execution was on the other side of one of my courtyard walls. I was not, however, spared from lying awake all the following night thinking about the event that had taken place next door.

Fred told me of the tough struggles the white railway workers had had against the BSA Company, the owners of the Rhodesia Railways, and how he had Jackie Keller to thank for the reasonable standard of living he and his family enjoyed. Jackie, as I well knew, was the white railway workers' leader. To show me what the railway workers had been up against over the years, Fred brought me the report of the board of enquiry set up to review a dispute and strike that had taken place as early as 1927.

In evidence before the Board of Enquiry, the railway administration argued as follows.

> The fact that the native is exhibiting possibilities of development, and the fact that he is already encroaching, not only on the sphere of the unskilled white but also on the sphere of the skilled man, must be apparent to everyone who is living in Rhodesia and looks about him.

This was a warning to white railway workers against their excessive demands.

The railway administration was reiterating what was stated in 1926 by Brigadier General FD Hammond, CBE in his *Report on the System of Southern Rhodesia* (Vol. 1, p.38).

> There is a very large class of so-called skilled work, which does not require skill or knowledge of a high order and can be performed by natives under periodical supervision after a short period of instruction.... The work of firing a locomotive is easily within the scope of the native.... Work requiring a much higher degree of skill than the trades mentioned is being performed by natives in many parts of Africa.
> If education of a more skilled order was given, and the native was allowed to be employed as a fully skilled tradesman, still larger economies would be effected....
> The only aspects of the case which I can discuss are the economic ones.... against these are to be weighed the social and political views.

Clearly, the white workers on the railways had to be placated for *political* reasons and the BSA Company was prepared to play its part for European political supremacy, as long as these workers did not make excessive economic demands. The African workers, on the other hand, could be denied skilled work as they had no political clout while they did not have the vote! On the copper mines of Northern Rhodesia, Africans were similarly underused in skilled work for political reasons. The black-white ratio had dropped progressively after the end of the war, as European immigration increased. Whereas in 1945 there were 8.7 African workers to each European worker, in 1955 there were 5.5 Africans to each European, a ratio even lower than on the gold mines of apartheid South Africa.

Fred and his fellow white workers would go on extracting this political price until they were forced to give way, and this would not happen while the franchise was tilted overwhelmingly in their favour, as in the federal proposals. These thoughts strengthened my feelings that I had been right to fight against the proposals tooth and nail and made it easier for me to bear my loneliness, boredom and discomfort.

Grayling, my local lawyer, had lodged an appeal and my detention would last until this was heard. Bram Fischer came up from Johannesburg to visit me and to tell me that DN Pritt, QC had agreed to come out from the UK to take my appeal. Bram's visit was ostensibly as a legal advisor, but he cheered me up enormously. I was sorry, in years to come, not to be able to do the same for him when his wife Molly died so tragically in a car accident and later, when he languished in prison for ten years in apartheid South Africa and died of cancer. Bram and I met again in London in December 1952. I had the pleasure of meeting Molly when she visited London in the mid-fifties. They were both noble Afrikaners.

With nothing to do, the days were long and the nights longer still. The night would effectively start at five in the afternoon when Fred left and I was locked into my cell. However, there were the occasional visitors like Harry Nkumbula, who was allowed in for a short visit and Reuben Kamanga, who came down from Ndola when he was released from his imprisonment for contempt of court. From them and from the local newspapers that I was allowed to receive daily, I learnt that I had not been forgotten - far from it. But the main news was that the money needed for my appeal was slow in coming in. My personal funds were exhausted. I was later to hear that some of the contributions from Africans had been badly handled and misused. An appeal fund was opened by well-wishers in South Africa and handled by Dr Guy Routh, a trade union official and academic. In Britain, a fund was opened by Sir Leslie Plummer, a Labour member of Parliament, to enable me to appeal to the Privy Council.

Since I was kept in prison some eight hundred kilometres from home, my family found it difficult to visit me. Jake came soon after my imprisonment and later my parents travelled by train from the Copperbelt for a visit. My mother broke down when she saw me. I tried hard to reassure her that all was not lost, but to no avail. Instead of cheering me up the visit left me depressed on account of the sorrow I had caused my parents. A visit from my youngest brother, Abe, helped to cheer me up. He was on his way home from school in Cape Town and had brought greetings from many of my South African friends of all colours, people like Ray and Jack Simons, Kenny Parker, Rev J Ngwevela of Langa and others. Professor Julius Lewin from Witwatersrand University, who wrote to me frequently was also a great support.

Time was dragging until Mr Pritt arrived and we travelled by plane to Salisbury, with me under police escort. There the appeal was heard by Justice Robert Tredgold, a liberal man. But despite Pritt's able argument, Tredgold found that 'an appeal did not lie', or, in lay language, that the law in the Northern Rhodesian Penal Code, under which the government had proceeded against me, did not provide for an appeal. So I went back to gaol in Livingstone to await an appeal to the Privy Council.

With my personal funds exhausted, my appeal to the Privy Council in Britain was 'in forma pauperis', as a pauper! It would take some months to prepare the grounds for appeal and have them printed, as required, on special (and expensive) paper. In the meantime, the October heat and humidity was making life in the cell unbearable at night and it was quite a relief when I was informed that I would be flown to the UK to await my appeal there. So on December 4, after nearly eight months of incarceration, I was taken to Livingstone airport and flown to London on a first class ticket! (Kofie would, no doubt, have expected people in Britain not to say: 'Zukas came by first class', but that 'Zukas came by plane'!) Since the plane was touching down in Ndola my parents were informed and they came to say goodbye to me there, with my father bringing me one hundred English pounds to start me on a new life in exile.

Before leaving Northern Rhodesia I managed to smuggle out a statement to my colleagues on the Copperbelt. It included the following:

> Federation is only one of the things that confront us. We must look further ahead.... Our African workers are unable to live on their present meagre wages: *chilimba* is now universally practised on the Copperbelt because the African worker's monthly wage is insufficient to buy a single major item of clothing. This is all a result of the Cheap African Labour policy and as Lawrence Katilungu has rightly said, "the only solution to African cheap labour is to embark on continual industrial unrest"....
> The African worker is denied a future. He cannot become a skilled worker, or rather be paid as such, because of the industrial colour bar. How long can we tolerate this system?

CHAPTER SEVEN
A LIFE IN EXILE

> This is one of the great paradoxes of exile:
> The sanctuary I have found, the very sanctuary that guarantees that a voice has survived, simultaneously cuts that voice off from direct access to the land it is responsible for keeping alive, the voice that demands to be transmitted to others.
>
> *Heading South, Looking North,* Ariel Dorfman.

The travel document with which I arrived at London Airport on 5 December 1952, stated very clearly that it was for a one-way journey to Britain. It also gave a reference to the authority for this from the Colonial Office. Apart from being told to report to the Home Office in Regents Park, London, within a week, the only difficulty I had with immigration was that of providing them with an address. This was soon solved by the appearance of an old friend from Cape Town, Alick Ross, my welcoming party, who himself was on a short visit to London and whose sister, Mrs Eileen Denton, I had informed of my arrival. Alick rushed me along 'because', he said 'the smog was coming down fast', and we managed to get into central London while there were still a few metres of visibility. Percy and Eileen Denton had arranged for me to board with a landlady in St John's Wood, a suburb in North-West London. Our rapid exodus from the airport prompted the following piece in *The Manchester Guardian* on the following day::

> Mr Zukas Arrives:
> After eight months in detention pending his deportation from Northern Rhodesia Mr Simon Ber Zukas, European vice-president of the Northern Rhodesian African National Congress flew into London Airport today and vanished into the fog. At any rate, none of those here with whom he might have been expected to communicate had heard from him by this evening and the solicitor acting for him in his appeal to the Privy Council was even unaware that Mr Zukas was in this country.

Before the murk swallowed him up, however, Mr Zukas said to a reporter at the airport: 'I am going to fight against my deportation. If my appeal is successful I am going straight back to Africa'. The petition to appeal to the Privy Council was laid on Wednesday: at the moment Mr Zukas's counsel, Mr D.N. Pritt is defending Jomo Kenyatta.

The misconception that I was vice-president of the Northern Rhodesian African Congress had crept into the overseas press during my period in gaol and on seeing it now for the first time, I wrote to correct it, pointing out that the VP was Dauti Yamba, MLC. The correction was duly published by the paper.

Socially, I was welcomed by left-wing South Africans living in London and by Commander Edgar Young, whose wife had once lived in Broken Hill (Kabwe) in Northern Rhodesia. Politically, I was drawn in by the Union of Democratic Control (UDC), which, under the influence of Basil Davidson, had organised a fund to meet the legal costs for my appeal to the Privy Council. Sir Leslie Plummer, MP, headed the appeal for funds. The UDC had a history going back to the First World War, when it was started by E.D. Morel, famous for his exposure of atrocities committed in the Congo under King Leopold of Belgium, the philosopher Bertrand Russell and a handful of others. Sir Leslie had worked in Africa, where he was in charge of the Groundnut Scheme in Tanganyika, started by the Labour government after the '39-45 War.

Basil Davidson and I were working closely together against the imposition of Federation and he had also been working on this issue with Dr Hastings Banda, a Nyasalander, then in practice as a GP in the London suburb of Kilburn. When a delegation consisting of the Congress vice-general secretary, George Kaluwa, and Chief Mpezeni arrived from Northern Rhodesia to lobby the British government against Federation, Basil suggested that we all meet at Banda's residence. Back in Northern Rhodesia I had heard of Banda and had read a pamphlet which he had jointly authored with Harry Nkumbula. At the end of our meeting Banda asked me why I joined the African Congress to fight Federation, instead of forming up with 'fellow Europeans'. By way of reply, I asked him if he was worried about contamination. To this he did not reply, but my question obviously annoyed him. (Our paths only crossed again when we were both guests at Tanganyika's independence celebrations and I found he never forgave me for challenging his chauvinism). We were to interact again after both our countries obtained independence, but that was not to be face to face (see Chapter 9).

LH Gann, in his *History of Northern Rhodesia*, thought on similar lines:

> Zukas and Fox-Pitt would have played their cards better by keeping their Congress contacts underground.... both could probably have wielded much more influence by confining their overt activities to missionary circles, and to the powerful white settler community.

Banda's chauvinism can be more easily excused than Gann's reflections: the latter failed to appreciate that Fox-Pitt and I were acting on the principle of non-racialism, as did Sir Stewart Gore–Browne, who like me became a member of Congress. (Much later, non blacks were also welcomed as members of the ANC in South Africa on the same principle of non-racialism).

The UDC sent me as a speaker to many Labour Party branch meetings around Greater London to talk on Federation. Once, I was accompanied by Mbiyu Koinange, a close relative of Jomo Kenyatta, who spoke on the situation in Kenya. It amused me to hear him denying the existence of Mau Mau and explaining that these were sounds made by Kikuyu children when playing. (Mbiyu was made a deputy minister by Kenyatta, when Kenya gained its independence.)

My appeal to the Privy Council against the deportation order did not succeed, so I had no option but to settle down in Britain and seek a long-term job as a structural engineer. The conditions of my permit to stay in Britain provided that I had to obtain Labour Department approval before accepting an offer of employment. At first I did not understand the purpose behind this: surely, having been brought to Britain, not as an investor and not at the request of family in Britain, the logic would be that I should work for my upkeep. The purpose became clear as I found a suitable post and sought the obligatory approval.

An offer by a leading consulting engineer, Dr Hajnal Konyi in London, was not approved because the pay offered was too low and therefore deemed to undermine the living standard of British workers suitable for the same post. Yet an offer by Franki Piles Ltd was deemed too high, because it deprived a British worker of a job with good pay! I despaired in this Catch 22 situation. When I was later offered a post by the Trussed Concrete Steel Company, I mentioned my previous experiences with the Labour Department. So they pitched their pay offer low enough not to deprive a British worker of a good salary, yet high enough not to undermine a British worker's standard of living. This worked and I stayed with this firm of reinforced concrete design and construct specialists for eight years, rising to be one of their senior engineers. (Sir Hugh Weeks, the managing director, and I got on well and he came to our cocktail party when I launched our consultancy practice in London with two other partners many years later. Like Sir Leslie Plummer, Sir Hugh Weeks had also been involved in the ill-fated Groundnut Scheme in Tanganyika).

While working in London, I tried not to lose touch with the political situation at home and kept receiving newspapers and writing to Congress activists, like Jonathan Chivunga and Dixon Konkola. But gradually a good deal of my time was devoted to the South African situation. Harold Wolpe was in London and intermittently, so was Lionel Forman. Bram Fischer passed through on his way back to Johannesburg from a World Peace Council Conference in Europe and soon Duma Nokwe and Walter Sisulu of the South African ANC arrived, on their way to a youth festival to be held in Bucharest. Through these I was drawn once again into activities against racist oppression in South Africa.

At home the planned two-day general strike or national days of prayer, for which I had been working until my detention, was called by Nkumbula for 1 April, 1953. It was badly organized and had very limited success. Of the African civil servants only one hundred and six stayed away from work and seventy five of these were dismissed; it was not known how many stayed away from the private sector. Unfortunately, there was a belief in the Congress leadership that all that was needed was for Nkumbula to give the call and all town workers would return to their villages. Such a call came in a Coronation Day statement by Nkumbula. He called on 'all able–bodied Africans to go back to your lands and gardens during the next rainy season before the land-grabbing settlers have taken the last inch of your soil'. (*Northern News* 8/8/53). When I was still active in Northern Rhodesia I used to emphasise the need for organization for such an event and not to leave it to chance. I have little doubt that this was the main reason why the government sought my deportation. After the strike, Nkumbula called on the people to prepare for the 'long haul'. (11/4/53 President's Statement)

Congress made a last effort to persuade the British government *not* to impose Federation by sending a delegation to London. Chiefs from Northern Rhodesia and Nyasaland presented a petition to the United Nations in June. All to no avail: the British Parliament passed the Rhodesia and Nyasaland Federation Bill and it was given royal assent in mid July 1953. When the Order in Council establishing the Federation was laid before Parliament in Britain, Attlee, on behalf of Labour, promised to make the Federation work well: the Africans in the three territories could only promise to make it *fail*. They had one weapon in their armoury that would sustain them in the years to come: Federation was clearly being launched without any meaningful African *support*. This, as a result of *our efforts* over the preceding two years, could not be hidden, internally or externally. We could congratulate ourselves on a limited success. The African stand was that the Federation had no legitimacy.

This stand was clearly admitted by Northern Rhodesia's chief secretary, AT Williams, when he said that Federation was being 'imposed by the British government', even if Africans were opposed to the scheme, because this opposition 'does not itself turn a good scheme into a bad one.' He went on to threaten: 'I have heard that... Africans have shown a tendency to question the right of government to rule in this country. That will not be tolerated'. (*Northern News* 9/7/53). In Britain African opposition against the Federation gained wide support in Labour and Liberal rank and file circles as time went on and this would stand us in good stead in bringing about the Federation's eventual demise. However, realism dictated that we prepare ourselves for a long haul.

As part of the long haul strategy, I began to mobilize funds to assist militant trade unionists from Northern Rhodesia to come to Britain for short periods of study. I succeeded in getting Dixon Konkola to come over after his release from a spell in prison. He was sentenced for leading a demonstration in Broken Hill (Kabwe). He was in bad shape mentally and took his short imprisonment as a stigma. From his letters I could sense a growing defeatism in him. My attempt to get Jamieson Chapoloko, a leading mineworker, to come to Britain was frustrated when Mr Chapoloko 'was not allowed to board an aircraft'. In response to this report in *The Times* on 13 October 1953, 'the Northern Rhodesian government's legal department.... stated that no official action had been taken to prevent the departure for England and Vienna of Mr JM Chapoloko.' (*Times* 14/10/53). Whether the action was official or not,

Chapoloko did not make the trip even though he had the air ticket. I learnt from Jake, who was living in Ndola, that an officer from Special Branch was involved in blocking Chapoloko's departure.

In London I was not aware of being watched by anyone on behalf of the government of Northern Rhodesia. However, I got a hint in Lusaka at independence that this was the case. David Mulford, an American research worker, was allowed to look through official archival material which was being brought in from the provinces for destruction in Lusaka on the eve of the hand-over of British power to Kaunda. In the material there was a reference to 'police surveillance in London of Simon Zukas for the government of Northern Rhodesia'. Mulford became aware from this material that of the prominent trade unionists 'several were to continue to maintain their contacts with Zukas in London.' (Mulford, *Zambia, The Politics of Independence*.)

I met Harry and Noreen Webber through Lionel Forman and they introduced me to Cynthia Robinson, Noreen's younger sister, who had come over from Cape Town to do a post-graduate course in art-teaching at London University. Cynthia and I had overlapped at the University of Cape Town, but our paths never crossed. She had become politically active there by joining the Modern Youth Society, the successor to the Modern World Society, of which I had been chairman from '48 to '50. We soon found we had a lot in common in our political aims, if not in our social backgrounds. She was clearly a serious girl for her age, being only twenty-two. We became friendly and started going out together. She was going off to Bucharest to attend a world youth festival in 1953 with other South Africans and one Northern Rhodesian law student, Fitzpatrick Chuula. On Cynthia's return from Bucharest we continued our friendship, which even survived a trip she had to make to South Africa to be with her mother on the death of her stepfather, Louis Epstein. On her return to London from Cape Town we decided to get married. While she was in Cape Town, at my suggestion, Cynthia arranged financial support channelled through Ray Simons for Nephas Tembo, who was studying at Langa High School. She already knew Nephas from the Modern Youth Society and I had assisted him in 1951 to go to Cape Town. Nephas became a deputy minister in 1964 and, apart from a short break, he continued in that capacity until the end of Kaunda's presidency in 1991.

Our civil marriage ceremony on Saturday, 30 January 1954, in the St

Pancras Registry Office, was attended by Cynthia's sister, Noreen, our Rhodesian friend, Marjorie Chimowitz, and a few South African friends, including Brian Bunting, who was in London for a short visit from Cape Town, and Vella Pillay, a South African resident in London. (See plate 2) The ceremony over, Cynthia and I rushed off to our political commitments: Cynthia to a meeting of the South African Students Association, then led by Frennie Ginwala (who became speaker of Parliament on the ANC coming to power in South Africa in 1993) and I to address a Labour Party branch meeting on Federation. Not marking the occasion with a reception or lunch was not our only disrespect to custom: getting married on a Saturday is offensive to religious Jews. We intended no such offence: it was more a matter of ignorance of the tradition. In any case, the bigger offence was not to be married by a rabbi.

We did not seek permission from Cynthia's father, Julius Robinson, not out of ignorance, but out of fear of refusal. He was a prominent businessman in Salisbury and Johannesburg and friendly with Sir Roy Welensky. We felt he was bound to try to frustrate our plans. When I met my father-in-law some weeks after our marriage he was particularly concerned whether our marriage was 'in community of property' or whether we had entered into 'an antenuptial contract'. His mind was on the Roman Dutch law obtaining in Southern Rhodesia and South Africa.

These matters were of no concern to us, but to put Julius' mind at ease, we decided to obtain legal opinion. Our financial and property relationship, we were told, revolved on my domicile. Dr Lauterpacht of the University of London, an expert in international law, put various questions to me to ascertain my domicile. I replied it was Northern Rhodesia. 'How can you claim that', he asked, 'when you have just been deported from there?' I insisted that it was so despite my deportation, since I believed that I would be back in Northern Rhodesia one day, and certainly within ten years, as the country would win its freedom from the recently-imposed Federation. Dr Lauterpacht doubted my certainty, but accepted that my state of mind, together with some other facts, would probably settle my domicile as still being Northern Rhodesia. On that ground Cynthia and I were, in Lauterpacht's opinion, not married in 'community of property'. That made Julius happy. (This consultation took place in mid 1954: Northern Rhodesia broke from the Federation and I returned there, with Cynthia and our two children, some *ten* years later: in February 1964, although we did not take up residence there until early 1965.)

Cynthia and I became active in the *general* campaign against colonialism. With Dr Leon Szur from South Africa, Joe Murumbi from Kenya, and a few others, I was involved in forming the Movement for Colonial Freedom (MCF) under the chairmanship of Fenner Brockway, MP. Our South and Central Africa Committee used to meet regularly in a committee room in the House of Commons. On some occasions Fenner would invite members of the Labour shadow cabinet to our discussions. Barbara Castle spoke to us on her visit to Cyprus, for which she was being castigated in the right-wing papers. Jim Callaghann attended when a delegation from the Malawi Congress Party addressed us. We organized many conferences and meetings on colonial freedom. Tony Wedgwood Benn, MP was a prominent member and so was John Horner, general secretary of the Firemen's Union.

When Joshua Nkomo and his wife were brought over by Moral Rearmament for a visit to Britain and Geneva, Tommy Fox-Pitt, who had arrived in Britain to take over as secretary of the Anti-Slavery Society, was keen that Joshua and I should meet. Moral Rearmament had plans for Joshua and they certainly did not include a meeting with me. They went out of their way to frustrate Tommy's plans. Tommy did, however, manage to sneak Joshua away from them to meet me, and not only did we discuss the fight against Federation, but Joshua, Dauti Yamba, Pascale Sokota, George Kaluwa, Chief Mpezeni and I met and had a group photo taken. Moral Rearmament failed in their plans to win Joshua away from the freedom struggle and he told me that he had accepted their offer of the trip merely to give his wife some international exposure.

Joshua Nkomo was a moderate man and, at the time, stood for partnership with the white settlers. Earlier, after his return from attending an official London conference on Federation he addressed a meeting in Bulawayo where he said that 'Federation will not embrace all races, but will be only for Europeans... I think the Europeans must be told now that we are not going to wait as juniors and that there can be no seniors and juniors in a Federation of partnership'. Joshua had the stature of a moderate leader, yet even so he had no place in Godfrey Huggins' scheme of things in Southern Rhodesia. He was a rather earthy man. In Dar es Salaam, after the official independence celebrations for Tanganyika, Joshua and I and my sister-in-law, Yvette, were sitting together at a night show at our hotel. The show included a performance by a white female stripper. On being asked what he thought of the act, Joshua's reply was: 'What's the good of a naked woman in public?' It may not have been much good to him in one respect, but it did help him to take his mind off the thorny question of whether to go home or not. His ZAPU executive had just been detained by Prime Minister Edgar Whitehead and the same fate could have been awaiting him.

Another Central African leader who came to London in the mid fifties was Harry Nkumbula. When Harry and I met at an MCF conference in the seaside town of Margate, I formed the impression that his earlier fire was fading and that he would not lead us to independence. So, after our meeting, I started to encourage more militant personalities to head the ANC. For this I was seen by Doris Lessing and by Fox-Pitt as 'divisive' (only after Kaunda split off from Nkumbula did they change their minds and become as enthusiastic for Kaunda as I was.) Some years later, after a meeting at Fox-Pitt's house in London when Nkumbula spoke of Congress' latest policy of parity of representation in the territorial Legislative Council, Mainza Chona, then still a law student in London, told me how much this pained him and that he would have to 'beg for a personal dispensation from Nkumbula to go on supporting majority rule'. Not surprisingly, when he returned home, Mainza moved away from Nkumbula's Congress and later led a party which became the foundation for the United National Independence Party (UNIP).

One of our political activities was keeping Jack and Ray Simons in South Africa informed of international *political* affairs by regularly sending them press cuttings from *The Times*. As I read *The Times* during tea-breaks at work I would mark what I thought were relevant items with a cross and in the evening Cynthia would cut them out and post them once a week. After this had been going on for some time Cynthia began complaining that I was not sticking to political items. On checking, I had to agree with her. Clearly, while my back was turned at work, my colleagues would, as a practical joke, make their contribution to the anti-apartheid cause by marking up some *non*-political items! This ceased when I explained to them the reason for my odd habit.

Ray kept in close touch with us and when she arranged for Elizabeth

Mafekeng, a South African trade unionist to go to China, we put Elizabeth up on her return through London. We were amused to hear that, on being shown through a pineapple canning factory and seeing the poor working conditions, Elizabeth told the Chinese that their workers should have protective clothing, including gumboots, as the workers had in fruit canning factories in South Africa! Elizabeth was a representative from the South African Canning Workers Trade Union, (which Ray had helped to build up) and she was not prepared to let the Chinese authorities off the hook.

Occasionally we would receive confidential documents from South African activists for passing on to international organizations. On one occasion, it all went wrong when Ray sent such a document by *registered* post. It arrived while we were away on our annual holiday. After several attempts to deliver it, the postman left a note for us to collect the letter from the post office on our return. However, after our return it was no longer at the local post office and we had to try the main London post office, only to be informed that it had been sent back to the sender in Cape Town. I guessed that the sender was Ray Simons and immediately informed her through a clandestine channel. We were now in fear that it would be intercepted by the South African authorities, with serious consequences for Ray. She was equally worried, but by careful timing, Ray managed to retrieve it from the Cape Town central post office before any damage was done. The lesson Ray learnt was not to send similar documents by *Registered Post*!

Much of my political activity was devoted to the struggle against apartheid in South Africa. In 1954 I was asked by Ruth First (a leading South African journalist, later killed by a letter bomb in Maputo) who was on a short visit to London, to become one of three representatives in the UK of the newly reformed South African Communist Party. The others were Vella Pillay, working for the Bank of China as an economist and CF, a fellow in one of the colleges at Cambridge. The three of us were to keep in touch with South Africa through safe addresses. The re-formation of the Party was still very secret and we were to tell no-one, not even our wives! Ruth also asked me to contribute a regular piece to *Fighting Talk*, the mouthpiece of the South African Congress of Democrats, which was allied to the African National Congress. I did the 'London Letter', beginning with the April 1954 issue and my last contribution was in April 1955, on the rolling strikes on the Zambian

Copperbelt.

In 1955, Moses Kotane, of the South African ANC and Communist Party, was in London on his way to the first non-aligned conference in Bandung, Indonesia. An opportunity was thus provided to discuss the problems facing the liberation movement in South Africa and what assistance we could render from Britain. When Kotane was later lobbied at the conference by a Northern Rhodesian student from India, Munu Sipalo, Kotane put him in touch with me and we remained close friends until we parted political company in the eighties. Sipalo returned home from India in 1956 and became one of the most militant campaigners in Congress. In 1958 he split with Nkumbula and became general secretary of the newly-formed and short-lived Zambian African National Congress (ZANC). He was detained when ZANC was banned and, on his release, he became secretary general of UNIP. He was instrumental in pushing the nationalist movement to achieve radical constitutional change by 1960. Political frustration at home in the late fifties drove him to drink and despite widespread enthusiasm for his militancy, he lost support from his colleagues in UNIP and got sent off to London. Sipalo did, however, make a valuable contribution to ZANC and UNIP as their first general secretary. Douglas Edmunds, a white left-wing businessman, who worked with him in UNIP head office spoke of Sipalo as the best administrator and organizer that the party had in the late fifties. Sipalo had great difficulty in overcoming his drink problem and on his return to Lusaka he suffered burns when his house was petrol-bombed by his enemies *within* UNIP. On the party becoming the government in 1964 I assisted, at Kaunda's request, in getting Sipalo into a hospital in East Finchley, London, which specialised in drying out. This was successful and he was healthy enough at independence in 1964 to be made a minister in the first cabinet. Unfortunately, he later had a setback and was again sent to London, but at the last minute refused to be taken by me to the same hospital!

HA and Pauline Naidoo, old friends from Cape Town who had been working in Budapest on the Hungarian Radio, arrived back in London in mid 1955. When we met I heard what life in Communist Eastern Europe was really like. They, especially HA, had become totally disillusioned with communism and told tales of lack of freedom of speech, corruption, Party people on the make and devoid of idealism, some forming part of a super class with many privileges and so on. One had heard similar tales before and dismissed them as coming from Trotskyites or the reactionary press, but I knew the Naidoos too well as South African patriots and fighters against apartheid to dismiss their witness. Naively, thinking that Communist friends in South Africa did not know, I tried to share with them what I had learnt, only to find that I was soon being bypassed as one of their appointed London representatives. By the time the revolt against the Soviet system in Hungary came in October 1956, my eyes were fully open and I broke off my connection with the South African Communist Party.

For a long time I had thought that South African communists were different, that what mattered to them was the struggle in South Africa and not blind idealization of, or belief in the goodness of Stalin and the Soviet System. I now found that the leadership was not prepared to accept within their ranks open critics of the Soviet system and the Eastern European bloc, no matter if the critic remained committed to the struggle for liberation in South Africa. Some leading South African communists may not have known the realities of Soviet Communism, but that was because they had *made* themselves immune to such knowledge. Many, however, *did* know and found rationalizations so as to be able to live with the contradictions. Often, those leaders who travelled to Soviet Russia or Eastern Europe were given VIP treatment and never went off the beaten path to find out the real state of affairs. Many South African communists chose to ignore the realities of the Soviet and East European systems because they felt the need of the financial and logistical support of these regimes in the struggle to end the apartheid regime. This also applied to many non-communist members of the South African ANC. With these I tried to maintain links.

When our son David was born in July 1955, Cynthia went to the South African High Commission to have him added to her passport. They took her passport but failed to return it! Even with a backwoodsman like Verwoerd at the helm, the South African authorities could hardly have done this as punishment for having a child, so it must have been either as punishment for Cynthia's anti-apartheid activities or for getting married to me. Alas, we will never know, as they would not give reasons. However, their high-handed

The Zukas family home in Ukmerge, Lithuania
as found during our nostalgic visit
(Plate 1)

On our wedding day 31.01.54 at the Registry Office,
St Pancras, London
(Plate 2)

Inaugural Meeting of African Congress, Lusaka 10-12th July 1949
Back Row: Lipapile, Sokota, ?, ?, ?, I.B. Nkonde, S.B. Kofie, ?, A. Kazunga, ?,
Second Row: D.W. Siwale, G. Musumbulwa, R. Mumpashya, Richmond, Nalumango,
Rev. Mushindo, Chief Mulundu, Chief Mwase, ?
Front Row: Rev. Lucheya, ?, D. Yamba, ?, M. Kakumbi, G. Mbikusita, Rev. Kasokolo,
Laban Zulu, Joseph Mumba, ?
(Plate 3)

Dar es Salaam 1961 at Tanganyika's Independence Celebrations
S. Makasa, Dingiswayo Banda, Kenneth Kaunda, Author, Simon Kapwepwe, Lewis Changufu
(Plate 4)

London 1963
Justin Chimba, Author, Reuben Kamanga, Nalumina Mundia
(Plate 5)

With Dr. Jack Simons, Lusaka 1974
(Plate 6)

AFRICAN NATIONAL CONGRESS
(SOUTH AFRICA)

Tel. Nos.:

P.O. Box 1791
LUSAKA
ZAMBIA

26/5/79

Dear Simon,

I am leaving for 'DAR this morning, for the meeting for which you so kindly helped us prepare reports.

I regret I totally failed to call on you after that or since. But I do want to say MANY THANKS.

I shall see you on my return.

Warmest regards to Cynthia.

Oliver

Letter from Oliver Tambo
(Plate 7)

With Professor René Dumont, Chungu Irrigation Scheme, Lusaka
(Plate 8)

First MMD Convention, 1991
(Plate 9)

The pontoon bought by the three Kalabo MPs for transporting relief maize in the '91/'92 drought across the Zambezi River near Lealui
(Plate 10)

Agricultural Show, Lusaka, 1993
Prize Giving by Minister of Agriculture, S. Zukas.
(Plate 11)

The Family, 1999
(Plate 12)

With my late brother Jake, London 2000.
(Plate 13)

As Interim Chairman of FDD with Lt/General Tembo
addressing a rally in Chawama 2001
(Plate 14)

action was, for us, not all that disadvantageous. Since South Africa was still in the Commonwealth, Cynthia applied for and was granted British citizenship and did not put her foot in South Africa House again until Mandela became president. To travel to see her mother in Cape Town in 1959, Cynthia had to go on a British passport, with special entry permission from Pretoria, obtained by her mother. By then she had also added on to her British passport, our second son, Alan, born in October 1957.

Cynthia devoted herself to anti-apartheid activities, first with the South African Freedom Association and later as secretary of our local Finchley Anti-apartheid Committee, much of her time being spent in fund-raising. Anti-apartheid activities in Britain increased after the 1960 Sharpeville massacre and South Africa's departure from the Commonwealth. Cynthia was involved in organizing the boycott campaign of South African goods. At one stage the Finchley Labour Party considered nominating her as a Justice of the Peace (JP) but by then Macmillan had delivered his wind of change speech in Cape Town and our long exile appeared to be nearing its end. In between having babies, Cynthia had to find time to look after visitors from the Rhodesias who came to stay in London for short periods. These visitors included people like Dixon Konkola, Robinson Puta, Moses Mukwaya, a journalist and Charles Mzingeli of the Southern Rhodesian Reformed Industrial and Commercial Workers Union and others.

Since I was working as a design engineer in structures, I joined the appropriate trade union, the AESD (Association of Engineering and Shipbuilding Draughtsmen) and became a branch treasurer and attended some conferences at national level. At one such conference I met Jimmy Young, a past general secretary of the association, who was a member of the Dalgleish Commission, which in 1947/48 had investigated the colour bar in industry in Northern Rhodesia and made progressive recommendations for African advancement in industry. We had a lot to talk about and it turned out that Jimmy was responsible for writing the Commission's report.

While working at Truscon, I was part of a team doing research on flat plate construction in concrete. The firm was introducing a system of construction for multi-storey flats, which had become popular in the USA. The system departed from the traditional beam and slab construction by omitting beams and having the floor slabs sitting *directly* on the columns: this saved much labour on the formwork to the concrete floors. A full-scale bay was constructed and loaded in stages up to the point when collapse took place. I was made responsible in 1958 for writing up our findings, but this was not fully published at the time. However, in 1987 I participated in an international conference on structural failure in Singapore and presented a paper on the above work. (See: International Conference on Structural Failure, Volume 2)

As chief engineer with a firm of consultants, I was part of a multi-discipline design team for a factory complex, where tractors were to be assembled, at Fords, Dagenham. During the design process I was discussing with the client's representative the width of the large doors to the building, through which lorries would have to drive in to deliver parts to the assembly lines. He kept on asking for the width of the doors to be increased beyond what I thought quite adequate for trucks. Extra width had cost implications and I told him that I was very surprised at his approach as Ford was very cost-conscious. 'Ah' replied Mr Amey, 'you don't know the factory people we are dealing with: the people on the assembly line will arrange with the truck driver for him to get stuck through the door so that they can idle on the assembly line while waiting for materials. A wide door will obviate that trick.' The atmosphere at Dagenham was never a happy one and this applied not only to workers and staff but also between departments.

Around 1960, with the Cold War still raging, my employers had a commission for establishing observation posts throughout Britain for pinpointing the centre of explosion in the event of an atomic bomb being dropped. Reports from such posts would enable the limits of the contaminated area to be established and prevent rescue teams going into it. The work was suddenly brought to an abrupt end because the atomic bomb was superseded by the hydrogen bomb and the devastated area expected would be so much greater that the observation posts became obsolete. If I did not join CND (Campaign for Nuclear Disarmament) in the protest marches, it was only because I was in Britain as an exile! The threat of nuclear weapons to our civilization was brought home to me, not least, by this engineering work that we were involved in.

*****

Soon after our marriage we had moved to South London near Crystal

Palace and lived there in a flat for two years. Since we were outside the London underground system, our friends and visitors from home found it difficult to reach us, so we moved back to North London, East Finchley, where we lived very comfortably for some eight years in a house of our own. During our stay there we made friends with neighbours; we were within easy reach of our South African friends; our two boys attended a good local primary school and we were gradually losing our exile mindset. My younger brother, Abe, came over for further education and kept in touch with us and Cynthia's parents were frequent visitors to London.

When Cynthia's mother came over annually we would accompany her to theatre or opera and there were many occasions for eating out in good restaurants with her and also, separately, with Cynthia's father. We took annual holidays at the coast with the children and often stayed in the country when my work was outside London. While supervising construction of a building in Stratford-upon-Avon I took the family with me and Cynthia and I were able to go to many Shakespeare plays there. Life was good and I was enjoying living and working in Britain. It was very tempting to forget Northern Rhodesia and its problems.

CYNTHIA'S POSTSCRIPT

In my last year at Cape Town University, in 1952, I became very active in student anti-apartheid politics. I joined the Modern Youth Society, which was mainly a left-wing discussion group and I became involved in the ANC-led Defiance Campaign. It was in MYS that I first heard of Simon Zukas. Simon, I heard, had been arrested in, what was to me, a very remote part of Africa, Northern Rhodesia, and we decided to organize a party to raise money for his defence. Simon's young brother Abe was at school in Cape Town and so was Nephas Tembo, my first friend from Northern Rhodesia. They both joined us in our efforts at fund-raising.

Soon after that, I proceeded to London to do a post-graduate art teachers' course. I joined my sister Noreen, who was already there and recently married. To my amazement I found that this hero from a distant land was in London and friendly with my sister and brother-in-law. Our paths appeared destined to cross and with so much in common: friends, beliefs, commitments, it was just a matter of time before we fell in love and got married.

With a speedy return to either South Africa or Rhodesia seeming out of the question, we settled down to a happy and comfortable life in London. Once our children were born I gave up painting and became a full-time housewife and mother.

However, Simon and I both kept up our campaigning for an end to apartheid and oppression in South Africa and independence for Northern Rhodesia. We were always sure that though it might be a long haul, our future would be back in Africa.

From the late fifties I was meeting more and more 'Zambians' who came to London for training or studies or as UNIP representatives to attend conferences and I enjoyed being able to give them some home comforts and hospitality. Our sons enjoyed meeting young Makasa and young Kapwepwe, who came over to school in Britain and stayed with us during their holidays.

Chapter Eight
THE RISE AND FALL OF THE
CENTRAL AFRICAN FEDERATION

The Federation was established in 1953 without the Dominion Status which the Europeans would have liked. Southern Rhodesia, a self-governing colony since 1923, continued to come under the Commonwealth Office, as did the Federation as a whole. Although Nyasaland and Northern Rhodesia retained their status as colonies/protectorates under the Colonial Office, its writ in the two territories applied only to subjects defined in the Federal constitution as 'Territorial'.

For the first three years of the Federation Europeans were consolidating their newly-won powers, while African nationalists were licking their wounds and confining their active opposition to such local issues as competing with the provincial administration for the support of chiefs and organizing boycotts against pigeon-hole shopping in the towns. Chiefs, militants thought, had to be put on a knife-edge, as some of them tended to be afraid of losing government recognition if they were seen to be pro-Congress. Congress, through well-organized boycotts and picketing in Lusaka in January 1954, succeeded in putting an end to segregated shopping. Discrimination was also practised in shops in the first-class shopping areas and boycotts of these took place successfully in Lusaka, Livingstone, the Copperbelt and Mazabuka.

On the industrial front, government had gained the support of Katilungu, who was becoming an accepted establishment-figure. He kept a grip not only on the African Mineworkers Union, but also on the TUC. For a time there were good benefits for the Northern Rhodesian mining companies and from Federation. But not for long. By mid 1956 the Africans in the northern territories had licked their wounds long enough to restart their struggle against white rule.

On 11 September 1956 the government of Northern Rhodesia declared a state of emergency in an attempt to deal with African unrest, manifested in a series of rolling strikes on the copper mines. Police arrested fifty-four leaders on the Copperbelt, including the entire leadership of the Mineworkers Union, except their president, Lawrence Katilungu, who flew off to Southern Rhodesia. Ignoring a prohibition on gatherings, thousands of African men *and women* demonstrated against the arrests and the police used tear gas and baton charges to disperse them. In Ndola, not a mining town, African demonstrators were fired on. As part of the Federal internal security system, Southern Rhodesia immediately offered to the Northern Rhodesian government up to one thousand policemen, three hundred white and seven hundred black. Aircraft were used to spot and intimidate prohibited gatherings. Clearly, the spirit of resistance was reviving and I was very encouraged on receiving news of these events. The detainees included Matthew Nkoloma, who had been in correspondence with me. Also arrested was my old colleague of the Anti-Federation Action Committee, Mungoni Liso.

Nkumbula was in London at the time and he attended one of our MCF committee meetings in the House of Commons, chaired by Fenner Brockway, at which I presented a paper on the situation on the Copperbelt. Nkumbula did not appear to know what was going on at home or to regard the events there as of political significance. (In Lusaka, at Congress' annual conference, Nkumbula dissociated Congress from these strikes).

Yet these events *were* politically significant. During July and August, branch executives had called unofficial strikes on the mines, including Broken Hill, which is outside the Copperbelt. These did not have the blessings of Katilungu, who was away in England. The official strike issue was the mine companies' recent recognition of MASA, the Mines African Staff Association, and the transfer to it of many skilled mineworkers. The union had fought for their advancement and was now to lose them as members. Even before the State of Emergency was declared, the demonstrations spread to the Copperbelt commercial townships and to Ndola. Clearly, these events went beyond industrial matters: the declaration of the State of Emergency was in itself a recognition by government that they were confronted by a complex political-industrial situation. The London *Observer's* Lusaka correspondent recognised the political element in these events, when he reported that 'the situation can only be judged against the background of suspicion and friction that has been building up steadily since the establishment of the Central African Federation'. (*Observer* 16/9/56)

In October, a commission of inquiry was held while the union leaders were still detained and late in November the detainees' application for habeas corpus was heard by the Northern Rhodesian Chief Justice. The emergency was finally lifted at the end of 1956, but this did not bring stability to the Copperbelt or to Northern Rhodesia as a whole; unless one agrees with the view held by Mr Keith Ackutt, a former director of the Anglo-American Mining Corporation, who claimed after a strike at the Southern Rhodesian Wankie Colliery that 'a riot or two does not make for instability'. Nevertheless, these events were more than 'a riot or two'!

Disturbances were not confined to the main urban areas on the line of rail. Tear gas and bullets were used by the police to disperse demonstrators in several parts of the Northern Province and Luapula, as well as in the Eastern Province in 1957. There were further violent confrontations in the Gwembe Valley in 1958, at Chilubi Island in Lake Bangweulu in 1959 and again in the north in 1961. The last, part of the campaign known as Cha Cha Cha, was the most serious of the disturbances. The Cha Cha Cha was a popular and energetic dance at the time. Its use as a code name for the resistance campaign implied vigorous action.

An event of great political significance was the way the Federal and territorial government handled the resettlement of the people to be displaced by the flooding of the Kariba reservoir, as a result of the construction of the dam wall at Siavonga. On the Southern Rhodesian side Minister Fletcher went to persuade the Tonga people to move, by taking with him beads and rolls of calico, as if he was still in the last century. On the Northern Rhodesian shore of the Zambezi, 29,000 Tonga were moved to new villages in barren agricultural areas with low rainfall and were paid compensation at an average of eleven pounds per person. When police attempted in 1958 to force the Valley Tonga people to move to higher ground, the people retaliated with spears. Eight of them were killed and thirty-four wounded. More attention seemed to be paid by the authorities to resettling the wildlife than the people. These events, combined with white settlement in the Mkushi Block, focused attention on African land insecurity in the white-controlled Federation. This lesson was to give a new momentum to the struggle to undo Federation. I came to the conclusion that, despite the low density of the population in Northern Rhodesia, it was the land question that was the Federation's Achilles' heel. This became a mobilizing force, first with the people of

Southern Province and later in the rest of the country.

Sir Roy Welensky took over the premiership of the Federation in 1956 from Lord Malvern and started the drive for increased powers for his white electorate and the Federation. The result was the Constitution Amendment Act of 1957, enlarging the Federal Parliament from thirty-five to fifty-nine members, with a resulting increased European advantage over Africans. Welensky then obtained the agreement of the Tory government in Britain to convene a Constitutional Review in 1960 and he made it clear that he was expecting Dominion Status for the Federation out of this review. This open drive for Dominion Status gave a further impetus to our movement, for we realised that unless we organized ourselves in time to prevent it, our country's fate would be sealed.

Meanwhile, Dr Hastings Banda's return to Nyasaland had given an extra spurt to the Malawi Congress Party in their struggle to pull Nyasaland out of the Federation. The British government could not resist the pressure and began moves to accommodate Dr Banda, while still hoping to keep Northern Rhodesia in the Federation. This did not work as in Northern Rhodesia the tempo of struggle was also accelerating.

Within the ANC in Northern Rhodesia, Nkumbula was trying to hold back growing militancy. In 1956 he vetoed a proposal in the Congress executive, that Congress should demand universal adult suffrage for Northern Rhodesia. Under Nkumbula's leadership the ANC was weak and compromising not only on votes for all, but also on self-government, on majority representation and the issue of independence from colonial rule. This weakness led to breakaways. Simon Kapwepwe walked out, to be followed by other militants, including Kaunda after some delay. On 26 October 1958, these dissidents launched the Zambia African National Congress (ZANC) with Kaunda as president, Sipalo as general secretary and Kapwepwe as general treasurer. On hearing from Sipalo of the formation of ZANC, I immediately applied for membership. ZANC organized a boycott of the territorial elections that were about to be held on the basis of a new constitution, which did not provide for non-racial, majority representation. As a result, ZANC was banned in March 1959, a state of emergency declared and its leaders arrested and deported to various areas within the country.

ZANC's suppression did not still the new militancy which was developing;

if anything it made it grow faster as a result of the internal deportation and restriction of militants to relatively slumbering areas. Kaunda was sent to Kabompo; Kapwepwe and Nephas Tembo to Mongu; Robert Makasa to Solwezi; Sikalumbi to Namwala; etc. In each case the restrictee was sent far from his own tribal area. Makasa in his book *March to Political Freedom* gives us an account of the political activities that took place under restriction:

> we were so determined to keep the flame burning that we immediately formed... Advisory Committees through which we co-ordinated our political action.... these [also] served as vehicles of information.... we cultivated a good working relationship with both the ordinary folk and the civil servants.... we worked and succeeded in reaching as many people as possible in this area through our clandestine contacts.

In June some of the leaders were tried and sentenced, Kaunda receiving nine months imprisonment.

With ZANC suppressed, its leaders in restriction or in gaol, and Nkumbula's ANC compromised by its pacts with non-nationalist parties led by white liberals like Sir John Moffat and Dr Alexander Scott, leading Africans who remained unrestricted started to launch several alternative political parties. (One such party, The United National Congress Party, led by Dixon Konkola invited me to take up (in absentia) one of the posts in their executive. I declined this offer because I had by then lost confidence in Konkola as a leader). Mergers were taking place between the multiplicity of parties, resulting in the United National Independence Party (UNIP), first under the presidency of Konkola, then Kalichini and then of Mainza Chona, on his crossing over from Nkumbula's ANC. Mainza Chona later handed over to Kaunda when he was released from prison and new elections were held.

Feeling confident that in UNIP we had a party and leadership that would pursue the end of the Federation and work for independence, I got together with other Northern Rhodesians in London, including Thomas Fox-Pitt, Fitzpatrick Chuula, 'Chico' Kamalondo and Richard Zimba and we formed a branch of UNIP. The branch was later recognised officially and my membership card is dated July 1960.

Nationalist militancy at home was also coming to the fore in the schools. In October 1959 there were disturbances of a political nature in Northern Rhodesia's elite secondary school, Munali, and it was closed down by the territorial minister of African education, Mr Gabriel Musumburwa. Some of the students did not return when the school was reopened and were sent out by the nationalist movement for training abroad. Disturbances followed in other educational institutions in 1960. The Reverend Mervyn Temple told me that he had trouble at a school in the Eastern Province, where students wanted to name a dormitory after me! These events were not easily dismissed by the authorities because at that time the students in secondary schools and teacher training institutions were already adults in their twenties.

The Federation was now under threat both in Northern Rhodesia and Nyasaland. Even Southern Rhodesia was in turmoil, if not against Federation, then on territorial issues. To some extent, the increased pace of resistance to white rule in the Federation can be attributed to inspiration from the All African People's Conference held in Accra in 1958 and attended by delegates from Central Africa. However, Welensky's drive to achieve Dominion Status by 1960 was the major driving force behind the African revival. Starting with ZANC, and continuing under UNIP, the militants agitated that: 'We must get self-government before 1960 or face the prospect of Dominion Status under white majority rule'. Harold Macmillan's wind of change speech in Cape Town on 3 February 1960, while being a recognition of the new African spirit, also acted as a spur to accelerated liberation from colonial rule.

With the Federal constitutional review conference due in 1960, the Tory government set up at the end of 1959 a commission, under the chairmanship of Lord Monckton, to assess opinion in the two northern territories. To placate Welensky the African members chosen were all moderates, so UNIP refused to give evidence before the commission. Nevertheless, when the commission reported in October 1960, it could not conceal the hostility to the Federation in Nyasaland and Northern Rhodesia and described the opposition to it as 'widespread, sincere and of long standing'. Political events in the Federation did not stand still while the commission was gathering evidence and preparing its report. Militancy under the leadership of UNIP was growing daily. Unfortunately, the militants' campaign went beyond the control of Kaunda on 8 May 1960, when rioters near Ndola stopped a car and set it alight after dousing it with petrol. Inside the car were a white woman and her children. Mrs Lilian Burton died from the severe burns she received.

Belatedly the British government published, in February 1961, proposals for self-government for Northern Rhodesia. The two nationalist parties found the proposals acceptable, but Welensky, the *Federal* Prime Minister, in a series of dramatic moves, forced the British government to rethink. When it published in June 1961 its *revised* proposals for constitutional change for Northern Rhodesia, they proved far less than had been conceded to Malawi. This triggered off very strong action by militants all over the country. By October, nineteen people had been shot by the authorities and more than two thousand arrested. The proposals had clearly been tailored by Ian Macleod to placate Welensky. Though Macleod claimed that the two sets of proposals (known as the 15/15/15 Proposals) varied in form, not in intention, I analysed them in a paper for Kaunda before he left London. This was also done in Lusaka by a European Maths teacher from Munali School. It was clear to us that Macleod was using his prowess as a contract bridge player to cloak the advantage he was giving to Welensky's side (those few in Northern Rhodesia wishing to remain federated with Southern Rhodesia) in the proposed territorial election.

To counter Welensky's pressure on Macleod, UNIP started the Cha Cha Cha campaign in the north. Kaunda gave the impression to the authorities and the media that Cha Cha Cha was not under his leadership or control, but the impression I got from UNIP members was that he was distancing himself only for tactical reasons. Indeed, when he came to London on the eve of the campaign he told me that the campaign was about to start and left me in no doubt that he was not all that distant from it. Kaunda's tactic paid off, as it left him in a position to talk to those people in Britain who wanted to see change, but would not have been prepared to talk to him as a leader behind the disturbances.

New British proposals followed under Reginald Maudling, who took over from Macleod at the Colonial Office, and the result was that in the election the two nationalist parties gained sufficient seats together to form a government. Strong attempts were made by Welensky and company to ally Nkumbula and his ANC to the Federal Party and prevent a nationalist coalition. However, under pressure from leading African personalities, Nkumbula co-operated with Kaunda and formed a government.

Another election, on a wider franchise, followed in January 1964 and this time UNIP was able to form a government on its own. In February the new

Legislative Council passed a motion demanding 'secession from the Federation now'. On 29 March Britain conceded this demand. It was now a matter of weeks before the Federation was wound up at a meeting in Victoria Falls, presided over by RA Butler, to divide the assets between the territories.

Federation proved an expensive exercise for Northern Rhodesia. According to Richard Hall, 'it was officially stated that there had been a net loss of revenue of approximately £10 million a year since 1953 and that Southern Rhodesia had been the main beneficiary'. (See: *Zambia* by Richard Hall). Many Northern Rhodesian Europeans did not regret the collapse of the Federation because of this loss, although they had been ardent supporters of Federation in the fifties.

Obituaries on the Federation followed. *Welensky's 4000 Days* by Sir Roy himself and *The Sudden Assignment* by Lord Alport, minister of state in the Commonwealth Office in 1957 and since March 1961, High Commissioner (governor) of the Federation. Alport recognized Britain's folly:

> The crude fact was that Britain had launched the federal experiment in Central Africa without being sure that those who were to be responsible for its success knew how to make it work or were convinced that it was possible to do so. Further, Britain had divested itself of the powers necessary to keep it on the right lines, or correct the distortions which local prejudice, fear and animosity produced. (*Sudden Assignment* by Alport)

I was impressed with Alport's memoir. What struck me was the British government's blind naivete which, surprisingly, was shared by Sir Andrew Cohen, who was heading the Colonial Office at the time Federation was being hatched in London. The British Colonial Service should have known more about white settler intentions and how the settlers would use the extra powers that were being given to them in the Federal Constitution. There was, after all, the solid record of the all-white legislature in Southern Rhodesia in handling the land issue. The Land Apportionment Act allocated fifty per cent of the country, including all the best land, for *white* settlement only! Alport went on to admit that 'African opponents heavily outnumbered the handful who were in Federation's favour' (p247) a far cry from what Tory ministers, like Henry Hopkinson (later Lord Colyton), insisted in1953!

Lord Alport reveals that Katilungu's death was a big blow to those who hoped to save the Federation. Clearly, Lord Alport hoped that Katilungu would be able to offset UNIP's success in mobilizing African opinion and action for the termination of Federation. What is not clear is whether it was also hoped that Katilungu would be able to get the African mineworkers to back Federation, which would have been most unlikely.

Welensky blamed the demise of the Federation entirely on the British government: 'I say that Britain has lost the will to govern in Africa and is utterly reckless of the fate of the inhabitants of the present Federation'. He castigated the British government for saying that 'consent of the inhabitants' was a requirement for the continuation of the Federation and said he reminded them that such consent was required only for radical change in the status of the Federation.

> I pointed out that the preamble [of the Constitution] only required the consent in two cases: first, if amalgamation were proposed; and second, if and when the Federation came to full, independent membership of the Commonwealth and Britain's direct control over the affairs of the two Northern Territories was to be relinquished. (*Welensky's 4000 Days*)

Clearly, while the British government were by 1963 mindful of the new climate of world opinion requiring consent of the governed, Welensky, in his Rhodesian isolation, thought he could still have gone on governing without it, just like his neighbour to the South.

As far as I could see, there was nothing in Welensky's memoir to show that he thought he could have offered anything to the northern territories, once they became self-governing under African majorities, to entice them to continue with the Federation. As an experienced politician with the white voters, he probably knew that the almost all-white Southern Rhodesian electorate would not have accepted such an option! The sad truth was that Federation had been imposed on unwilling African populations in 1953, because, in Welensky's words, 'Britain had lost the will to govern' and chose, at Welensky's behest, to renege on past pledges and promises. Now Welensky was complaining of similar treatment because it came to his turn, in 1963, to be abandoned.

In looking back on the rise and fall of the Federation and looking forward to emerging independence for Northern Rhodesia, I tried to assess for myself what I had contributed. I felt that my contribution had been in turning the emerging political movement in a militant direction: away from begging the

Colonial Office for continued protection towards demanding universal suffrage and self-government, based on majority rule. Anti-Federation was only one aspect of this. In 1951, Africans in Northern Rhodesia were still very frightened of the colonial government. I tried to overcome this by adopting a visibly militant stand in politics, which I thought would encourage others. I tried to help the African trade union movement in their fight against the mining companies for better pay and conditions and for advancement into more skilled jobs and, at the same time, help them play a leading role in the nationalist movement. My activities resulted in heart-ache and some suffering for my parents and brothers, for which I was sorry. For my own suffering from detention in gaol and deportation I had no regrets, as I felt that the cause I was supporting was a just one and the steps I had taken were fully justified. My only regret was that I came out from these experiences a much harder person.

Chapter Nine
GOING HOME

Although I had predicted in 1954 that I would be home within ten years, Cynthia and I did not live in London with our bags packed ready to depart at short notice either to Northern Rhodesia or to South Africa. On the contrary, we put down roots in Britain. With money which Cynthia had been left in her grandfather's will, we bought a four-bedroom house in the Hampstead garden suburb, in North London. Cynthia joined the local arts school for evening classes, while I worked as a structural engineer and made moves up the professional ladder.

By 1960, I was encouraged to start my own practice in London as a consulting structural engineer. A loan of five hundred pounds from my father-in-law was of great assistance. During my eight years in the UK construction industry, first as a design engineer with a design and build firm and later as chief engineer with a firm of consulting engineers, I had built up contacts in the industry, which made me confident of obtaining commissions in my own right. I took offices in Bloomsbury, Central London (a professional address) and there I was later joined in partnership by AS Magasiner and we practised as Zukas and Magasiner, Consulting Engineers. Our early work included the structural design for a prestigious office block in the Haymarket (near Piccadilly Circus), the steelwork design for the grid of a television studio in Cologne, West Germany, the steelwork design for the stage complex in the Lincoln Centre in New York; and the conversion of a building in Savile Row, London, as a musical studio for the Beatles. Our practice employed several assistant engineers and we had a reasonable flow of work.

Structural commissions normally come on recommendation from architects, but occasionally the appointment is subject to the choice of the would-be contractor. On one occasion I had to be interviewed by the managing director of a London construction firm before he would accept the architect's recommendation. I was very nervous about this interview and wondered whether I would be examined on my competence as a structural engineer and my ability to design for ease of construction on site. I calmed myself by recollecting that I had worked for many years not only in the design office, but also on sites as part of a construction team and was familiar with the contractor's problems and point of view. I was ready to tell my would-be interlocutor all that. However, to be on the safe side, I consulted a friend of mine who was working under this managing director as a project manager, on how to conduct myself.

To my surprise, this friend advised me not to talk of structure or construction, unless asked. He went on: 'wear a *dark* suit, white shirt and white handkerchief in the breast pocket; polka-dot or plain tie and black shoes; no pencil, pen or slide-rule to be visible in any pocket'. I took his advice and went along, still nervously, to the interview. After an introduction and exchange of a few pleasantries the MD said he would be pleased to have me on the project and that was that. When the project was in full swing I met this MD again, now on easier terms, and one of his remarks was that he accepted me because he liked my turn-out! I did not volunteer that I had been groomed by one of *his* men, who knew him rather well!

Another system of obtaining commissions was to indulge in entertaining clients in London night-clubs. My partner and I were pleased not to have to resort to that and so were our wives, although we could not avoid some wining and dining as part of professional life.

The London Office of UNIP, which Mainza Chona had established while in the UK to avoid arrest in Northern Rhodesia on a charge of sedition, had remained in existence after his return home in 1960. It was for a while run by Munu Sipalo and later by Chiko Kamalondo with a supporting committee consisting of Richard Zimba, Bitwell Kuwani, Fitzpatrick Chuula, Tommy Fox-Pitt and myself. We published a monthly newsletter – *The Voice of UNIP*. While Sipalo gave us problems resulting from his alcoholism, Kamalondo gave us problems resulting from girl friends that felt let down. At one stage we could not hold meetings in the UNIP office without the telephone being rung repeatedly by a girlfriend. (Cynthia, too, had to cope with frequent phone calls as a result of Chico's unsolved matrimonial affairs).

I had a surprise visit from Arthur Wina, our UNIP representative in the USA, who impressed me very much. He left me with the June '61 copy of the *Northern Rhodesia News Survey*, published by himself. Arthur was studying in Los Angeles and was on his way back after a visit home. He briefed me on events at home. He was to play an important role in post-independence politics. We formed a bond, then, which would last until his untimely death in 1996.

Simon Kapwepwe started passing through London in the early sixties and asked me to arrange a place in a secondary boarding school for his *deaf* son, Paul. Cynthia took it upon herself to find a solution and discussed the problem with the secretary of the National Institute for the Deaf. On her recommendation, Cynthia went to Brighton to look at a school there. She booked Paul into it, and later took him down there when he was brought to London by Kenneth Kaunda. Paul would, thereafter, come and stay with us for his short school holidays and sometimes bring with him for company a deaf Egyptian boy, Abdullah. One Sunday, while they were staying with us, we found ourselves being flooded from the ceiling when preparing breakfast. The bedroom above, occupied by Paul and Abdullah, had its own wash basin with hot and cold water taps. The boys had left the taps turned on and were unable to hear the running water! This incident made us very sympathetic towards the problems of the deaf.

Reuben Kamanga, one of the co-founders of our Anti Federation Action Committee, came to London from Cairo in 1960 and when he obtained a donation of some thirty thousand pounds from the Ghanaian High Commissioner, he entrusted it to me for disbursement on instructions from himself or from Kenneth Kaunda. I kept the money on deposit at my bank and disbursed or remitted from it when instructed. I accounted fully to Reuben Kamanga when we met again in 1964.

In 1960 Kaunda arranged for me to be invited to the Tanganyika independence celebrations in Dar es Salaam as one of the UNIP delegates. It was a very exciting moment for me to land on African soil after an absence of eight years and to be able to witness the birth of a free Tanganyika. After the celebrations there was another treat in store. I drove with Robert Makasa and Victor Zaza to Mbeya, near the border with Northern Rhodesia, in the hope of meeting my old colleague, Justin Chimba, who was to be driven up from Northern Rhodesia. Although the rainy season was on and the gravel road had many muddy stretches, I immensely enjoyed the drive through the African bush and the appearance of a giraffe standing on the road some fifty metres in front of us. Unfortunately, Chimba did not manage to get to Mbeya, but I did come across my old army buddy, John Harvey, the son-in-law of Sir Stewart Gore-Browne. John had driven up from Shiwa to collect his mother who had travelled down from Kenya, where she was a schoolmistress. I had not seen John since the war and was pleased to join them for lunch at the Railway Hotel and catch up with some home news: UNIP's Cha Cha Cha campaign was causing problems to the authorities in some areas, especially along the Luapula and on the Copperbelt..

The hotel's name must have reflected wishful thinking, since there was at the time no railway passing through Mbeya or anywhere nearer than four hundred kilometres! (The railway did reach Mbeya in 1970 with the construction by the Chinese of the rail link between Kapiri Mposhi in Zambia and Dar es Salaam.)

While in Dar I spoke at a local UNIP rally with Kaunda and had my first experience of the frequent use of slogans, a practice which had developed since my departure in 1951. The audience must have thought me a very mundane speaker. I also addressed a meeting at a political school in Kivukoni, run by Dr Colin Leys and there met Rankin Sikasula, later Kaunda's secretary and a deputy minister. We have remained close friends ever since and when he was ambassador in Maputo, Mozambique, I was his guest during a visit in September 1981. On returning from Mbeya, I stayed on in Dar and anxiously awaited the arrival of my parents and Jake and his family. I had not seen my parents and Jake for eight years and had not yet met Jake's wife, Yvette, and their children! It was an emotional get-together for all of us.

Joshua Nkomo stayed in the same hotel as I and we discussed whether he should return home and face being jailed by the Whitehead government. Hastings Banda also stayed in the same hotel and though we would greet each other, he kept his distance. Frenny Ginwala was living in Dar at the time and publishing *The Spearhead*. At her request, I contributed an article to her publication on the theme of 'Uhuru na Kazi or Uhuru na Kupata?' (Independence and Work or Independence to Receive).

In the article I urged that the people forgo immediate increases in consumption and start to create national savings by national restraint. Trade union restraint can become a corollary of national liberation 'only when there is a government policy, applicable to the whole nation, of restraint, of austerity, of saving today for investment towards a better tomorrow.' I went on to address myself to the trade unions:

> After independence the trade union movement has a duty to ensure that the national savings, resulting from.... the elimination of foreign political control, are not appropriated by the already-established internal commercial classes, plantation owners, foreign trading establishments, foreign industrial concerns and, above all, foreign finance institutions.

I laid out my thinking for post-independence policy, which should also apply to our own country: all sound economics, even if Marxist-sounding stuff, but spending restraint did not become general policy in post-independence Africa, either for workers or governments.

DN Pritt, QC was one of the invited guests to the ceremony and Kenneth Kaunda, who was meeting him for the first time, made a point of thanking him for taking on my case in 1951.

I was pleased to meet Oscar Kambona and Zwai Poliso, both ministers in the Tanganyika government, and Rashid Kawawa, the vice-president. I detected no strain in the relations between the ministers, but it was not long before Oscar was exiled after being suspected of having a hand in an attempted army and air force coup, which was put down with the help of British troops flown in from an aircraft carrier.

For Kenya's and Uganda's delegations it was certain that their independence would soon follow, but for Northern Rhodesia and Nyasaland the road ahead would still involve struggle. The Cha Cha Cha campaign was, however, having some impact and there were signs that the British government was coming to the conclusion that the Federation was beyond saving.

During the celebrations I noticed three Dakotas of the Federal Airforce of Rhodesia and Nyasaland, parked on the apron at Dar airport, ostensibly standing by in case of anti-white disturbances in newly-independent (but disturbed) Congo. They certainly brought no Federal government guests to the celebrations as none were invited. However, they may have had a more sinister purpose, as I soon discovered: Welensky was assisting Moise Tshombe in his attempts to split off Katanga from the Congo.

A journalist friend revealed to me on my return to London that at an off the record meeting organized by the *Economist* at their flat in Piccadilly, Reginald Maudling, then Foreign Secretary, said that support for Welensky had to be abandoned because he was causing Britain embarrassment internationally with his interference in the Congo. (Britain had retained responsibility for the Federation's foreign affairs. In 1990 I was told by Valentine Musakanya, who had been representing the Federal government in Katanga during the Tshombe attempt at secession, that Welensky had been working towards attracting Katanga into his Federation. No doubt, this is what was embarrassing Britain internationally and to what Maudling was referring at the *Economist* meeting).

The moment I heard of Maudling's views on Welensky, I guessed we would soon see the unwinding of the Federation. I rushed off the information to Makasa, UNIP's resident representative in Dar es Salaam, for onward transmission by road to Kaunda in Lusaka and this enabled Kaunda later to play his hand more confidently in his negotiations with Britain. It was not long before it would be Kaunda's turn to meet the editorial staff of the *Economist*.

When Kaunda was about to form the first UNIP government and was visiting London, I was asked by a member of staff of the *Economist* to arrange for Kaunda to have dinner with the editor. During dinner Kaunda told the gathering how Tshombe was working with Welensky and Harry Nkumbula to interfere in Northern Rhodesian politics. Not only was Tshombe supporting Nkumbula financially; he had also donated a huge American car to Mwata Kazembe, the paramount chief in Northern Rhodesia's Western (Luapula) Province in order to influence the chief to support Nkumbula. After dinner Mr Tireman, the editor, invited Kaunda to sit in a chair which he went on to describe as one that Welensky, Maudling and Macleod had sat in and discussed Central African affairs off the record. An interchange of views took place, after which Mr Tireman posed this question: 'Mr Kaunda, you are a *good* man and good men do not make good heads of state. Have you considered this?' Kaunda hummed without replying, but the point Mr Tireman was making sank in. Mr Tireman had probably been taken in a little by Kaunda's soft manner and had not allowed sufficiently for the educational process that was ahead for Kaunda; or perhaps it was Mr Tireman's purpose to initiate this educational process? I thought, then, that although Kaunda might be a good man, he was not lacking that *other* quality, which would enable him to be a head of state! (And so it later proved).

Events in Northern Rhodesia were moving fast. On the formation of the UNIP government in February 1964, with Kaunda as prime minister, government resolved to allow the return of all the people who had been excluded or deported on political grounds, *providing each complied with immigration regulations*. This decision was immediately followed by a telegram to me from Mainza Chona, general secretary of UNIP, saying: 'Red Carpet awaits your arrival'. I had been waiting for this moment for eleven years and was overjoyed. Cynthia and I decided on an immediate trip, but thought it prudent for her to fly out first with the children, and for me to follow after she had arrived. They went to Ndola to stay with Jake and family and experienced no problems and I followed a week later. My plane landed in Ndola for a short stop on its way to Lusaka as was the practice at the time. Although I was booked to Lusaka, customs and immigration had to be cleared at Ndola.

Before being allowed outside the terminal building, where there was a huge crowd assembled to welcome me, I was issued by the immigration officer with a prohibited immigrant's notice, allowing me to stay in Northern Rhodesia for one month only and requiring me to report to the police. On emerging from the terminal building I was carried shoulder high and then asked to address the crowd. Banners welcoming me were on display. I was so overcome that I could say only a few words in reply to the words of welcome, before I was called to the plane as the last passenger.

It was explained to me at the time that the technical reason for my being treated as a prohibited immigrant was the fact that I had arrived without a visa. Only as a British subject could I enter without a visa. (The officials were clearly sticking to the literal wording of the cabinet decision and they, no doubt, through the secretary to the cabinet had an input in the wording.) The joy of my welcome was soured by this notice and the sourness was to turn to bitterness when a white immigration officer later insisted, on my arrival at Lusaka Airport, that I report to him in his town office. However, I soon saw through the game that was being played by these old hands. So I went to the Ministry of Home Affairs, where the UNIP minister, Simon Kapwepwe, gave instructions to his white permament secretary to issue a document freeing me from the need to report my movements to immigration. (This was later followed, after independence, by my becoming a citizen of Zambia by registration, and being issued with a Zambian passport).

At Lusaka Airport I was met by a smaller crowd than in Ndola, led by my old colleague, Reuben Kamanga, the country's first prison graduate and now a cabinet minister. With him was Mama Julia Chikamoneka, who anointed me with flour and gave me a cowrie shell. Mama Julia was famous for having led a crowd of middle-aged UNIP women in a demonstration in front of Ian Macleod in Lusaka, with all the demonstrators having bared their breasts. This was a local African tradition of defiance or protest, a tradition probably arising from the insistence by missionaries that African women should cease going round bare-breasted.

So after eleven years in exile I was home, if for the time being only on a visit and on a prohibited immigrant's permit! I was impressed with the way Lusaka had grown: even though the main street, Cairo Road, still had many empty plots on its east side, it had been provided with drainage and been tarred. There was now an area, some kilometres to the west, laid out for heavy industry in addition to a light industrial area adjacent to the main shopping centre. I visited friends in Matero, the township where most Africans lived, and I remembered that this had been proposed in the Jellico Town Plan, but not yet developed when I was last in Lusaka in March, 1951. Jellico, a well-known town planner from Britain, had debated in his report whether to site the township for Africans on the west or east side of the town. He justified his recommendation to site it on the west side, down wind from Lusaka, so that the sound of 'tom-toms' would not keep people in Lusaka awake at night. He did not appear to take into consideration that this township for Africans would also be downwind of the heavy industrial area with its smoke-stacks and industrial fumes. I recalled that when I read this report I wondered whether Jellico had not been influenced by white settler racial thinking, which prevailed and was dominant in the pre-Federal period and during the life of the Federation.

My family and I had to go back to London for the children to return to their school, and Cynthia and I then wrestled with the difficult question of whether to uproot ourselves from London and shift to Lusaka.

Independence Day was scheduled for October 24 and an invitation soon arrived for us to fly out to attend it as guests of the government. Naturally, it gave us great pleasure to accept it. The independence celebrations filled me with joy and I felt that I shared some responsibility for bringing about the event. There were many reunions with old friends from Ndola and even from Southern Rhodesia, like Robert Chikerema. From Malawi came Bridger Katenga, who had inspired several of our independence leaders in the struggle in Ndola.

While in Zambia for the pre-independence visit, I met my old political friend and engineer colleague, Harry Chimowitz, who came up from Southern Rhodesia and we agreed to set up the consulting engineering practice of Simon Zukas and Partners in Lusaka, associated to the practice of Zukas and Magasiner in London. Harry was to be resident partner.

Chapter Ten
ONE ZAMBIA ONE NATION

When Harry Chimowitz found a suitable house for us to buy in Lusaka, Cynthia and I began the painful process of packing up our household in London. After letting our house, we flew out in April 1965, to settle in Ngumbo (Maybin) Road, Lusaka. Our son David was ten years old and Alan was eight. We came to settle in Zambia (in my case-resettle) with a continued interest in working for the ending of white domination in the whole Southern African region. We cherished our ties with the liberation movements of Rhodesia and South Africa and remained committed to them. We also wanted to play our full part in the political, cultural and economic development of Zambia.

As an active member of UNIP and one well-versed in disciplined party procedure, one of my first tasks after our arrival in Zambia was to go to UNIP headquarters to find out which branch of the party we should join. Mukangano branch in Rhodes Park was the appropriate one, and we were soon welcomed into it. After a few meetings I was elected its chairman. I had to chair evening meetings twice a week: on Friday night, of the whole branch; on Tuesday night of its executive committee, referred to as its cabinet. It promised to be very exciting.

At one branch meeting a member complained that he was still being stopped at night by the police for questioning, even though the night curfew had been abolished by the UNIP government: this must be taken up with the authorities he insisted. The complaint was echoed by other members and so it was taken to our cabinet meeting on the following Tuesday, where it was again discussed by, more or less, the same people, since there were so many cabinet positions that almost every branch member either held a substantive post or that of deputy.

At another branch meeting a member recounted for twenty minutes how he was stopped by a European plot-owner when he tried to take a short-cut to go to the Longacres shops, for the purpose of 'eat some more'. I suspected that this was some code-phrase for 'helping himself, without paying' and so I was reluctant to allow that complaint to go to cabinet. Was he always taking this short-cut, I asked tongue in cheek, rather than posing to him the question of whether it was right to help himself without paying. 'No', he answered, 'before independence I used to pass around the plot, along the road for the purpose of eat some more, but that was too long.' My reluctance to take this complaint to cabinet surprised the members and they could sense some misunderstanding. My position was, however, not helped by the lengthy explanation of the significance of 'eat some more'. It turned out to be a biscuit made in South Africa and marketed under the label of Eet Sum Mor. Trespassing was, clearly, the real issue and that was a difficult matter to deal with, even by cabinet, and the complainant never got satisfaction. Through discussions such as this, Cynthia and I got to know the local custom of going into great chronological detail before getting to the point, but we also got to know the matters, minor to us, that were of issue to the people living as servants in the low density suburbs.

Officials from UNIP Provincial Office were not above exploiting the simplicity of our members, who were, in the main, house servants working in European households. In order to convince our members to attend a rally in down-town Lusaka on a Sunday, one official addressed our branch, emphasising that the speaker will be: 'Doctor, Doctor, Doctor Kaunda!' (He was referring to Kaunda's three honorary doctorates).

Cynthia and I regularly attended branch (and cabinet) meetings for a year or so before we decided that we should try to get a branch going in the town centre where we could have members from the professional and business community included and so be able to raise the level of discussion. Mainza Chona, the party general secretary was against this. It appeared to me that the party leadership were quite happy with party life remaining at the Mukangano branch level, but Cynthia and I were finding that level somewhat tiresome and decided that we should allow our membership of Mukangano branch to lapse. The branch did not exist for much longer and became defunct after several members obtained employment in state enterprises such as the Tourist Board. Lapsing our branch membership did not mean, however, that we stopped considering ourselves as members of UNIP.

Mulungushi Rock, near Kabwe, was the holy of holies of UNIP. I had attended two Mulungushi conferences in early 1964 as a delegate from the

London branch and I was also there for two days and a night at the crucial conference when the delegates were voting for party vice-president. The competition was between Kamanga and Kapwepwe. Much canvassing was being done beforehand. I was staying in a grass hut with Jimmy Skinner, the party's legal advisor and Zambia's first Attorney-General, when Mainza Chona rushed in to say that Kapwepwe was walking between the huts, greeting delegates and that something ought to be done to counter this. Clearly, Chona and Skinner were in some anti-Kapwepwe camp. This was generally known, but news to me.

During the vote for party vice-president old Mama Julia Chakemoneka tried to stage a pro-Kapwepwe demonstration, but was grabbed by Dingiswayo Banda, one of the members of the Central Committee, and he held her firmly in his arms until the result was announced in favour of Kamanga. It could not escape my notice that there was much tension between the two camps and this division was to persist for many years and eventually led to a split in UNIP. Kapwepwe once related to me how he had groomed Kaunda for political leadership when the latter was still a stutterer. Now that Kaunda was at the top, Kapwepwe expected to be, at least, the number two. But there was more to it than Kapwepwe's feeling about his rightful place in the UNIP hierarchy. (Kaunda conquered his stutter, according to Kapwepwe, with the use of a walking stick, which he would stamp against the ground whenever he got into speech difficulties).

There were two camps: one mainly from Bemba-speaking areas supporting Kapwepwe and one mainly from non-Bemba-speaking areas supporting Kamanga. The next party conference at Mulungushi Rock took place in 1967 and there the Kapwepwe camp won the day and Simon Kapwepwe was elected party vice-president to replace Kamanga. I wanted to attend that conference but I was not included in the Lusaka team. I suspected that it was because it was thought by the provincial leadership that I was in a camp not of their liking. The truth was that I was in no camp at all. I had avoided allying myself with either. Rumour persisted that Simon Kapwepwe was really in competition, not for position number two, but for position number one. I tended to dismiss that and focused on the national issues for which he stood, which I saw as no different from those motivating Kaunda. (In 1990 I heard from Valentine Musakanya, who was cabinet secretary in the years immediately following independence, that Kaunda always thought I was in Kapwepwe's camp).

Had I followed the local tradition of gearing one's politics to personal friendship, I should have, in fact, been in Kamanga's camp, for we had been friends socially and politically since 1951. Whereas I had been friendly with Kapwepwe only from 1960 and at only a superficial level, at that. However, my political alliances have always been based on principles and personal friendship would follow politics, rather than the other way round.

I kept in touch with Jimmy Skinner, the Attorney-General, who lived close by. He invited my views on the appointment of consultants for the new railway workshops in Kabwe. It turned out that the government was faced with a threat of legal action from a British firm of consultants: a double commitment had been made to a British firm by the Ministry of Transport and to a French firm by the Ministry of Development and Planning. To resolve this problem I was invited to State House one evening to give my views; present were Kaunda, Kamanga (then vice-president) and Skinner. The issue was resolved by sticking to the appointment of the British firm and placating the French by awarding them the consultancy for the Maamba Colliery development. This was the *only* occasion when my views were sought by President Kaunda, yet a widespread view persisted in Zambia that I had an entrée to State House as an advisor. My advice was not sought and I did not offer it.

Towards the end of 1964, after being established for half a year with only minor commissions coming from government (the main source of consultancy work) our firm was appointed by the director of buildings, Mr Baldwin, as structural consultants for the new parliament building. My partner, Sascha Magasiner, and I both took it in turn to work on this project and we were joined by Julian Siann, an engineer from Cape Town, who applied to work with us in independent Zambia. We set about training Zambian structural draughtsmen and were the first firm to do so.

Our next government commission of interest was from the Development and Planning Commission (it was then not integrated with the Ministry of Finance) for a bridge across the Zambezi at Sesheke and an associated harbour. Up to Sesheke, western Zambia lies on both banks of the river and the road south from Mongu, while following the left bank until Senanga, then avoids the heavily watered left bank and runs along the drier right bank until Katima Mulilo, which is across the river from Sesheke. This road or, as it was then, track in the Kalahari sands, was developed by the labour recruiting agency, WNLA, for transporting Africans from Barotseland for work on the South African gold mines. Once the route crossed, by pontoon, from the left to right bank of the Zambezi at Senanga, it was joined by a branch from Kalabo, which, while still in Zambia, acted as the concentration point for recruits from Angola. This route, though all on Kalahari sands, was traversed before the Second World War without four-wheel-drive trucks, by the simple device of placing grass in the wheel-ruts in the sand. On reaching Katimo Mulilo, the recruits would be driven south through Botswana after a short trip through the Caprivi Strip.

To proceed to Livingstone, which is some two hundred kilometres downstream, Zambians would have to enter South Africa which was then occupying the Caprivi Strip, at Katima Mulilo, and pick up a boat or barge on the right-bank harbour and proceed downstream. Crossing to the left bank by dug-out canoe, would take Zambians back to Zambia at Sesheke and from there a track had been developed through the Kalahari sands to the forestry station of Mulobezi, which was also a railhead for a railway to Livingstone. The overland route from Sesheke to Livingstone was some three hundred kilometres: not only a hundred kilometres longer than by river, but also much slower.

The established traffic routines then involved no customs or immigration formalities at Katima Mulilo. Zambian traffic by river barge from Kazungula would disembark and offload at the harbour in the Caprivi Strip and proceed, through a nominal border barrier, to a post on the right bank in Zambia and from there to Senanga by road. To proceed further upstream continuously with river transport was not possible because at Katima Mulilo there were a series of rock barriers, creating rapids and there was a further obstruction in the form of the Ngonye Falls at Sioma, one hundred and thirty kilometres upstream. Earlier in the century barges did proceed upstream and were towed on sledges to bypass the rapids at Katima Mulilo and Ngonye Falls.

The Development and Planning Commission thought that South Africa might deny Zambia the use of the harbour in the Caprivi Strip. It therefore asked us to design a harbour on the left bank at Sesheke, and a bridge

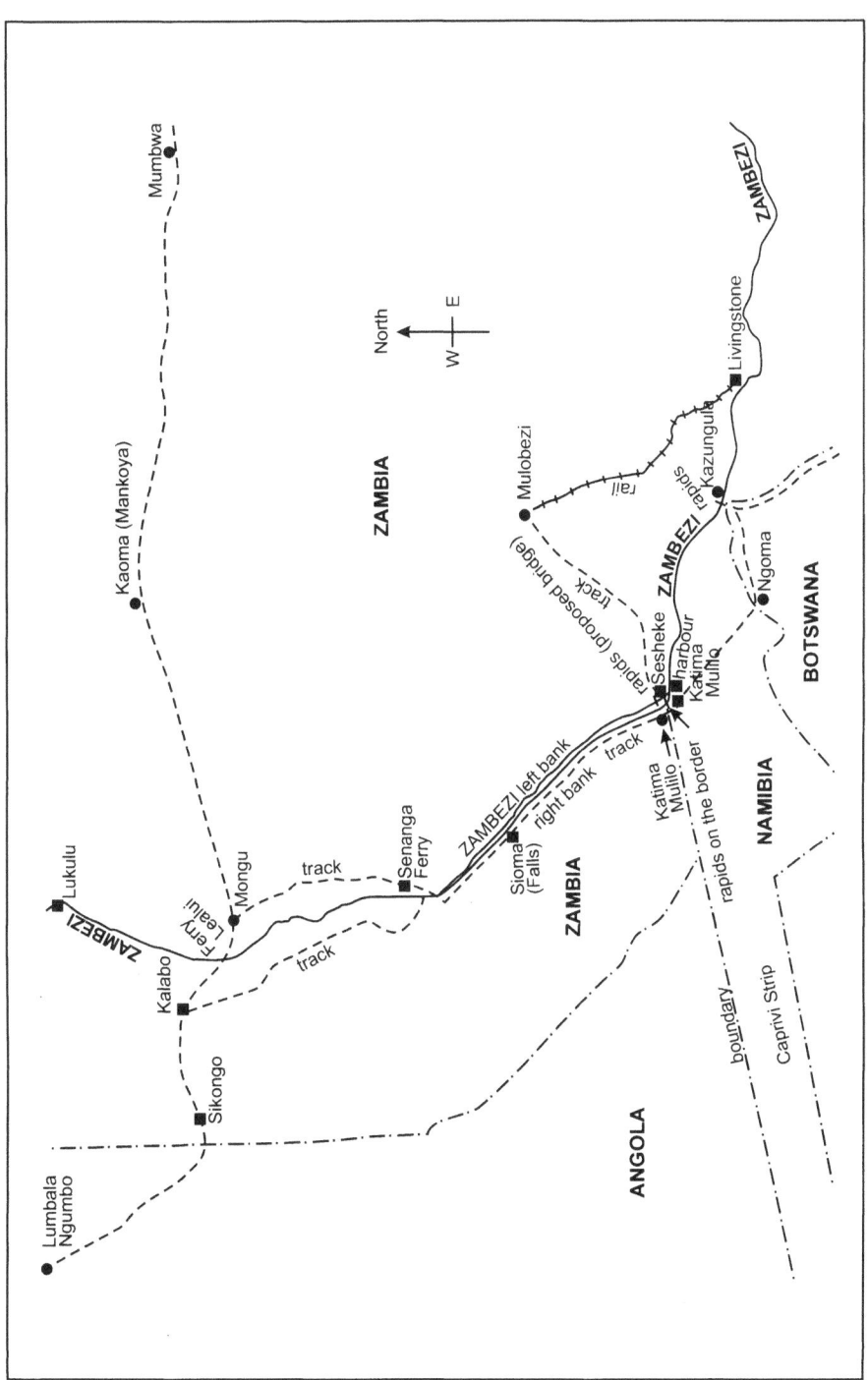

crossing, founded on the rock outcrops upstream, to enable Zambian traffic to cross to the right bank, all within Zambia. For both political and professional reasons I found this commission of great interest and my partner, Harry Chimowitz, and I threw ourselves into it with great zeal. For our initial reconnaissance we travelled up from Kazungula to Katima Mulilo by the barge of Zambezi River Transport and disembarked at the harbour in the Caprivi Strip. I did this with some trepidation as this was in South African territory, where I knew I was unwelcome. However, nothing untoward happened and we walked unhindered from the harbour through the border to Zambia on the right bank of the Zambezi. We spent a few hours there observing the rocks, which jut out in several broken bands across the river and decided to locate the bridge not on the band, which coincides with the border, but on one further upstream. We did this to avoid having to negotiate with the South African authorities, and so that Zambians could cross without border formalities. The bands consist of basalt dykes and each appears to have many outcrops at low water suitable to found piers on, without involving work in deep water. We decided we would need to return for a week with survey gear to plot these outcrops and the bank approaches and then decide on suitable spans.

We did return some weeks later, albeit through routes different from that which brought us the first time. Our final recommendation for the bridge consisted of prestressed concrete bridge beams spanning some twenty-five metres and supported on concrete piers. The total length of the bridge was about one kilometre. For the deck I recommended the use of teak sleepers, which were being manufactured at nearby Mulobezi for use on railroads. The local teak is very strong and very durable and can be used economically to carry road traffic. I did this in order to utilise local material, and also to minimise the importation of aggregates over long distances at great cost. Roads Department had other views and in any case the bridge was never built and came back on the agenda only after Namibia gained its independence. Although I was again involved, it was in a different capacity. Harry and I did return for our survey work: he by Land-Rover via Mulobezi and I separately, by Land-Rover via Mongu and Senanga.

For the survey, I arrived at Katima Mulilo in the company of my old friends Tommy Fox-Pitt and Basil Davidson, having set out from Lusaka and travelling to Mongu via Mumbwa and Mankoya (now Kaoma). Basil had wanted to research Lozi oral history and Tommy, having just done a post-independence stint in Mbala to assist the provincial administration in Zambianization, was keen to do a nostalgic trip before leaving Zambia to return to the UK for proper retirement. Tommy had once been acting provincial commissioner in Barotseland. I stopped off at Katima Mulilo, while they carried on through Mulobezi to Choma and then to Lusaka. Tommy provided his Land-Rover, which he had used for his year in Mbala and was to sell on completing this trip. We started our trip on the tarred Great North road and turned west at Landless Corner and then never saw any tar for the next 1600 kilometres.

At Mongu we visited Lealui for an audience with the Litunga, Sir Mwanawina III, who had tea served to us in a very fine china tea set, a gift from the Queen, and told us that he was coerced by the colonial authorities to support Federation. I have heard otherwise from my old friend Peter Fraenkel, who was at the time in the Northern Rhodesian Broadcasting Service: that it was not so much coercion as inducement with a promise of being sent with a Lozi entourage to attend the coming Coronation of Princess Elizabeth. Peter thought that Mwanawina only agreed to urge peaceful opposition, not acceptance.

Basil had a session at Nalolo with a Lozi historian, recommended by Munu Sipalo. The historian went over well-trodden ground, which started with the myth 'Nyambe and his wife-daughter begat the first Lozi king (Nyambe was God)'. He went on to list the Lozi kings up to the then ruling Mwanawina III and recalled the Makololo conquest, their rule and eventual defeat. I do not recall Basil using this research in a book. He remembered this trip when he wrote to me in July 1995 on hearing that I was an MP in the Western Province. (See: Zukas Papers, Zambia Archives.)

Tommy Fox-Pitt left Zambia after this trip to settle on a farm in Devon and soon after his departure he and I were given Zambian awards by President Kaunda, at the 1966 independence anniversary celebrations. We were each appointed Officer of the Companion Order of Freedom, third division, (OCF), for having 'given great service in the national cause which resulted in the attainment of independence'. There was also a well-deserved award for a former mineworkers' leader who had remained a staunch nationalist fighter and even suffered imprisonment, Robinson Puta.

I was happy with the award: it represented recognition of my contribution. However, one visitor to the country, Ralph Schoenman, an associate of Kaunda's and mine from pre-independence days in London and secretary to Lord Bertrand Russell, thought that I should have been asked, on my return, if I would be prepared to serve in the cabinet. He posed the question to Mainza Chona, who replied that 'South Africa might bomb the Copperbelt if Simon were included in the cabinet'! The new president and his cabinet were certainly in fear of South Africa at the time and even hesitated to give asylum to Jack and Ray Simons when they arrived in Lusaka after fleeing from South Africa. It took a strong intervention by Simon Kapwepwe to overcome this hesitation.

That the South African government might have had an exaggerated view of my importance in the struggle against apartheid would not have surprised me. I was, however, surprised that this should have somehow been passed on to the new government of Zambia. During our years in London, Cynthia and I were under South African surveillance. When my brother-in-law, Dr Harry Webber, returned to South Africa from London in 1956, he found that the government suspected his political bona fides since it was recorded in his file that he was at a dinner with Simon Zukas at a London West-End hotel. It happened to be nothing more than a family occasion, but the South African government had not yet discovered our family relationship.

The illegal regime in Rhodesia posed a greater threat to Zambia than South Africa at that time. In 1967 four Rhodesian residents were detained in Zambia on suspicion of spying for Rhodesia. One of these was a Mr Cecil Swift, a quantity surveyor and partner in the firm of Hood and Swift, which had offices in Zambia and Rhodesia. While I had worked on projects with Adam Hood, I had not met Swift, but I was aware that he came up frequently to Lusaka to attend to partnership business. During a search, carried out at Swift's house in Lusaka by D/Inspector Norman of the Zambian Police, several documents were found, which were later produced as evidence at the tribunal set up to review the detentions. Amongst these documents was one in Swift's handwriting which read as follows:

1. Every 2 weeks
2. Major construction projects Govt. & private

3.   Foreign interests in bldg. industry
 *4.   Simon Zukas
   5.   Harry Chaimowitz [sic].

The list contained a total of 21 items, including 'Military/Police activities' and one, Item, no 17, saying, 'Destroy letters'. (Exhibit P22, Report of the Tribunal on Detainees, GRZ cabinet Office Paper, 1967)

Harry Chimowitz was a Rhodesian by birth. While Harry and I were not surprised to discover the Rhodesian government's interest in us, we were not able to discover the significance of the asterisk against my name. Perhaps it implied special attention? However, we did not stop our frequent contacts with Chikerema, Nyandoro and Silundika, the ZAPU leaders in exile, and Simpson Ntambaningwe of ZAPU. We already exercised prudence in our contacts with other Rhodesian Europeans. (The tribunal was satisfied that this was a 'list of Swift's activities and duties in connection with obtaining by him and passing on information to Rhodesian Intelligence' and Swift was deported).

My links with Chikerema caused me some embarrassment on one occasion. ZAPU was co-operating with the South African ANC in the fight against the Smith regime and wanted to show this to the world. A filming-team was brought to Lusaka and Cynthia and I were asked to allow them to interview Chikerema and Oliver Tambo, president of the ANC, in our garden. Unbeknown to us, the filming crew were then taken to the Zambezi valley to film camps where fighters of the two organizations were training. Chikerema was later shown to the world as speaking from these camps. This caused embarrassment to the Zambian government, who had been claiming that no such camps existed on Zambian soil. This pretence had the purpose of enabling Zambia to condemn Rhodesian military incursions across the border in the Security Council. As time went on this game wore thin, but at the time the Zambian government was furious with Chikerema. As a result of this incident, Cynthia and I took a decision not to lend ourselves to liberation strategies passively: we would want to know the whole move before agreeing to be involved. We also took the view that we would ask no questions from those involved in covert actions against Rhodesia or South Africa as long as we were not being asked to assist.

Cynthia and I were enjoying our life in Zambia. Having placed our two sons in a UK boarding school, we found ourselves with a lot of spare time and not enough to do over weekends, so we decided to spend a long weekend at Lake Malawi in 1966. At Blantyre Airport our booked car was waiting and we set off for Lilongwe immediately we were through immigration, as we had four hundred kilometres ahead of us. We were driving most of the day and reached Lilongwe after dark. As we parked in a hotel carpark, an African police officer approached us, checked our number plate and asked us to accompany him to the police station where he showed us a telex from police HQ, Blantyre, that he was to apprehend us and return us forthwith to Blantyre. We were bewildered. Being pretty tired and hungry we asked whether we could stay the night in the hotel, where we had a booking. He felt he could not agree to that, in view of his telex. So we were made to drive through the night back to Blantyre, with the police officer as guard and passenger. When I was too tired to continue driving, he allowed us to pull in at a police station on the way and take a nap for an hour or two in the car. On arriving in Blantyre as it got light he directed us to the house of the chief immigration officer, an Englishman, who made his bathroom available to us and gave us breakfast and then told us that we would have to leave for Lusaka on the afternoon plane. 'You slipped in through the airport, but the Doctor does not like you', we were told. The Doctor was, of course, Kamuzu Banda, the Life President, whom I first met in London in December 1952 when he questioned why I had not formed a white anti-federation party instead of becoming a member of Congress. No doubt he had also heard of our left-wing activities. The chief immigration officer told us we could lodge an appeal to the Doctor. Since the Doctor had recently forced into exile all the leaders of the Malawi Congress Party who had prepared the ground for his homecoming after an absence of some forty years, I did not take up the offer. He murdered some of them, inside and outside Malawi, while he was on excellent terms with Britain and even the apartheid regime in South Africa.

As a result of this episode and my desire to see even the less accessible parts of Zambia, I attempted, some years later, the exploration by foot of a route to the Nyika plateau, up the escarpment from Muyombe in Zambia. This would remove the need for tourists and Zambians to have to reach the Zambian part of this beautiful national park by road *via* Malawi. However, a road up the escarpment *direct* to the Nyika Plateau from Muyombe would be very expensive and is something for the distant future.

Simon Kapwepwe was vice-president from 1967 until 1970, when he resigned. He formed the United Progressive Party, (UPP) in 1971. Although I was on close personal terms with many of the UPP leaders (Chimba, Chambeshi, Chapoloko and Kapwepwe) I was not in sympathy with the moves to form this party as I saw it mainly as an expression of Bemba nationalism. On expressing my unease about the coming split to John Papworth, who was then working in State House as an assistant to Kaunda, I was told that Kaunda thought 'It could be contained'! Indeed, it was contained, and so was tribalism. The UPP was banned and its leaders arrested in September 1971, with the exception of Kapwepwe, their president, who contested and won the Mufulira parliamentary seat. However, in February 1972 Kapwepwe was also arrested and Kaunda announced his intention of creating a one party state.

Our son David, who was only sixteen and at boarding school in the UK, wrote a letter to President Kaunda protesting at the imprisonment of Kapwepwe and the moves towards a one-party system. David concluded with the 'hope that my father will withdraw his support from UNIP....' I came to know of this letter only when Kaunda's principal private secretary, Mark Chona, sent me a copy of the letter and his reply, in which he says: 'Presumably your father may have already informed you about the exact state of affairs....' Although I regretted the steps being taken to 'contain' the UPP, I was, at the time, still a supporter of a one-party system for Zambia, but I did not try to explain to David 'the exact state of affairs'. This one party system appeared to be the solution to the tribal schisms that were threatening to tear Zambia apart.

This point of view I retained for another decade and when, after their release from detention, Chimba, Chapoloko and Chambeshi, leading officials in the banned UPP, came to see me to ask for financial support, I had to remind them that they did not come to see me before deciding to split off from UNIP and I castigated them for supporting in Parliament the bill for a referendum to put an end to the provision in the constitution for referenda on certain crucial issues. The bill also empowered Parliament to remove, by simple majority, entrenched clauses from the constitution. They were now suffering the consequences of their own short-sightedness. We parted as friends but they went away empty-handed. During Chimba's detention Cynthia and I had given some financial assistance to Mrs Chimba.

Kaunda's next move to contain sectionalism was the introduction of the one-party participatory democracy, after appointing a commission to go round the country to take evidence and make recommendations. The recommendations were then heavily modified by government and in August 1973 we had a new constitution and went into the Second Republic.

In 1970, before writing *In the Eye of the Storm*, his book on Angola, Basil Davidson was staying with us while waiting to be conducted by MPLA cadres into Angola. One night, on returning home after dark, Cynthia noticed a grey volkswagen parked in the street opposite our house, with its lights off. I decided to investigate and the car started driving off. I gave chase in our car and caught up with it, only to be given the slip at a traffic light, when the escaping volkswagen went through on the red. I reported this to State House and gave the car number in a statement to the detective who was sent round. There were many Portuguese living and working in Lusaka, and some were spying for the Caetano regime. Despite this surveillance, Basil was taken safely by MPLA into Angola to observe the guerrilla war being conducted by Dr Neto's forces. Basil came back safely from the trip, if in a very emaciated state. He had to be fed back to some normality by the Chimowitzes, with whom he stayed, as we had gone off to the UK before his return. On a trip like the one described in his book, he could hardly have given us a firm return date! Zambia could not escape being affected by the struggle against Portuguese imperialism in the region.

When in 1969 the chief justice, Jimmy Skinner, supported a white judge who had given a judgement in favour of the release of some captured Portuguese soldiers who had crossed into Zambia in pursuit of freedom fighters on our south-eastern border, riots broke out in Lusaka. The rioters demonstrated at the High Court and tried to force open Skinner's door when he locked himself in. They then marched to State House, where the president addressed them and instead of condemning their behaviour as a serious breach of law and order, commended their reaction and said that in future he would 'give them guns'. He was, no doubt, trying to calm the crowd and to control the situation that was being instigated by pro-Kapwepwe elements, who were taking advantage of the widespread emotional dissatisfaction with the judge's ruling and Skinner's support for it. It was rumoured that a minister had even gone to solicit support for the proposed demonstration from an armed National Service unit in Kafue. When I confronted Chimba with this, he claimed that it was Grey Zulu, not he, who was that day in Kafue. To me, it appeared that on that day power had passed to the street and that Kaunda was trying to placate the rioters with his address to them because he, too, sensed that *even* elements of the state machine appeared to be on the side of the street. Indeed, that was so: the para-military guard, normally brought to the houses of ministers and judges every night was not provided to the chief justice that night! This proved the last straw for the Skinners and they decided to fly out from Zambia the next day, leaving their main belongings to be packed by friends.

Mr Skinner may have been right in principle to support his judge's unpopular decision, though, with his past political experience, he should not have neglected to phrase his remarks to take account of the strong feelings that had by then grown amongst the Zambian people against the Portuguese. The Skinner statement provided an issue around which the Kapwepwe supporters were able to create a united front with the pro Kaunda tendency, before Kaunda realised what was going on.

As Cynthia and I were going to the UK a few weeks later to be with our boys during their school holidays, we made a point of going over to Dublin to see the Skinners. Jimmy was in a very bad state of nerves and we felt very sorry for him and the family. He felt let down by his president, whom he had served loyally, not only since independence, but also in the run up to it. But what rankled him even more, was that not a single Zambian had come to see him or telephoned him to express sympathy. A Zambian legal colleague and minister, whom he had assisted in professional development, gave him the cold shoulder in the airport VIP lounge while waiting for departure. This colleague hid his head in a magazine. Only after seeing that Kaunda had come to say goodbye, did this colleague feel confident enough to come up to shake Skinner's hand. (Skinner was subsequently assisted by Kaunda financially with a lump sum.)

I learnt from Skinner that the split within government had reached a point where ministers were hardly in their offices and civil servants were told to send matters to cabinet and yet cabinet was not meeting. The split nearly came to a head at the time Simon Kapwepwe's son, Paul, died from injuries received in a motor accident, but the period of mourning took the heat out of the crisis and things simmered down. Clearly this split manifested itself in the riots against Mr Skinner.

*****

In May 1972, I transmitted to Kaunda a recommendation by Basil Davidson, Lord (Jock) Campbell and Canon John Collins to appoint a left-wing economist to do research on South African military and economic imperialism in the region. The person they recommended was appointed and did a considerable amount of work on this subject. But on seeing the numerous demands for funds to pay for this research and seeing relatively little new in it, I consulted Jack Simons on its worth and he, too, saw little in it. I then wrote to Davidson that I was recommending to Kaunda that the arrangement be terminated.

On that occasion, in May, when I went to State House to see Kaunda, I also discussed the request by Mark Chona (principal assistant to the president) to release Joseph Nyaywa, one of my firm's engineers, to work on some secret projects for State House. Joseph was a young structural engineer, who had come to us from the Roan Antelope copper mine and he was training under me. He already had a degree in structural engineering from the University of Bristol and was showing great promise. I went to discuss this request with Kaunda as I thought that Joseph still needed to acquire more practical experience, as he had just failed in his interview for membership of the Institution of Civil Engineers (of Britain) and I felt that he should have another try at it shortly. Kaunda thought that the national interest was such that Joseph should switch immediately. I never asked what the projects were in this national interest and nor was I told! After leaving us, Joseph built up an institution with a high technical capacity and was also involved in the supervision of the construction of escape tunnels at State House as well as an underground command post and several other secret projects. Although we kept in touch, Joseph never mentioned the tunnels to me or the nature of the other projects. I did, however, get to know what his projects were from other sources downtown and they were certainly technically ambitious and impressive, given Zambia's state of development. One of the tunnels got flooded soon after construction and, fortunately, Kaunda did not have to make use of any of them during the UDI raids. It is equally fortunate that Zambia managed to see the collapse of Ian Smith and his illegal regime in Rhodesia without having to rely on some of the ordnance systems that Nyaywa was developing! Joseph was not only one of Zambia's most able engineers, but one of very high integrity and dedication to the national cause. Our firm lost a valuable member, but we were satisfied that, in the position he moved to, he was making a big contribution to Zambia.

MPLA had received support from the Zambian government for their struggle against the Portuguese regime in Angola, yet when the latter's collapse came in Portugal and in the African colonies, Kaunda was to start supporting MPLA's enemy: Savimbi's UNITA. Zambia called for the formation of a government of national unity in Luanda, while allowing Tiny Rowland's Lonrho jet to fly arms to Savimbi via Lusaka Airport. Also, there was proof 'that... a Zambia Airways plane laden with ten tons of arms and ammunition from the Zambia Army had taken off for Huambo, UNITA's headquarters in Southern Angola. The consignment also included radio communication equipment as a donation to UNITA'. (See *Downfall of President Kaunda*, by BS Chisala).

One night in 1977, Jack Simons came to tell me as a member of the University Council, that students at the university were very restive about these goings on and asked what could be done to make government aware of the unpopularity of its position on Angola. I could only suggest that the students demonstrate, providing they did so peacefully. Next morning there was a strong demonstration against this policy from many students at the university, but Kaunda appeared to take no notice of this pressure *at the time*. The police detained some lecturers, including Robert Molteno, who was kept in detention for some weeks and then deported to the UK. I was not aware at the time that an underground Marxist group had been formed in the university and that it was based on a cell system with three members to a cell, with some expatriate lecturers heavily involved. It took a long time for Kaunda and his cabinet to come back on the side of MPLA and when they did, they tried to get Zambians to forget that UNIP had ever been pro-UNITA and Savimbi.

In his memoir, *Years of Renewal*, Henry Kissinger has confirmed what some of us thought at the time: that Kaunda and the cabinet had switched their support to Savimbi in 1975 when they saw that MPLA had active Soviet support in taking over power in Luanda, the Angolan capital. What we did not know at the time was that a state visit to Washington was used by Kaunda to lobby President Ford to provide American military assistance to Savimbi in his fight against the MPLA. Kaunda thus accomplished a 'change [in] American national policy' towards Angola. 'Kaunda persuaded Ford that Soviet arms deliveries were threatening to help the Angolan Marxist MPLA... seize power and that American assistance was essential to frustrate Soviet designs'. Kaunda's meeting with Ford was on 19 April 1975, well before the date projected for Angola's independence, which was 11 November 1975.

Our president was asking for *far more* than support from the US for Savimbi, in order to level the playing field in the coming election: he was actually suggesting to Kissinger the anti-democratic position that 'Regardless of the outcome of the elections, Savimbi should be the president'! The result of this intervention by Kaunda was not only the intensified involvement of the CIA in Angola with massive arms deliveries: it also led to the American encouragement of the South African invasion of Angola. South Africa made use of the MPLA dissident, Daniel Chipenda, whose splinter group had been supported by Kaunda in an attempt to be 'involved in the internal politics of the MPLA'. (See Kissinger *Years of Renewal*).

That the UNIP government under Kaunda was supporting Chipenda against Neto in the schism that was developing in the MPLA in 1974 was known to some of us in Lusaka at the time. Chipenda was an Umbundu, and he played the tribal card with our UNIP politicians, who usually understood such schisms in tribal, rather than ideological terms. Some Zambian ministers believed that Neto had turned against Chipenda and company, as freedom came in sight, merely because they were Umbundu. As a result, Chipenda was being protected by Zambian plain-clothes police officers while he was in hospital in Lusaka. He was refusing to go to our western border, as demanded by the MPLA command. I was given a document by one of Chipenda's supporters in July 1973, in which Chipenda put questions pertaining to difficulties that had arisen in the MPLA:

> why the militarism
> the lack of cooperation between the people and guerrillas, and guerrillas and leaders. abuse against the population

executions without trial
difference in standard of living amongst militants
no real participation of the population in the life of the organization in the liberated areas

The document was a response to Chipenda' suspension from the MPLA, announced in a notice by Dr Neto dated 10 August 1973. I had some sympathy for Chipenda but no knowledge that Kaunda was behind him and encouraging a split in the MPLA.

Kaunda's real position was not merely that of advocating a government of national unity for Angola and was a far cry from neutrality. Much later, as a result of Western foot-dragging on removing the Smith regime in Rhodesia, he changed his position and co-operated with the Eastern European bloc. But before that time, he appears to have feared Soviet influence on our western border to the point of soliciting American intervention in Angola, supporting Unita in its fight against MPLA and supporting Chipenda against Neto *within* MPLA. Daniel Chipenda later collaborated with the South African forces that invaded Angola and he appeared in a white uniform at the head of their column that was nearing Luanda before it was thrown back by Cuban troops.

I heard from Elijah Mudenda in 1974 that Dr Neto was out of favour with our government, while a meeting of the MPLA was taking place in Lusaka under the auspices of the OAU. The meeting was surrounded by a unit of the Zambian Army which had orders to stop a walk-out by any of the factions. Unity was not achieved at this conference. Mudenda was blaming Neto for not being able to handle traditional chiefs, but I suspected there were other reasons! There was also Zambian condemnation of torture by the Neto faction of MPLA near our north western town of Zambezi and the execution of some MPLA dissidents on Zambian soil, near the border. My friend Jethro Mutti, the minister of state in the North Western Province, also talked to me of 'MPLA's lack of understanding of the tribal factor in their politics'. I thought these remarks of some significance and spoke to Liz Mathos, who arranged for me to brief some of the MPLA leadership in Lusaka. (Jethro has historical links to eastern Angola as he is of the Ankoya people who settled in Zambia after emmigrating from Angola.) Vernon Mwanga and Rupiah Banda, who were both friendly with Tiny Rowland of Lonrho, once boasted of having been major players in swinging Zambia against the MPLA and in favour of Savimbi.

After the MPLA took control of Luanda, a journalist who had been there and was passing through Lusaka gave a lecture on the state of affairs in Luanda at the house of Marjorie and Harry Chimowitz. I attended and found the lecture of some interest: the main point made was that there was in Luanda a power parallel to the MPLA which was controlling the poverty-stricken masses in the shanty towns and competing with the MPLA. It was not a pro-MPLA meeting, though those attending were, no doubt, all in sympathy with it.

The next morning I heard that Harry Chimowitz had been taken in by the police for questioning about the meeting: 'who organized it and who attended?'. Although Harry mentioned me as one of those attending, I was never approached or questioned by the police. We had been living in a one party state since 1973 and now it was becoming clear that this state was developing elements of thought control. Fortunately, Harry was released that same afternoon, while I was still preparing to petition Kaunda for it.

In November 1974, my father passed away in Salisbury where my parents had been living since the mid-fifties. Through the help of a relative, permission was obtained for me to be allowed into Rhodesia on condition that I made no statement to the press. At the airport Jake and Abe had no immigration problems; I was issued with a 'Notice to Prohibited Immigrant', but allowed to enter and stay for the funeral and a few days after it. My father was seventy five years old when he died of heart failure while locking the gate. My mother was left to live alone in the house, which they owned. She was seventy four and since I was a prohibited immigrant, I could not visit her. It was very frustrating for us and after she declined our offer to live with us in Lusaka, we arranged for her to emigrate to Israel. We settled her in a flat in Haifa where she spent the last five years of her life.

One government project which my firm worked on during the late seventies was a complex to house our intelligence services. We were the consulting structural and services engineers; the architects were Erhard Lorenz & Partners. The complex, generally known as Red Brick, is essentially a multi-storey office block with a basement. The basement houses a practice range for revolver shooting practice by personnel who protect VIPs. This is no different from that provided in Europe in many banks for practice by their security personnel and tellers. On completion and occupation, rumours developed that the complex contained dungeons. Even my friend Rankin Sikasula, who was very much part of the Kaunda system, thought so until I enlightened him to the contrary. During the MMD campaign in 1990/91 the rumour gained strength and it was even claimed that in the basement were torture chambers. This was countered by Kaunda saying that 'Simon Zukas should be asked since he was the architect'. BS Chisala wrote:

> Former Minister of Home Affairs in the UNIP government, Lewis Changufu, said there were no torture chambers. He said Simon Zukas was the architect of the Red Brick and he should know if provision was made for such chambers. (Chisala *The Downfall of President Kaunda*, p157).

Although, for professional reasons, I issued no statement, I denied that there was provision of dungeons or torture chambers in the complex whenever I was asked about it.

In March 1978, while I was driving back from visiting Jake and his family in Ndola, and bringing back our house-servant, Esther Ncube, from an operation, we had a car accident. Esther was killed outright and Cynthia sustained severe injuries to her back and ribs. It took her several weeks to recover and many months after that for us to get over this event. We were very grateful for the support we received from friends of all races. President Kaunda wrote that they were 'praying for her [Cynthia's] speedy recovery'. (See letter dated 31/3/78, Zukas Papers at National Archives) Zambian women friends came daily to visit Cynthia in hospital in such numbers that the matron had to start limiting them for the sake of Cynthia's health. Cynthia's sister, Noreen, and her husband, Harry, flew up from Cape Town to be with us and as soon as Cynthia was able to travel, we flew to Southern Spain to have a holiday with them.

The South African ANC had offices in Lusaka and I kept in touch with Oliver Tambo. In early May 1979 I assisted him with the preparation of a document for presentation at a meeting in Dar es Salaam* but then lost touch with him for a while. A considerable time later came the news that, in order to clear the way for progress towards independence for Namibia, an international understanding was reached whereby the ANC would have to leave Angola. I then immediately received an approach on Oliver's behalf to assist urgently

---

* See Plate 7.

with the design of a prison, to be built wherever the ANC would move to. 'I am an engineer and not an architect', I explained. 'No matter! Can you do it in secret and in great haste' was the reply. Since no fee would be involved and since it was to be secret, I could not use my office staff or seek advice from my long-time friend, architect Erhard Lorenz. There was no option but to spend several nights working at home for long hours, relying on my painful eight months experience of Livingstone prison and drawing up a scheme in my own fair hand. I provided blocks of cells, ablution blocks, kitchen facilities, an administration block and several exercise yards.

My brief was to cater for quite a number of inmates, both male and female and of several categories, to be housed in separate blocks of cells. Apparently, over the years, the ANC had detained some criminal elements that it discovered in its ranks in Angola, some dissidents who knew too much to be released and some suspected spies that South African intelligence had managed to infiltrate. All these would have to be taken with them on the ANC's departure from Angola. Hence the need for the prison.

Cynthia and I are a very close couple and we have few secrets from each other. Yet, I did not reveal to her at the time what I was working on for those few nights, just as she did not reveal to me that she was paying, from her own personal account in the UK, the school fees for Chris Hani's daughter in Lesotho! (Chris Hani was a prominent member of the South African Communist Party who was murdered during the transition to majority rule in South Africa.)

AN ATTEMPT TO FORCE A CHANGE OF COURSE

When one looks through the intelligence files of the First and Second Republics, i.e., of the Kaunda era, one cannot but be impressed with the meticulous attention which they received from Kaunda, in person. Anything he thought important in a report he noted in red ink in the margin, and referred to someone appropriate for noting or action, usually for his assistant, Mark Chona. He gave great attention to internal security and to the security of his person and, of course, to the security of the country from outside threats.

From the moment Kaunda became prime minister, he was confronted with the kidnapping of a white South African refugee from Lusaka and his transportation to South Africa in the boot of a car, without interception at the border. As president, he had to face many security infringements by Rhodesia after UDI and even the infiltration of one of their agents, John Brummer, as a resident of State House. Harold Wilson, then British prime minister, told Kapwepwe in London on 9 September 1966 that 'the South Africans and Rhodesians had infiltrated [the Zambian government] and that they will do great damages [sic] to us'. (See *The Kapwepwe Diaries*) Because of these events Kaunda was vigilant on security matters throughout his presidency and he set up a formidable machine for the purpose. Yet, in October 1980, a few days after Zambia's sixteenth independence anniversary celebrations, with the threat from Ian Smith and from South Africa not yet over, a coup attempt nearly succeeded. Preparations for it had been going on for many days within a few kilometres of Lusaka.

Kaunda had stood up to Smith and despite economic hardship and raids of various sorts which resulted in killings of freedom fighters and many Zambians, he managed to carry the nation with him for fifteen years. However, many people were becoming restive towards the end of the seventies, especially the elite, whom Kaunda had helped to create through the policy of nationalization of business, industry and mining.

I accompanied Cynthia to Livingstone for one meeting of the Museums Board, of which she and Edward Shamwana were members. At the evening social get-together Edward told me of his supply difficulties as a furniture manufacturer. (He was also a leading lawyer). He could no longer get springs for the manufacture of beds and easy chairs, which used to come up from Rhodesia. He felt that it was time 'Kaunda and Co were told that we had suffered long enough for others in the region'. Since I was of the view that our freedom was meaningless until the whole region was free from white domination, I did not agree with Edward and we drifted on to other matters. I did not then see any significance in his remarks as I had heard similar views from other members of the Zambian business elite. State propaganda attributed our economic ills, largely, if not totally, to the consequences of our valiant support for Zimbabwean freedom. The response of some of the elite was that 'we had better see a peace dividend when Zimbabweans get their independence'. Many Zambians were beginning to doubt that Kaunda's line was the whole truth: some felt that our economic ills were also due, to no small extent, to successive UNIP governments' mismanagement of the economy. We were supposed to be in a participatory democracy, yet changing course seemed impossible through the ballot box while a one-party state obtained.

In mid 1979 Kaunda got wind of the general mood against his policies. After the successful conclusion of the conference of Commonwealth heads of government in Lusaka, when steps to settle the Rhodesian problem were agreed on, Kaunda promised 'shortages to go within six months'. No doubt he was hoping that by then a friendly government would be in place in Rhodesia and goods would flow in from the south. (*Daily Mail*, 13 August 1979). Yet even nine months later there was no improvement in our economy and there were rumblings among those elements of the elite frequenting the Lusaka Flying Club. Kaunda lost his cool in April 1980, when Elias Chipimo was the guest speaker at the annual dinner of the Law Association. In discussing democracy, Chipimo advocated the multi-party system as the surest way of avoiding coups. He went on to ask 'Where is there going to be order if the only change in leadership is to be the death through the assassin's bullet?' Chipimo was referring to the assassination of the president of Liberia in the coup led by Sergeant Doe, but Kaunda saw this as Chipimo's recipe for Zambia and demanded his dismissal from chairmanship of the Standard Bank of Zambia. (*Times of Zambia*, 23/4/80)

The bank obliged and Elias was shattered and on the verge of a nervous breakdown when Cynthia and I went to see him. Cynthia and I knew Elias well enough not to suspect him as an active plotter and we went to see him out of solidarity with the views he had expressed and because we felt he was being unjustly dealt with by Kaunda. We found that Chipimo was seeing himself in Biblical martyr terms, but regretted his not expressing himself more obtusely. He had worked on his speech until the early hours of the morning and had not been alert enough to spot that he could be misinterpreted. I would like to feel that our visit helped Elias to regain his self-esteem. Kaunda named several others as part of the group of dissidents against his policies: John Mwanakatwe, Andrew Kashita, Valentine Musakanya, Francis Nkhoma, Lewis Changufu and Emanuel Kasonde. All of these had held high office in government since independence.

A half year later, I was shocked and upset when I heard that there had been some odd goings on in the Chilanga area, close to a farm in which I had purchased a one third share in 1975, and that a coup had been planned. Edward Shamwana was one of those arrested. What did upset me even more was being castigated by Stella Shamwana, Edward's English wife, a few days later, for 'what your friends had done in suspecting and arresting Edward'. I could offer no defence for the behaviour of my friends, as we sat down to dinner at our mutual dear friends' table, but agreed that Edward was a mere critic of the system and did not deserve to be treated as a security risk. Later Stella got to know the truth that Edward was a key player in the attempted coup, but I know from mutual friends that she had no inkling, at the material time, of his involvement, let alone leading role.

While proof was still being offered in court of Edward's involvement in the attempted coup and while this was being challenged by his defence, and while many doubted the court's impartiality, I was discussing the issue with my friend Arthur Wina, a former minister of finance and by then, like myself, a critic of the UNIP government. I learnt from him that there must be some truth in the allegations, as Edward had at one stage been sounding out some people for cabinet posts. I kept this bit of information to myself but wondered what I would have done had it reached me before government became aware of the plot!

One of the other accused was Valentine Musakanya. He was severely tortured by his interrogators and never really recovered his self-confidence and well-being. He was found not guilty. Although Valentine and I had not been on close terms, we had developed a mutual respect for each other. When I returned to Zambia he was chief secretary to the cabinet and had at one time been the Federal representative at Lubumbashi (Elisabethville) in Katanga, a post which involved his working closely with the British Consulate, as foreign affairs was not yet under the Federation. Valentine and I worked together when he was in charge of the Commission for Technical Education. He was high up in the civil service and responsible for the creation of our system of technical training, including a school for training pilots and aircraft technicians. He himself had qualified to fly and was an inspiration to many Zambians to take up flying. He served Kaunda from the months prior to independence until he and Kaunda no longer saw eye to eye. He was then appointed governor of the Bank of Zambia for the period following nationalization of most of the existing large enterprises, replacing the previous governor, Dr Justin Zulu, who was not in sympathy with the nationalization terms and the consequent outflow of foreign exchange. After a spell at the bank, Valentine was offered a post with IBM in Paris, but before finalizing the offer IBM wrote to Kaunda to ask whether they were in order to employ him. Kaunda's reply was 'He is a good man, but was not good to me'; they could go ahead and employ him. Clearly, Kaunda and Musakanya had differed on important issues.

Cynthia and I had no sympathy with the coup because we saw no mass movement behind it and because we suspected that one of its objectives was the withdrawal of support for the struggle in Rhodesia and South Africa. But we were sympathetic with the dissidents' desire to re-introduce the democracy we had enjoyed at independence. During Valentine's incarceration, Mrs Flavia Musakanya made an application for a building society mortgage to develop a small commercial plot in Lusaka. This came up for approval at the loans committee of which I was chairman and I persuaded the committee to approve it, only to find it later being withheld by management, after political intervention. I also made a point of helping Flavia to keep up her spirits when we met socially during that period. (Soon after our approval of the loan, Musokotwane, then minister of finance, reconstructed the board of the building society and removed me).

A key ingredient of the coup plan, which gave it a high chance of success, was the reliance on a group of around sixty five trained Katangese dissident soldiers under the command of their leader, Deogratias Symba. These were against the Mobutu government and had been living in exile in Zambia's

North-Western Province after being thwarted by a French expeditionary force in a foray into Katanga from Angola. It was the reliance on these foreigners, with no local tribal affiliations, that resulted in the plot's late discovery only days before they were due to strike. Discovery took place when one of the plotters, Mundia Sikatana, informed the government of the planned coup. Had the plotters relied on local dissident junior soldiers, discovery would have taken place much earlier through the informer system and the tribal grapevine.

In September 1981, on my way back from an ascent up Kilimanjaro, I visited Maputo and stayed for a few days with my old friend, Rankin Sikasula, the Zambian ambassador to Mozambique. When I made contact with Aquino Braganza at the Eduardo Mondlane University, he asked me to give a talk to some lecturers on the attempted coup in Zambia. I pointed out to them that had it succeeded it would have resulted in Zambia's withdrawal from support for the struggles in Namibia and South Africa. Present at the lecture were also Albie Sachs and Ruth First. It was not long after my return to Zambia that we heard the sad news of her tragic death while opening a parcel containing a letter bomb. Aquino was in the same room and suffered injuries. Later, Albie lost an arm and nearly his life, when opening a car which had been booby-trapped by South African agents.

I concluded my talk at the university with the observation that the attempted coup resulted from a schism similar to that which had arisen between Trotsky and Stalin in the late twenties: Trotsky for world revolution – Stalin for building socialism first in the Soviet Union. Kaunda stood for the liberation of the whole region: the plotters wanted Zambia to concentrate on rebuilding Zambia's economy, leaving the nationalist forces in Namibia and South Africa each to wage their own struggle.

Kaunda dealt with the plotters and continued ruling, without changing his policy of supporting the struggle against the apartheid government in South Africa and for independence in Namibia. Unfortunately for Zambia, when independence came to Zimbabwe, no peace dividend for our shattered economy seemed to be forthcoming. The coup plotters saw in this a good reason for isolationism. Kaunda, on the other hand, tried to persuade the nation that we still could not relax, since the South African apartheid regime was raiding us and we remained a Front-line State. If he had then started a process of structural adjustment of our economy, as advocated by the IMF and World Bank, and re-introduced democracy, he might have been able to avoid several further attempted coup d'etats.

On Musakanya's release, he went back to his several businesses, which included a farm in the Northern Province. At his request, I flew up there with him to give him technical advice on the possibility of installing a micro-hydro power plant and we focused on Zambia's economy and Kaunda's inability to get us back on a growth course. He referred to various goings-on in State House and revealed to me that Kaunda was of the view that I had sided with Kapwepwe rather than with himself and that I even kept a portrait of Kapwepwe on a wall rather than one of him. Kaunda's informers must have invented this one, as Cynthia and I did not follow the post independence tradition of hanging portraits of leaders on our walls. We displayed the works of local artists and a few of Cynthia's paintings! Although I have nothing concrete to go on, I have remained with the impression that Valentine was not without some role in the events discussed above. Although I do not support coups which have no basis in mass action, I remained close friends with both Valentine and Edward until their untimely deaths. In Valentine's case, I cherish the memory that I was able to visit him in the intensive care unit of the Royal Free Hospital in London and say a few words to him before he expired a day later. Flavia, who was by his side, thought from the expression on his face that he recognised and heard me.

Kaunda's mistaken view about Cynthia and myself notwithstanding, it was difficult to keep a balanced view of the rivalry between the two camps. But we did find it manageable because we did not adhere to the view that personal friendships should decide our politics and because we could see that a good deal of Simon Kapwepwe's following was really nothing but a push for Bemba-speaking hegemony: hegemony of Northern Zambia, in combination with the Bemba-speaking Copperbelt. We appreciated that Bemba-speakers were the most numerous group in Zambia, but didn't accept that power in Zambia must always reside with them: tribalism was abhorrent to us from whatever quarter it came. Cynthia and I were very upset by the undemocratic treatment Simon Kapwepwe received from the UNIP machine when he tried to challenge Kaunda for the party presidency in 1978 and by his being beaten up by UNIP thugs in Lusaka when he subsequently broke away from UNIP. When he died from a stroke in January 1980, we were overseas; had we been in the country we would have travelled to Chinsali to attend his burial.

Simon Kapwepwe sometimes took a simplistic view of events and we differed on several occasions. He was a successful minister of agriculture as he could inspire peasant farmers while taking advice from his officials. He was a man exuding power and often he used it unnecessarily. Had he had the chance of leading the nation, he might have galvanised the peasants and workers into higher economic productivity, but I doubt whether he would have mustered a following from our intellectuals. It is sad that our democracy did not give him that chance. Whether he could have achieved the degree of national unity that Kaunda achieved is uncertain. Despite many dictatorial pronouncements and actions, Kaunda achieved to a high degree our national motto: 'One Zambia One Nation'.

Cynthia and I had allowed our UNIP membership to lapse in the early seventies. We disliked the UNIP slogan 'It pays to belong to UNIP' and the strong-arm tactics used by UNIP youths on women at markets during elections. We disliked the purchase of Mercedes-Benz cars for ministers and the rent-a-crowd charades at the airport on Kaunda's arrivals and departures. Above all, we disliked one-man rule, which, in effect, obtained. However, we did not join any clandestine opposition groups and remained friendly with our numerous old friends in UNIP.

CYNTHIA'S POST SCRIPT

I was helped to settle in by our good friends Harry and Marjorie Chimowitz, who were already living in Lusaka. Also, Simon's brothers Abe and Jake and Jake's wife and children were living in Ndola and we visited each other frequently. The children soon fitted in to Lusaka Boys' School and made friends. An additional joy was that David, who had suffered severely from bronchitis and asthma during the English winters, improved dramatically in Lusaka's clean air and warm climate.

It is hard to look back and try to summarise one's feelings then. For so long we had been fighting against racism, colonialism, prejudice, apartheid, etc, and here was a chance to do something positive: to be involved with the creation of a nation and to be among equally enthusiastic friends. Here was a chance for me to prove to my South African relatives that we, black and white, could all live in harmony, and to show how utterly ridiculous their prejudices were. We were both delighted to be asked to join various committees. On my part, I was soon teaching English to a group of UNIP women in Kamwala, taking art classes, and joining the Red Cross. Most exciting of all, I was inspired by everything I saw to get back to painting. I started working seriously for the first time since leaving art school, and some of those early paintings were among the best I have ever done. In fact, life was great! Obviously the euphoria couldn't last, and life in Zambia has had its ups and downs, but never for one minute have I regretted our decision to come and live in Zambia.

In addition to going back to painting and etching, I had the opportunity to get involved in the cultural life of Zambia. Soon after we came to Lusaka I was nominated to the National Museums Board of Zambia. Our regular meetings were held in Livingstone at the Livingstone Museum, and they gave me a chance to broaden my knowledge of all aspects of museum activities, and to meet so many interesting people. I became secretary of the Lusaka Art Society in 1965, which organised annual group exhibitions, among various activities. Some years later, I joined two friends, Joan Pilcher and Ruth Bush, to become a director of Mpapa Gallery, the only commercial gallery in Lusaka at that time. I think our gallery played an important part in encouraging talented Zambian artists who exhibited in the gallery. We also organised workshops, and became a sort of home from home where artists were always dropping in for advice, help, or just a chat. Lechwe Trust, which I chair, is also able to encourage artists with grants and scholarships. From 1997 to 2002 I have been a member of the National Arts Council of Zambia, which has given me the opportunity to work with people involved in music, drama and traditional arts and crafts. I hope that in a very small way all these activities have helped to create the lively cultural scene that we have in Zambia today. I was proud to have my contribution recognised by the Council with an award in 2001.

Chapter Eleven
WORKING PART TIME WITH STATE INSTITUTIONS

Although I became disenchanted with UNIP policies and ceased to be involved actively in Zambian politics, I retained an interest in national affairs. On a part-time basis, while working full-time as senior partner in my practice of consulting engineers, I was involved in the following: University of Zambia (UNZA), Industrial Development Corporation (INDECO), Zambia National Building Society (ZNBS), Commission for Technical Education (CTE), National Council for Scientific Research (NCSR), Export Board of Zambia (EBZ) and Kariba North Bank Company Ltd (KNB).

UNZA

When we arrived in Zambia in 1965, the university had already been launched, a provisional council was in place, a vice-chancellor and registrar were appointed and construction of the Great East Road Campus was in full swing. Cabinet was in a great hurry to see the university get off the ground in order to produce graduates to fill the civil service, since there were only some sixty-five graduates to start us on the road at independence. Richard Jolly of the Commission for Development Planning had produced a report giving graduate requirements and this was used in the physical planning of the university project.

However, by early 1967, when I was appointed to join the Provisional Council under the chairmanship of Mr Henry Makulu, the project was in a crisis. Construction had got bogged down and targets for opening of schools and intake of students were not going to be met, especially in the completion of students hostels. At its June meeting I was asked by Council to take over the chairmanship of its building committee and I accepted this responsibility. I was approached beforehand by the minister of education, John Mwanakatwe, and the question of being in practice as a structural engineer and a resulting possible conflict of interests came up. I took the view that although my firm had so far not been involved in the university project, I would hesitate to accept this chairmanship if it meant the exclusion of the firm from future university commissions. I would, of course, not participate in any discussion if my firm was the subject and I said I would not use the chairmanship for my firm's gain. (I remained chairman, with a short interruption, for some twenty years and have not heard of any complaints of bias from members of the engineering professions in Zambia, who might have felt unfairly treated; nor have I heard of any allegations that I pursued personal financial gain).

If there were complaints, they were from some of our professional firms of architects and planners, with whom I had to deal harshly, because they had, in my opinion, got the university project into the crisis that was facing us when I assumed the chairmanship of the building committee. Not only was the project in crisis in terms of completion targets, but Council was also facing a huge claim for extra costs from Messrs Costain Ltd., the main contractor. Their claim was based on alleged delays by various members of the professional team in delivering construction drawings and information. In view of the time scale, the contract was awarded on the basis of parallel planning, which required the professional architects and engineers to do their work while the contractor was already on site. This had worked to a large extent, but a contractor can always make out a case for being delayed if he is determined to make a claim. He can always arrange his schedule so as to show that he needs the very information which he knows the design team is behind on. It then needs a lot of dribbling to get to the truth.

The professional side was arranged in a somewhat unusual way. There was a planner, Mr Anthony Chitty, who operated from the UK on a visiting basis and under him was a local architect, Julian Elliott, who was responsible for doing the feasibility studies and sketch plans. To prepare working drawings, a different firm of local architects would be appointed for each building or group of buildings. *All* members of the Zambian Institute of Architects were to get a commission. The supervision, it was understood, would be done by an employee of the university, the resident architect, who was assisted, in the normal way, by a clerk of works. There was, therefore, a considerable division of responsibility on the professional side. While the architects scale fee included supervision, no deduction was being given (or made) for their delegation of the supervision to the resident architect.

Planning of the university was based on the concept of schools of study rather than departments. Most of the incoming senior staff were familiar with the latter and were convinced that departments comprised the proper system. Planning on the basis of schools of study required the provision of a single, central library, but senior academic staff wanted *their* schools to have their own libraries and similarly with car parks and lecture theatres. There were cases where a school dean would try to get his own school lecture hall, instead of the provision of centralised multi-use lecture halls. In terms of utilization efficiency, schools of study appeared to be capable of achieving the best results and I supported the planners on that, but I then had to fight hard against all attempts, overt and covert, by academic staff to circumvent it. Centralised lecture halls required sophisticated, computerised time-tabling of lecture periods, but our registrar, Lindsay Young, was, though very hard-working, a Renaissance man, trying to programme it all in long-hand.

In terms of construction, the contractor was complaining that the split levels within the buildings, a design favoured by Mr Elliott, was a major cause of lack of speed in constructing the concrete frames. The system required concrete columns between floors to be cast not for the complete storey height, but to be interrupted for the construction of an intermediate level. Although the contractor did not raise the issue, I observed that walls were being constructed in concrete even when, for structural purposes, they could have been specified as brick or blockwork infill, between concrete columns. A concrete wall has to be constructed as part of the concrete framework, whereas a brick or blockwork wall can be done later, without interrupting the construction of the concrete frame, leading to speedier construction of the building as a whole. There was another good reason for replacing concrete walls with brick or blockwork. There was a shortage of skilled 'site carpenters' for making shutters for concrete and no shortage of skilled bricklayers.

On taking on the responsibility for the university's building programme I had to take all these factors into account, from the concept behind the planning of a building to its completion. I had to carry with me members of the building committee who had served on it from the beginning of the project and had been responsible for it up to my arrival. I was not very popular with many of the academic members to start with. I set about reorganizing the project by recruiting in 1968 a new resident architect. From several applicants we selected IO Horvitch, a South African political exile, who was then working with a well-established firm in London. I knew of his abilities as an architect administrator from the time I was still in London and he handled the construction of the London Hilton. I also knew that he would be sympathetic to Zambia and what we were trying to achieve for the university in terms of speed and cost.

When 'Ike' Horvitch arrived, we analysed the project and could see that there was not much we could do with the *ongoing* contract, except to deal with the massive claim for extra cost by the contractor. While Horvitch took over the briefing of our legal team and marshalling the defence, we started a review of the approved master plan to see where we could make savings and simplify construction of buildings not yet out to contract. The master plan provided a concrete deck, a storey-height above ground level, between the library and the spine comprising the schools. This was intended to serve as a place for students to intermingle socially while they walked between the schools and library. The deck would have been hundreds of square metres in area and represented a major cost element. It would have been open to the sun. We could see no justification for it. We then battled with the old academic members of the building committee until we got a decision not to proceed with its construction. Instead we provided a grassed area on which students could mingle. For students to cross from the spine to the library we provided two bridges over the ground level road which was serving the spine of schools.

To change the mode of construction and move away from the brutalist style of architecture we selected the local firm of Lorenz and Pearce to design a new hostel complex. These would be in load-bearing brickwork, with only the floors in concrete. They were constructed much more quickly than the first set of hostels, in which concrete was specified not only for floors but also for walls. Erhard Lorenz had designed an interesting hostel in Sailsbury for Chancellor House before settling in Zambia after a spell in Southern Rhodesia, and had worked with internationally famous architects like Alveor Aalto in Finland and Arne Jacobson in Denmark. We had confidence in Lorenz providing the desired result. Naturally, we had strong opposition from the chief architect, Julian Elliott, responsible for the original concept for the campus.

As far as student numbers were concerned, planning of the university was almost entirely based on Richard Jolly's Manpower Report which reflected Zambia's *need* for graduates to deal with an assumed rate of economic growth. It did not take into account the nation's financial ability to pay for the university's expansion nor the ability of a Zambianised university administration to cope with the numbers of students, which were projected to reach five thousand by 1975 and ten thousand by 1985. Lack of funds for capital development became chronic in the mid-seventies and the administration's inability to cope with resident student numbers above three thousand soon became apparent when that threshold was reached. Larger numbers could have been coped with, but only by changing over to a halls of residence system, each hall with its own dining facility, instead of two centralised canteens. It became clear to me that the concepts associated with schools of study, when also applied to residences and dining facilities could, in our present state of development, only lead to a logistical breakdown.

At the beginning of one year the newspapers reported a crisis in student accommodation: more students had arrived than there were hostel beds. I knew that the available rooms and beds had matched the allocation of the student intake and I went one night to check with the dean of students. I found him in a large room surrounded by a circle of files on the floor and having great difficulty in sorting out the problem. It turned out that the dean had no card system to assist with the logistics. After a considerable amount of physical checking it was found that some rooms had been occupied on a single basis, whereas all were supposed to be occupied on a double basis!

In a foreword to a Report On Physical Development made by Mr Horvitch in 1971, I described the history of the university's physical development as falling into the following three distinct phases:

I   Conception and part execution as a grand, monolithic ensemble of austere, exposed-concrete buildings, linked by a concrete deck for pedestrians - 1965 & 1966.

II   Reaction adversely to the first crop of buildings; a self-critical reappraisal and wrestling with the problem of 'how to change direction without doing violence to what has already been erected'; then the laying down of new guide-lines, both administrative and physical - early 1967.

III   Going forward with a revised programme, on the new lines, to meet the University's growing needs with simpler buildings and forms of construction and with increased economy and speed - 1968 to 1971.

I went on to comment that:

> .... the Building Committee succeeded in consolidating and yet going forward: without loss of pace; with increased efficiency in the preparation of briefs; keeping costs reasonably steady in a period of heavy increases in building prices; with increased functional efficiency in the buildings and, we are confident, with increased beauty. (See: Report on Physical Development, I.O. Horvitch, University of Zambia, 1971)

As a member of Council I took an interest in the general development of the university and in March 1968 I was a member of the sub-committee appointed to select a new vice-chancellor to succeed Dr Anglin, a Canadian, when his contract expired. The brief from Council was to seek 'a new vice-chancellor from within and outside Zambia, bearing in mind that all things being equal a Zambian should be appointed'. We had applications from outside and two from within Zambia: one Zambian and one New Zealander, both of high calibre. We selected Professor Lameck Goma and he led the university successfully for many years until he joined the cabinet. His successor was appointed not by Council, but by Kenneth Kaunda and it was never clear whether he did so in his capacity as Chancellor or as President. Council members were called to State House for the occasion and we were told by Kaunda of the appointment of a new vice-chancellor and registrar. As it happened, the choice of vice-chancellor was a good one: Jacob Mwanza. However, the university was now, clearly, less autonomous than it was in its earlier days. Professor Goma, before departing, proposed the setting up of two other universities, one in Solwezi and one on the Copperbelt. The looming logistical problems of dealing with the expected growth in the student intake above the three thousand level must have been uppermost in his mind. In the mind of government, was the search for a way to reduce student power, as there had been demonstrations which the university administration had failed to control, followed by closure of the university.

In the university's early days the police asked us to cede a piece of land to them on the Great East Road for building a police post. The post would be between the university buildings and Parliament and enable the police to stop student marches on Parliament. As chairman of the building committee, I opposed this strenuously (and successfully) as did Dr Anglin, the vice-chancellor, not because the university was short of land, but because we wanted to preserve our autonomy and to obviate student feelings that political control was being imposed on them. We wanted a student body that was free to think and develop self-confidence. We never envisaged police invading the campus and dealing with students *inside* the campus, as regrettably, was to become an event of some frequency.

In 1965 the Provisional Council took the view that academic staff should be housed both on and off the campus in order to avoid insulation of expatriate staff from Zambian society. It therefore bought many houses and vacant plots in one of Lusaka's prime suburbs: Kabulonga. Many of the plots were built on by the university in the sixties, but those that had high cost development clauses were left for later. Many of the plots thus left vacant were in highly desirable locations and only became available for purchase because their owners were leaving the country after independence. When in 1976, land reforms decreed that land had no value and unless developed could not be sold, but could be repossessed by the state, the university was faced with the loss of these plots as it lacked the finance to develop them at the time.

It took a lot of effort by the building committee to protect these plots from predators. In one case, the predator was no other than a prime minister, Kebby Musokotwane. He wanted one of these plots for building his private house and kept on applying pressure on the administration to assign it to him. The administration, understandably, found it difficult to refuse the request. They brought the matter to the building committee which was discussing it when the vice-chancellor, Dr Jacob Mwanza, received a long-distance phone call from the prime minister, who was then in New York. As chairman of the committee, I asked the vice-chancellor to tell the prime minister that unless this pressure stopped, I would go public on the issue. The prime minister found another plot for his house: not a university plot! There were further attempts by ministers to grab these plots.

I was re-appointed to the University Council in 1973, then reappointed every three years or so until February 1991, when on expiry of my term, I received a letter from President Kaunda, thanking me for my past services. I had served on the Council for twenty-five years. No doubt, my public political position from 1990 had a bearing on the termination. This notwithstanding, I maintained my interest in the welfare of the university and was able to be of assistance to it in early 1995.

INDECO

Justin Chimba, minister of commerce, trade and industry appointed me in 1966 to the board of INDECO, the state industrial development company, the chairman of which was Andrew Sardanis. While a board member could make a contribution that would often be acted on, the INDECO set-up created by Andrew Sardanis was very monolithic and policy was being decided by Sardanis, in consultation with President Kaunda, outside the board. INDECO management would allocate one of its men to chair a board of a subsidiary and the members of the subsidiary boards were appointed without reference to the INDECO board. Loans for acquiring commercial and minor industrial enterprises were being provided by INDECO, usually to people who had recommendations from State House or the UNIP hierarchy. Most of these loans would become non-performing in a very short time.

On joining the board, I found that it had previously given out loans to politicos. Since most of these loans were *not* being serviced, I pressed the board that the secretary should send strong letters to the defaulters. The board agreed and the secretary acted on the decision. The chairman later showed me one reply from a politico, who was being recommended by our minister for membership of one of our subsidiary boards. The reply was written diagonally on the original letter as follows: 'You there sitting on your arse stop threatening me with legal action. You leave the money with me where it is safe'. Clearly, this person thought the loan was a reward for his past political contribution and it did not deserve servicing. There were many others of similar, if more subliminal mind.

Major enterprises in which INDECO was investing were the TAZAMA oil pipeline from Ndola to Dar es Salaam and the refinery in Ndola; the Intercontinental Hotel in Lusaka, the grain bag factory in Kabwe, the glass bottle factory in Kapiri Mposhi; the fertilizer factory in Kafue and the associated industrial township. It also had under consideration a small steel rolling mill for small sections at Kafue, the feasibility study for which could not establish a big enough market, when attention was diverted to an integrated steel plant, using our deposits of iron ore, first from Sanje, not far from Kafue and later from Solwezi. Fortunately, INDECO did not proceed with this project when nafta, the fuel on which the studies were based, jumped in price in 1973, making the project uneconomic. The fiasco associated with the project's successor, TIKA, does not lie at INDECO's door.

The status of INDECO changed dramatically in 1969, with the announcement by Kaunda that he was asking designated enterprises to sell to government 51% of their shares. What was now to follow, as part of the reforms, was a take-over of control of Zambia's economy. Many of the designated firms were owned by Rhodesians and South Africans and were controlled from Rhodesia and South Africa. As a result of UDI, their owners were unsympathetic to Zambia and the take-over was in the national interest. Some, however, would be taken-over to the disadvantage of our future economic growth, but this was not apparent to many Zambians at the time.

To achieve the take-over, INDECO was to become not only the negotiating vehicle for the transfer, but the *owner*, on behalf of the state, of the share being taken over in all enterprises, except mining. 51% was a controlling share, but management was to be negotiated in many cases with the previous owners. The take-over would be paid for, but there would be no payment for any goodwill: it was all to be at book value. Firms, which had not been in the habit of re-valuing their properties regularly found this approach punishing.

Some enterprises had owners who were only too keen to be taken-over, not only in part but in total. Examples of these were Zambezi Sawmills with its teak-cutting and processing at Mulobezi, near the Caprivi Strip, and Steel Supplies. The owners of these enterprises were even canvassing a take-over by INDECO before the reforms were announced! In the case of the former, the operation was on a low-tech basis and was only just surviving. When INDECO came in and brought in new sophisticated sawing equipment from Germany, and was soon advertising to recruit saw doctors it was not long before losses mounted. In the case of the latter, imported steel sections were being handled in open yards: when INDECO came in, large sheds were built both in Lusaka and Ndola, in which the steel sections were to be handled. For the shed in Lusaka an alternate usage had to be sought on completion: it was never used for the purpose for which it was built. Availability of capital in INDECO resulted in decisions being made often without adequate study of the market and on the basis of inadequate experience.

Some of the original owners found the new partnership unworkable when the new majority shareholder started applying non-commercial political criteria to pricing. They then pressed to be bought out in total. This was the case with Susman Brothers and Wulfsohn. This group, INDECO found on taking control, was the most profitable trading chain of all those it took over. Once it became a 100% parastatal it was merged with other trading outlets to mask their lack of profitability. The trading conglomerate soon went the way of all flesh.

A positive result of the take-overs was increased employment and training for Zambians at all levels, especially for Zambians with education. Unfortunately, State House used this opportunity too often for political patronage, to the neglect of economics. Managers were often appointed by State House and, as often, dismissed by State House. I saw the letter of dismissal of Mr Robert Chiluwe, who was managing director of Zambia Steel and Building Supplies. The letter, signed by the President, accused Chiluwe of 'disloyalty to me'! Although employees of parastatals did not always serve in the economic interests of the nation, they developed a sense of ownership which they would use frequently when it came to improving their own positions; workers would sometimes reject the appointment of a general manager not to their liking, as happened in the case of the parastatal construction company, ZECCO, when Josaiah Songolo was appointed.

A few private factories, ostensibly with the aim of import substitution, had been started precisely to use *imported* raw materials. The intention was to enable commissions from overpricing to be left outside the country, and thus to overcome exchange control regulations, which limited dividend remittance to outside shareholders. INDECO tried to reverse this tendency in Zambia's industrial development. However, the new pineapple - canning factory had to rely on imported cans, which made up the major cost element in the final product. The grain bag factory which was started with a view to eventually utilising locally-grown kenaf, even if, initially, this was to be imported from Bangladesh, finished up importing polypropelene as its main raw material! I soon learnt that state ownership and generous capital funding could produce many white elephants and was not necessarily assisting meaningful development in a developing country.

The next major step in the economic reforms was the taking over of a 51% share of the mining companies. Again Andrew Sardanis did the negotiations and when it was all agreed he came to the INDECO board for ratification. Dr Justin Zulu, who was governor of the Bank of Zambia and a member of the board was critical of the deal, especially of the terms which would allow the mining companies to externalise their profits freely. He argued that it would result in capital flight. I was also against *ratification* because the board had not been involved at all up to then and, more importantly, because I was of the view that the mine owners were being paid too much! After a drawn-out discussion, I moved, as a compromise, that the board *only* take note of the agreement and this was passed. Dr Zulu was soon replaced as governor of the Bank of Zambia with Valentine Musakanya, at the time a close friend of Andrew Sardanis. (Dr Zulu then went to join the staff of the IMF and returned to Zambia only in the late nineties.)

Over the years I had a good deal to do with parastatals, under INDECO and ZNBS and came to be disenchanted with state ownership as a basis for an economy in a *developing* country. I would argue accordingly with my friend Ben Turok, who was then on the staff of UNZA and of the opposite view. (See *Development in Zambia*, edited by Ben Turok) I saw much waste of resources, corruption, lack of work discipline and lack of transparency in state-owned enterprises. The 'buyer' in each enterprise, unless very carefully selected and supervised, would be corrupted by suppliers with under-the-counter commissions, which were then built into the price. Often the lines purchased made no sense in our local situation and amounted to dumping of slow-moving goods by the sellers. Zambia Steel and Building Supplies was a conglomerate full of such lines.

Premature Zambianization could also bring ruin to a state enterprise. In the case of the Nega-Nega Brickworks, an expatriate manager supplied by the tunnel kiln manufacturers, was replaced *prematurely* by his understudy, before the expatriate's contract had gone even half-way. Whereas the expatriate was constantly checking kiln temperatures and adjusting the coal feed accordingly, a less-diligent approach by his Zambian replacement resulted in the collapse of the kiln roof over the critical mid length of the tunnel and the new brickworks came to a standstill. It was never refurbished and an investment of over one million dollars went to waste.

While initially the Zambian economy expanded, the bad investments and inefficiencies soon started taking their toll on the state-owned conglomerates of INDECO and ZIMCO. With the president as chairman of ZIMCO, it even became difficult to hold regular board meetings. At board meetings of the parastatal companies much time would be spent correcting minutes and very little on discussing policy. In contrast, private sector companies rush through board minutes and spend most of the board meetings discussing policy and profitability. Another preoccupation of parastatal board meetings was the discussion of staff matters, usually the wrangles between staff and management and within management.

Corruption was widespread in the parastatal enterprises. It is often assumed that corruption goes with developing countries, yet insufficient attention is given to the fact that it is firms from the developed world that are equally or even more responsible. When bids were advertised for design and supervision for duplication of the oil pipeline from Dar es Salaam to Ndola, I tried to persuade a leading British firm, with experience in this field internationally and in East Africa, to put in a bid. I found them reluctant to do so on the grounds that those judging the bids would be influenced by bribes. In the event, a bid put in by two British firms, in joint venture, failed to corrupt the Zambian manager with a bribe. To his credit, the manager, Lishoma Muuka, had set up a tape recorder and the offer of five per cent to him was recorded and the bidders' representative was kept in gaol for many months as a result. One of the firms was a leading British consulting firm in civil engineering and the other had been practising in Central Africa for many years. I tried to get the latter hauled over the carpet by the Zambian Association of Consulting Engineers, but without success.

ZNBS

At independence there were two building societies in Zambia and they operated well for many years after independence. They each had some Zambian directors before they were taken over by the state and amalgamated into the Zambian National Building Society, with Elias Chipimo as the first chairman. I was appointed to the new board and for many years I chaired the loans committee.

When the UNIP government brought in the leadership code we started referring applications from leaders for more than one mortgage to the secretary general, Grey Zulu, for his approval. His response was to tell us, more or less, to mind our own business! Despite UNIP's public declarations on limiting acquisitions by leaders, many applied and were given multiple mortgages, yet when reviews were made of non-performing loans leaders were in the majority. Management failed to exert pressure to achieve repayments for fear of being dismissed by their political appointing authority. Edward Shamwana who would raise criticisms resigned from the board.

On one occasion I was handed a note from the minister of finance, recommending that a bridging loan be approved for Veritas Trust (a Kaunda family trust) for the acquisition of the firm City Radio Ltd. As chairman of the loans committee I declined to consider it, and to the minister's credit, I suffered no consequences. I later heard that the Trust achieved its objective by using another state-owned institution. President Kaunda praised one of the country's leading accountants for the operation. Kaunda referred to the accountant as 'my financial wizard', when he inaugurated the Chair of Human Relations at UNZA, on behalf of the Trust. There was no wizardry involved, only manipulation of funds at the expense of parastatals. City Radio Ltd was bought by the Trust with a bridging loan from State Insurance and, almost immediately, was resold to State Insurance for a higher price. The margin was kept by the Trust, which was not a state enterprise.

When Kebby Musokotwane was minister of finance my long term service on the board of ZNBS came to an abrupt end. Officially, this was on the basis of the minister 'wanting new blood', but actually because the loans committee had approved a loan to Mrs Flavia Musakanya. Harvey Golson, who was a recent appointee to the board and a member of my committee suffered the same fate, also, officially, on the same basis although he had served for less than a year!

NCSR

The National Council for Scientific Research was formed to supersede a federal institution. I was appointed to the Council and became chairman of one of its committees, concerned with the building industry. The Council, under the chairmanship of Simon Kapwepwe, had a reasonably-sized complex built, but very little research or development has been done under its auspices. My committee started a building centre, but with a low level of locally - manufactured building products to exhibit, the centre soon flopped.

In 1969 I persuaded the Director, Dr Gad, to support a proposal for a rural development project in the peri-urban area, some twelve kilometres from Lusaka: the Chunga Irrigation Scheme. Zambia's desperate desire to end rural non-development had given rise to some bold policy decisions by government: massive encouragement of formation of co-operatives, liberal provision of loans, wholesale distribution of tractors to co-operatives and the intensive development zone programme, none of which had met with much success. I thought it would be worthwhile to encourage some existing small-scale vegetable growers to grow for the Lusaka market by helping them to construct their own irrigation system. Harry Chimowitz, and I looked around for such a possible project when our firm was designing and supervising the construction of a sewage works near the Chunga stream in Lusaka West. We came across some subsistence vegetable growers who were carrying water to their small plots by bucket from an incised river-bed, some eight feet below the banks. The lifting of water could have been done more efficiently and with less human exhaustion by *shaduff*, the bucket on a level as still used in Egypt, but this ancient technology had not yet reached Zambia.

The Chunga stream had a flow of water only during the rainy season so vegetable growing used to be done only then and this was the most difficult time to grow vegetables because of pests and diseases. The sewage works was going to discharge, initially, five million and eventually, twenty-seven million litres of effluent into the stream daily. Since the project area was several kilometres downstream and the design of the works was to modern international standards, there was an opportunity for utilising some of this flow for growing such vegetables as are used in cooking.

Harry Chimowitz surveyed and subdivided some eight hectares on the Chunga's north bank terrace in the Mungule Tribal Reserve into twenty plots, which could be irrigated by gravity from a canal, if a small weir were constructed to raise the water in the stream to terrace canal level. The NCSR provided the finance for a contractor to construct the stone weir and Harry and I mobilized the small-holders to construct a two kilometre-long canal with free labour, on the basis of self-help. Plots were allocated in February 1971 and the growers started growing vegetables and selling to markets in Lusaka. By the time President Kaunda visited the scheme on 6 July 1972, it was a going concern. (*Times of Zambia*, 7/7/72) The project continued with a considerable degree of success and without loans or subsidized inputs until the late eighties when the weir developed a leak at foundation level and the participators were unable to get it repaired from their own resources.

Until I got involved again in national politics, I maintained a close interest in the scheme and visited it regularly once a month. I encouraged the growers and helped solve some of their organizational problems. Meetings would be held every Tuesday to discuss common problems: furrow maintenance, crop selection, etc. When Professor René Dumont visited the scheme in the company of John Papworth he was favourably impressed and said 'the only problem is how to replicate it on a widespread basis'. Delivery to market was a problem and farmers had to cart their produce by wheelbarrow until marketeers started coming out in their vans to buy at the farm gate.

Small schemes like Chunga have a good chance of success, but they were not in favour with the politicians of the time, who were looking to large-scale projects for the solution to the country's agricultural development. Yet such large schemes had no success with peasant farmers. In discussions, at grass-roots level, I found that the peasants were against government policy of forming themselves into a co-operative, even for marketing their produce.

At an early stage I noticed that those growers who could do well were held back by fear of jealousy from their colleagues. On one occasion I found that a farmer who had been doing well as a result of experience gained while working in domestic service in Southern Rhodesia was accused of witchcraft and fined by Headman Kakoma! From then on, John Phiri's plot dropped production to below average! To avoid a similar fate an educated, young go-ahead farmer put up a sign at the entrance to his plot with the inscription 'SANJE MULEKE' (Nyanja: 'without jealousy').

With one or two exceptions, the participators in the scheme relaxed after reaching a modest level of income. When I found that I could not inspire them to go further and make maximum use of the land allocated to them and the abundance of free water available, I withdrew from the scheme and left them to their own devices.(See: *Zambia Geographical Association*, no 27 July 1974: *Appropriate Technology* Vol. 2, No 2)

EBZ

In 1989 I was interviewed by Dr Waza Kaunda, the president's son, and then appointed a member of the Export Board of Zambia, under the chairmanship of Joseph Nyaywa, a former employee of mine. Although during my membership I became a founder member of the Movement for Multi Party Democracy, Joseph, to his credit, fought those in government who wanted me removed from the Board on political grounds. When MMD came into government and I became a deputy minister I resigned to give the minister responsible freedom to reconstruct the EBZ.

KARIBA NORTH BANK

When Fitzpatrick Chuula was minister of power he appointed me to the board of Kariba North Bank Company Ltd., the company set up in parallel with the Central African Power Corporation so as to enable the construction of Phase II of Kariba, without needing the official involvement of the Smith regime under UDI, when raising a loan from the World Bank. The loan was then guaranteed by the Zambian government only. However, on completion of construction the power generated was shared with Rhodesia/Zimbabwe.

Zimbabwe had to pay KNB for the power supplied to it in US Dollars. When the Wapta, the unit of currency of the Regional Grouping was introduced, Zimbabwe insisted that they be allowed to pay in Wapta. When this came before the board, I spoke in favour of the request and I supported my argument with the need to encourage regional integration, only to find myself in a minority of one! Arthur Wina and Joshua Lumina, the other two non-official members spoke against and joked that 'Simon is too pan-Africanist'. The government and Zesco members were also against. They argued that Zesco, to whom some of the money would be passed, needed the US dollars to be able to procure equipment from outside the WAPTA area. One could also discern an element of brotherly dislike of the new Zimbabwe!

Requests came to the board for donations to the construction of the new UNIP headquarters complex and even to the UNIP conferences at Mulungushi Rock. These were presented and supported by management and passed without debate or objection at the meetings, but Arthur and I would lament afterwards between ourselves, of not being able to object for the time being. We should, of course, have objected inside the board meeting and taken the consequences, whether removal from the board -no discomfort- or being marked out as active dissidents, with consequences on our livelihoods. The one-party participatory democracy system that we were under would certainly not have tolerated such objection without some punishment. We judged the time not yet ripe to speak out against the party's milking of the public sector and later we would speak out. We should have spoken out much earlier than we did.

The pressure for donations to the UNIP HQ project was being exerted even outside the parastatal sector. To my surprise, my partner, Peter Miller, normally not involved in local politics, asked our firm to make a donation to the HQ project and he thought my objections unjustified. I criticised it on the basis of luxury and waste of resources. When Mainza Chona, then ambassador to China, discussed the project with the Chinese government they thought that we should first concentrate on building up industry before building a grand party complex. However, Kaunda would not be deflected and the Chinese went on to design and construct the complex as paid designers and contractors. The project cost was to be some two hundred million US dollars and in the event it was not completed in time for UNIP to enjoy its planned luxurious facilities.

The First Republic lasted for nine years from independence to 1973, when the one-party system was inaugurated. The Second Republic lasted for eighteen years. The First Republic did not start with an ideology: it had money from accumulated sterling balances and taxes from copper and got on with developing the country. The Second Republic started with the sterling balances exhausted and falling copper prices, and relied heavily on the ideology of humanism, a philosophy which was somewhat nebulous and certainly lacking a work ethic! Economic hardships soon developed from lack of prudence and production in the parastatal sector, coupled with over-consumption and subsidies. These were based on habits developed in the First Republic, and misuse of surplus from copper earnings, which should have been reinvested in exploration and maintenance of the mines. Economic ills were officially ascribed to the consequences of supporting the struggle against UDI until 1981, when Zimbabwe achieved majority rule and independence. I remained loyal to the ruling party and defended it until then and perhaps for a year or two afterwards. I then became a critic, although not a loud one. I saw that not all our economic ills were the result of such support: much was due to economic mismanagement and lack of political will to restructure the economy.

OTHER INTERESTS

While I was building up my consulting engineering practice in Lusaka and had spare time on my hands, Fitzpatrick Chuula invited me to join him in buying a plot in Roan Road, Kabulonga, Lusaka, and building some flats by direct labour. A two-storey block of six flats was designed for us by an architect and Fitzpatrick and I raised a loan from a building society. We acted as our own contractors and engaged Zambian artisans and labourers. These flats were later rented by Simon Zukas and Partners (later ZMG Consulting Engineers) for staff accommodation. Chula sold his share to the partnership when he decided to go farming and the firm added more flats on the plot. Today the development is owned by Cynthia and myself.

The partnership also built its own six-storey office block, Design House, in Dar es Salaam Place, Lusaka, also by direct labour and moved into the top two floors on completion. This construction was also financed by raising a loan from a building society. The building was sold when the partnership was reconstructed, after Harry Chimowitz and Sacha Magasiner retired.

Since resettling in Zambia I had been interchanging, periodically, with Sacha Magasiner who was running our London office of Zukas Magasiner. Cynthia and I had sold our house in East Finchley in 1966 and we later bought a mansion-flat in Hampstead, after staying in hotels for several visits and finding that unsatisfactory. In 1973, with the collapse of secondary banking in the UK and with it the property market, a vacant plot in Church Row, Hampstead, came up for sale. Cynthia spotted this and arranged for our family trust to purchase it. Our architect friends Ike Horvitch, Ted Levy and Issy Benjamin designed a block of three flats for us and, despite objections from an influential neighbour, were successful in obtaining council planning approval for it, because of their design fitting in so well into the neighbourhood. When the trust was ready to sign a contract with a builder, there was family pressure not to proceed, in view of the collapse of the UK property market. I was able to persuade the trustees to go ahead, on the basis that in property you have to take a long-term view. I had learnt this from the many successful property developers I had worked with while in practice in the UK and I have been proved right. The trust kept one flat for our family as a base in London.

My involvement in the Chunga Irrigation Scheme led to an interest in agriculture and in the mid-seventies I became a 1/3 shareholder in Balmoral Farm, a more-or-less virgin farm, some fifteen kilometres from Lusaka. My two partners and I started developing it and this proved an uphill battle. Before long, one of the partners left to settle in Sweden and I had to take over the enterprise with its debts! I had, by then, invested in it all I had saved from my years in consulting engineering practice in Zambia. I engaged a manager and continued the struggle to develop the farm, a process that is still going on to this day. Balmoral is a mixed farm with irrigated coffee as the main enterprise and, to my delight, our son Alan is now managing it.

This interest in farming came to the notice of Edwin Wulfsohn, who invited me to become a director of Zambezi Ranching and Cropping. Later I became its chairman, a post which I held until I resigned in 1993, on being appointed minister of agriculture. Under my chairmanship we built a small residential training school on one of the group's farms in Choma and I encouraged our general manager, Rodney Clyde-Anderson, to train a team of Zambians to take over as ranch managers when expatriate managers completed their contracts. Mr Clyde Anderson, a South African, did this very successfully and he has Zambian managers in all the ranches under him.

Chapter Twelve
'THE HOUR' CAME

His success in blocking the attempted coup in 1981 did not appear to cause President Kaunda to examine the reasons that led to it. No doubt, he would have explained it to himself as Shamwana and Musakanya seeking *power* and, after all, there was no declared programme by the suspects. That it might have had as its purpose a change to a multi-party system or privatisation of the nationalised enterprises was, evidently, not a conclusion that Kaunda came to, or if he came to it, he appeared in no hurry to change course. Economic reform was certainly not discernible until the second half of the decade, when Gibson Chigaga was appointed minister of finance. He was a businessman and farm owner and was ready to move forward to reform the economy. However, because he had to work within the established so-called socialist system, he had to tread cautiously and the economy continued on its downward path. There was widespread discontent with the state of affairs, not least amongst the elite, and even amongst the Parliamentarians, who were all UNIP. Kaunda lashed out at his critics from the elite.

To deflect criticism, Kaunda kept on ascribing our economic ills to the low price that the developed world was paying us for our copper; to our sacrifices made as a front-line state in helping to bring down the Smith regime in Southern Rhodesia; and to our still necessary support for the forces trying to end apartheid in South Africa. All fair reasons, yet not the only ones responsible for our economic plight. Had we concentrated on increasing copper production and started seriously, in the mid-seventies, on a structural reform programme, events would have moved differently. Our inability for a decade or so to come to some accommodation with the IMF had eventually started to be addressed positively, in the late eighties, by Chigaga and a team of reform-minded Zambian economists. However, by then much damage had been done and the economy was in the doldrums. Essential goods, like cooking oil, sugar and salt, were in short supply and subject to long queues and a black market. The copper mines, starved of capital, were producing less and less. The reform team began work in 1989 on NERP (National Economic Reform Programme) and was making some progress, yet not enough to turn back the tide of growing dissatisfaction with the one-party state. The country was restless and voices for change started coming from many directions.

Not only voices: a young army lieutenant, Mumba Luchembe, tried to take power on 30 June 1990, while the courts were still dealing with a suspected previous attempt at a coup, in which retired General Christon Tembo was the leading accused. At that time, Humphrey Mulemba, a leading member of the one-party Parliament, approached me for funds to help him in his campaign to move UNIP towards democracy and to assist in the legal costs for the defence of General Tembo. Humphrey and I had established a close relationship when, on the eve of independence, he arrived in London as part of a UNIP group that was to attend British party conferences. During the Second Republic Humphrey was, at one time, secretary general (then equivalent to vice-president) and held the deputy-chairmanship of the commission which recommended the introduction of the one-party constitution. However, Humphrey was never very comfortable with the lack of democracy within the system and even less with its socialist policies. In response to his request for funds, I contributed generously, only to find Humphrey's parliamentary moves inadequate and overtaken by that of others who moved outside Parliament.

When a national conference was advertised to take place on 20 and 21 July 1990, at Garden House Hotel to discuss the multi-party option, I decided to attend. However, I went there not without trepidation: we had lived too long in fear of speaking out under Kaunda for me not to worry about possible consequences to myself, and Cynthia questioned the wisdom of my going. I had not been aware of the plans in preparation for this meeting and assumed that was because I was regarded by its organizers as too close to UNIP to be involved. I was not a recipient of the letter of invitation sent out on 13 July. In fact, when a few days before this meeting I solicited support for Mulemba's moves from Mr E Chibwe, an uncle of Fredrick Chiluba, one of the original steering committee, I got a cold response. He told me later (after the Garden House Hotel meeting) that he thought, at the time, that I had got wind of their plans and I was fishing on behalf of Kaunda!

At the Garden House Hotel meeting I made a small intervention from the floor in support of the moves for multi-party democracy and apologised to the Zambian nation for supporting the one-party system in the past. I went on to say: 'the one-party participatory democracy was neither participatory nor democratic'. My intervention got me an unexpected ovation and my remarks hit the headlines the next day. (See *Daily Mail*, 21/7/90 and *Sunday Mail*, Harare, 22/7/90) Because of commitments on my farm, I did not attend the second day and was therefore not there to stand for election to any of the committees that were formed. I was, however, co-opted onto several later on.

At the conference the National Interim Committee was formed with Arthur Wina as chairman and Resolutions and Framework of Action, drafted by the national secretary, Akashambatwa Mbikusita Lewanika, were passed and the Movement for Multi-party Democracy was launched.

Someone recounted at the meeting that during a visit to China he had asked to be woken early by the receptionist at his hotel. When the phone rang in his room the next morning the Chinese receptionist announced: 'the hour has come' and he went on to tell us that here too the hour had come; not perhaps to get up to catch one's plane in time, but to change the government. So the MMD slogan was born: 'The Hour Has Come'.

Kaunda was meanwhile fighting vigorously to avoid dismantling his one-party system. I found his campaign distasteful, especially when he would tell critics 'to shut up'. He was proposing a referendum on whether to amend the national constitution to allow other parties to form. This was set for 17 October and later advanced to 13 August. UNIP councillors were to meet to approve this. Counting on my standing with some of the councillors, I had an advert placed in the *Daily Mail* under my name, pleading with them to drop the referendum and vote for democracy at their forthcoming meeting. In the event, Kaunda gave way, the proposed referendum was abandoned and, following amendment of the constitution by Parliament, the MMD became a political party and registered itself.

There followed a public meeting in Pope Square, Lusaka, and Arthur Wina, the interim president of the MMD, invited me to be one of the speakers. A crowd, estimated by the press at over 100,000, attended and the enthusiasm for change was palpable. Awkwardly, I greeted the crowd with the MMD slogan: 'The Hour' and the response came: 'Has Come'. There was no need to add: 'For Change', as this was now well understood. Other speakers started with the same greeting, but appeared less awkward than I. We were following a practice of slogan shouting, which started in the pre-independence era. It betrayed the fact that we had many ex-UNIP members in our ranks: it also foreshadowed the fact that MMD would follow other practices that obtained under UNIP: that we were not representing as clear and radical a change as we claimed!

In February 1991, the MMD held its inaugural convention and I stood for the post of national vice-chairman and was elected by a large majority. This gave me a place on the MMD executive, but apart from this, the role of vice-chairman was only as an *alternative* to the chairman. The chairmanship was won by Elias Chipimo, by default. It was generally assumed that whoever stood for president would stand for chairman as an alternative, in case of losing the former. Arthur Wina, the interim leader of the MMD, did not find this tactic palatable and thus missed becoming chairman when the vote for president went to Chiluba. This event went a long way to mar the future of the MMD, because Elias Chipimo's position became that of a lame duck chairman and he yielded to Chiluba the chairing of meetings of the National Executive Council, thus concentrating power in the hands of one man.

When it came to choosing candidates for the parliamentary elections I had declared to NEC (National Executive Council) my intention *not* to stand. (As a member of NEC I could have specified the constituency of my choice and I later heard that when the TUC had asked for me for one of the Copperbelt seats they were told of my decision). I then assisted in the campaign in the Western Province at the request of Mufaya Mumbuna, who told the NEC that the people of the Western Province did not believe him when he told them that white people were also in the executive of the MMD: they wanted to see if this was true! Our campaign in the Western Province was at this stage of a general nature, starting in Kaoma and proceeding north to Mangango and Lukulu and finishing in Shangombo and Sinjambela in the south. I used my Landcruiser and carried Walubita, Mumbuna and, at times, Akashambatwa. We even went across the Zambezi at Lukulu in August, when the dambos were still wet, to travel to Mtete along the Lungwebungu river, following a route covered by Dr Livingstone in the nineteenth century and by few whites in recent years, judging by the way young children ran away at the sight of a white man like me!

I was also learning fast other peculiarities of the Western Province. When, in Lukulu, people refer to the east they do not mean the Zambian Eastern Province near Malawi: they mean Kaoma, which is some two hundred kilometres to the east yet still in the Western Province. Often people spoke as if the Western Province was a national entity and not just one of the eight provinces of Zambia. However, they had at least this in common with the rest of Zambia: they wanted change. Change from what to what? They were waiting to hear from us. They were still to be convinced that there was need for a change of president and the party in power, but they knew that things had stopped working and were going wrong; that we were once a rich country and were now a poor country. Despite a police presence at all our meetings (except at Mtete, which was too remote even for them) we were being listened to, though perhaps with some mistrust. The common man mistrusted all politicians. I still regarded myself as not a *professional* politician and would take little notice of the briefing notes that were provided for me by the local MMD officials, telling me what would please the audience to hear and what to promise them that the MMD would deliver. I took even less notice of a note sent up at a meeting, south east of Mongu, from the husband of the headmistress of the school, that he wanted a new engine for his private truck, so would I promise to provide it! I did, however, respond favourably to a note which said that the people at Lukulu and west of the Zambezi needed reassurance that the Mbundu and Luvale who had immigrated from Angola would not be sent back by an MMD government. Evidently, UNIP were whipping up fears to this effect.

Many of these recent immigrants from Angola still had one foot in Angola. This became clear when, for a short while, there was peace between the warring factions in Angola in 1992. Zambia was then suffering from drought and there were worrying press reports that relief food was not reaching areas to the west of the Zambezi, with the result that people were so desperate that they were trekking into Angola across the closed border in search of food. Since these reports carried an implied criticism of the MMD government, I took it upon myself to investigate the problem. I found that, indeed, some immigrants had gone to Angola for a short period. However, it was not in search of food: they had gone to vote in the UN-supervised elections that were taking place and would result in a defeat for Savimbi!

Later, at a meeting on the way from Kalabo to Sikongo my co-speaker, Mrs Mumbwe, told the Luvale audience that whoever said that the MMD would send immigrants back to Angola was a scatterfool: I had learnt a new English word: scatterfool - a lovely combination of scatterbrain and fool.

Hunger and unemployment were the people's main concern at most of our meetings in the Western Province. One MMD youth said: 'we want the Boers back' (I think he meant the Afrikaner farmers) 'so that they will grow food, which we have failed to do'. One man in Mongu asked me if I had any MMD pamphlets to show that it would bring in investors to give employment. Clearly, as far as the masses were concerned the Kaunda era was seen to have failed in that respect, despite the nationalization of mines, shops and industries, and despite the creation of employment for educated Zambians. But did people appreciate that lack of employment may have been a result of nationalization? While the masses seemed not to worry who would own the enterprises to be privatised, some educated Zambians cautioned us to ensure that ownership should go to Zambians and not to outsiders. The general cry was for change: to create more jobs and more food, better schools and more clinics. I hoped we would not let them down.

While we were in Kalabo the local MMD district committee tried very hard to persuade me to stand for the Sihole constituency. I explained that I had decided not to stand at all in the next election, as I considered myself too old. When the constituency was later rearranged with Sihole being included in the Kalabo constituency and a separate constituency, Sikongo, formed to include most of what was before under Sihole, the Kalabo district committee repeated their request to me: to stand for Sikongo. However, the rearrangement of the constituency boundaries did not make it any more suitable for my age. The area along the border with Angola was as remote from Lusaka and as difficult to reach as it was when it included Sihole. The only added attraction (if there were any) seemed to be that the township of Sikongo was more substantial than Sihole and more accessible from Kalabo, the district centre. While Sihole had to be reached through sandy tracks, Sikongo could be reached by a fair gravel road from Kalabo. The road was built when the Sikongo border post was established after Angola's independence and a large police camp and immigration offices were built in anticipation of cross-border traffic. Not that Sikongo is actually on the border, there are some thirty kilometres to the border and only sandy tracks to take you there! Despite the local pleas, I put the matter out of mind and it was time to end the adventure and return to Lusaka.

The issue followed me to Lusaka, where Arthur Wina, who had chosen to stand in Kalabo, took the matter up again with me. The need for me in Sikongo had now an added reason: the candidate approved by the MMD national selection committee was unacceptable to the district committee and the man that might be acceptable to the latter was unacceptable to the former. This impasse could lead to disaster for the party's fortunes in Sikongo. Pressure from Arthur was difficult to resist and with Cynthia away on a visit to the UK, a decision was difficult to make. I told Arthur that even if I accepted and succeeded in getting elected I could stand the long distance travel for only half the term, until I was seventy. Since he did not think that an obstacle I went on to persuade Cynthia in a long and costly overseas phone call. I then decided to do another trip to Zambia 'Overseas' to decide on the spot.

When I got to Kalabo I found the atmosphere within the MMD camp very tense. In fact, there was not one camp but three and these were separated even geographically: there was the MMD district committee in its offices and the two other contestants, each with his supporters in separate encampments. There seemed to be no solution but for me to accept the nomination. One of the two contestants, Joe Sikongo, was prepared to accept me as the alternative, while the other decided to stand as an independent. After clearing my decision with Chiluba, I declared my acceptance of the nomination and persuaded Joe Sikongo and his supporters to join me as my election team. We then travelled the length and breadth of the Sikongo constituency in my Land cruiser campaigning: holding meetings wherever there was a school or even *a single* classroom.

Each school (and government guest house) has a book in which one is asked to make an entry after holding a meeting there. Most entries have comments on the attendance and the response from those attending. On reading through the comments made by UNIP leaders like General Masheke (the then vice-president) who had preceded me at some meeting places, I had to stiffen myself against becoming disheartened. Masheke would always write how well he was received, how all the people supported UNIP and that there was 'no doubt the people were with us'. I used to comfort myself by recalling the Zambian style that used to surprise me way back in Ndola: when I expected police informers to be shunned by my friends and found them, instead, being befriended. When I used to complain I would be told: 'don't worry, we will get them', followed by a curved sweep of the right arm, behind an imaginary figure, indicating "behind the back". Kaunda was being taken in by such reports from his campaigners that the rural areas were still with him. Perhaps General Masheke may have been taken in as well, by the people not showing him their true feelings while he was still a member of the government. In any case, I could not allow myself to become disheartened by these comments. They made me even more determined to convince the electors of the rightness of our programme.

Patiently, I would explain to the people how MMD would bring back economic prosperity. My knowledge of the vernacular was almost nil and I was being translated all the time. At one stage I spotted that my translator hesitated and appeared to be improvising while I was answering in simple English one questioner. The question was: why do we need two borders here, the international border with Angola and some fifteen kilometres to the east of it, another border, is this normal? 'Will you promise that when you get elected you will fight to do away with the second border—the Cattle Cordon Line?' To this I had replied:

> the cordon line is not an international or political line: it is a veterinary line to protect Zambia's cattle from dying from contagious bovine pleural pneumonia [CBPP] which has no cure. As a politician it would be irresponsible of me to go against the professional advice of veterinary experts who understand the seriousness of the problem. The MMD will help to bring peace to Angola and this should result in the restoration of veterinary services there. Then we may be able to do away with the second border.

I said the above despite the briefing notes from local MMD officials, which told me to answer such questions in the affirmative. Clearly, my interpreter thought I was throwing away my chances (and his) and decided to improve on my answer and make it more acceptable. Suspecting this, I asked him to interpret me precisely.

My answer would prove unpopular because the cattle owners in the zone between the border and the cordon line were disadvantaged and they were paying a social price in order to protect the cattle in the rest of Zambia. I was not unsympathetic and intended to do something to alleviate their hardships, which derived from lack of free movement of their cattle. I was, however, not prepared to take the easy way out.

In the event, I did get elected with an overwhelming majority, getting some eighty per cent of the votes cast, with UNIP getting less than twenty per cent and the independent losing his deposit. This result was not much different from that in most of the rest of Zambia, except in the Eastern Province, where UNIP retained its grip. The Zambian political style, which was revealed to me at Ndola, applied here also and perhaps even more so: the people did not reveal to the ruling UNIP, before the election, that they were going 'to give them the red card'.

The election over, I drove back the seven hundred odd kilometres to Lusaka for a rest and to be with Cynthia, only to find myself chairing a national victory rally near the Kafue roundabout, and introducing Chiluba as the main speaker. I told the crowd of over a hundred thousand, in siLozi, that in the west, from where I had just returned, we had 'cut off UNIP's tail' (UNIP, mukila bato) and that would remove their aggression. And so I was now the MMD member of Parliament for Sikongo.

When drought struck Zambia at the end of 1991 donor aid was made available in the form of yellow maize from the USA. However, we had a major crisis in delivering relief maize to the three constituencies of the Kalabo District. It all had to go across the Zambezi and the Kalabo District Council had only a small pontoon. A lorry coming from Mongu had to offload all its maize on the left bank then cross, empty, on the pontoon. The pontoon would then come back to pick up some of the load and ferry it across. After several trips the maize would be reloaded on the lorry and it would proceed to Kalabo. To remedy the situation, the three MPs of the Kalabo District, Arthur Wina, Amusa Mwanamwambwa and I clubbed together and procured, from personal funds, a pontoon large enough to carry a lorry and its full load across, without unloading. This enabled sufficient maize to be ferried across before the seasonal floods made the route impassable and ensured there would be no starvation in our three constituencies.

On going round the constituency as an MP I found that one was expected to bring development if not with government funds, then from one's own pocket or from what one could collect from well-wishers. The latter was a recipe for corruption, since well-wishers were likely to seek favours in return, unless these were friendly governments or international institutions. I resolved to press our government to bring essential development to my constituency, but I was determined not to fall into the trap of doing it on a personally-funded basis: the pontoon was an exception and it is operating to this day.

At the swearing-in ceremony of Chiluba as president, at the High Court, I was sitting next to Ms Edith Nawakwi, who was later appointed minister of energy and water affairs. She started telling me, in comparing herself to another minister to be, that she was 'making more money in her bedroom' than the other person will ever do. I was taken aback and admonished her not to talk so loudly as despite the new culture that has come with the MMD, Zambian society is not so liberated as to be able to accept that sort of talk from an MMD minister. For a while we seemed to be at cross-purposes, but I soon had to apologise for misunderstanding her: I had not read an article in one of our daily papers, wherein there was a description of Edith's successful tailoring activities in the bedroom of the flat that she was occupying.

When Chiluba was working on forming his cabinet he offered me the Ministry of Tourism. I was not happy with Tourism, as I doubted whether that would suit my abilities and told him I would think it over. I later accepted the post of *deputy* minister in State House. Some colleagues were astonished to hear this. However, I was quite satisfied, as I thought that this would still enable me to influence government policy: the status and remuneration was less important to me.

In the event, I was able to influence very little from that position. Although I had easy access to the president, meeting him often in State House and going with him on trips to the provinces, we never developed a close relationship. I was not part of any kitchen cabinet and since I lacked information on cabinet discussions I was unable to make any meaningful suggestions except perhaps on one or two important matters. I think he was more comfortable with his own age group.

As I was working in State House, on hearing the Kaunda family being publicly accused by the minister of works and supply (and also by a deputy minister in the Ministry of Finance) of having vandalised furniture in State House, I made a point of going round both State House and State Lodge to see what the problem was. I found no vandalism of paintings, furniture or property, except for a large opening that had been made through a wall in one of the houses associated with the State Lodge complex. This house had been used by one of the Kaunda sons as a recording studio. The hatch had been done professionally and in no way could be labelled vandalism.

Later I was shocked when it became known that when the minister concerned went to South Africa to purchase replacements, he insisted on going round doing the purchasing himself and using government funds without control by officials. As a result of the public outcry that followed, the minister was sacked by President Chiluba and I may claim some credit for this. Since this minister was his uncle and Chiluba had always stayed at his house in Lusaka during the campaign, the president's action came, understandably, only after considerable hesitation and it was done more in sorrow than in anger. Clearly, the accusation against the Kaunda family was made purely as a pretext for some planned non-transparent behaviour by the minister: the most that needed replacement were some mattresses! Once the president had dismissed the errant minister, I felt comfortable that, as a government we were in the right hands. I went ahead to sort out the mess left behind by the previous 'Party and its government' in the form of some building projects, where party and state were dubiously mixed up.

UNIP, as the sole political party in the Second Republic, had been allocated funds in the national budget for the construction of a new headquarters complex and this was still under construction when the MMD became the government. Clearly this was a national and not a UNIP asset, even though some funds were also collected for it from the public and by deduction from the salaries of top management in the parastatals. With the agreement of the minister of works and supply, I took charge of this project and worked with the director of buildings and his chief architect, both professional colleagues with whom I had worked in the past. I was able to guide them out of the impasse that they were in, since under the Kaunda era much was done on this complex on unorthodox lines and they were now not sure how to proceed. As more than one hundred million US Dollars was still required for the completion of the ambitious complex, I decided to complete only two buildings, which were of immediate interest and well on the way to completion: the Museum and a three-storey office block at the rear of it. On completion, I arranged to let the office block to the Privatisation Agency

(ZPA). More complicated for me was to get to grips with two other Kaunda building relics.

A trust had constructed an eye clinic and was in the process of constructing a temple, both within easy reach of State House and on state land. President Kaunda was said to be involved and so was some Indian guru. To deal with these building projects I had first to establish ownership. From Mr Shimabale, the controller at State House, I ascertained that *he* was the secretary of the trust. The trustees included the then chief justice (Annel Silungwe), Francis Kaunda, Grey Zulu, Mr Subulwa, later an MMD member of Parliament, and Mr Raganathan, the Indian guru, who had left the country immediately after the change of government.

I interviewed Mr Silungwe who explained to me how the trust, eye clinic and temple came about. Raganathan proved himself a great healer when he cured Kaunda's stomach ulcers and Mr Silungwe's eye cataract. Kaunda was impressed to the point of setting up the trust and having a clinic built for Raganathan to train healers on an international basis. I did not press, nor was I enlightened as to what the elaborate temple was, but I understood that Raganathan would have used it to exercise his spiritual powers. ZCCM (the state mining conglomerate) had been footing the bill for all this and now wanted to stop doing so. I got the clinic finished and handed over to the Ministry of Health. Since I was unable to find a tenant for letting the temple and funding its completion, I had further work stopped and ZCCM management were able to cease making payments to the contractor.

*****

After a victory rally in Mongu on 8 December 1991, two Indunas arrived at the government guest house at 2200 hrs and asked to see me privately. I was informed that the Litunga would like to see me at his palace and that next morning a Land Rover would be at hand. After consulting Arthur Wina, I agreed to be picked up at 0800hrs on the next morning and we arrived at the Palace at 0830. I stayed until 1030. I had met Ilute Yeta before the election in the company of Aka Mbikusita Lewanika and I remembered Yeta recalling Punabantu, Kaunda's press officer and close colleague, as saying: 'Many of us will die with our thoughts in our heart'. Did Yeta want us to know that under Kaunda, even those in his close circle could not express themselves freely?

Ilute Yeta started by assuring me he was 'not UNIP'. He said he had problems and needed help. 'The Nakatindis and Sikatanas are organizing people to throw stones on my roof at Limulunga and are even talking of replacing me'. He wanted me and President Chiluba to know: 'I am not UNIP. Masheke was the one who cooked it otherwise prior to the election. It was he who took the papers to the UNIP conference for me to stand as an MCC and it was he who wrote the statements purporting to come from the Ngambela'. I saw a sad man before me and felt sympathy for him. I thought that he must have been surprised by the MMD victory in his area and was seeking to come to terms with it.

We discussed how he could clear the false impression that he was still a pillar of the Kaunda era. I suggested a statement by the Ngambela or one from the Kuta, welcoming the MMD victory. I did not say it should come from him as I had learnt from my Lozi friend Aka that public statements do not come *directly* from the Litunga. In the same vein I suggested that he could follow tradition and blame and dismiss his Ngambela. I added that the statement should also reveal that he (Yeta) had resigned from UNIP. These moves would deter the Lozi activists within the MMD who might be bent on causing trouble. We parted on good terms and he indicated that I should expect some communication when I was back in Lusaka at State House which I could then announce at a press conference. At the least, I was left with the impression to expect some evidence of his resignation from UNIP.

A week or so later a letter from Lealui arrived for me at State House, brought by Induna Namunda. It provided no basis on which I could hold a press conference. It contained no hard evidence of a resignation; only a vague reference to it in a letter to Kaunda, dated 13 December 1991. I received a further complaint by phone from Yeta of people shouting for his removal from the Litungaship on 20th December and I had to tell him that there was nothing I could do in the absence of solid proof of his resignation from UNIP. The tensions then died down and Chiluba, the minister of works and I flew to Lealui and we discussed with the Litunga and the Ngambela the funding of various refurbishments to the palace buildings and the provision of electricity from the Zesco grid instead of by generator, which was no longer functioning. On our return to Lusaka I made sure that Zesco acted without delay. The refurbishing of buildings, however, got bogged down by delays in the release of funds by the Ministry of Finance.

Ilute Yeta regained his self-confidence when some leading Lozis, like Aka, started to peel away from the MMD. Yeta was seen to have been anti the MMD government for a considerable period. However, I kept up our relationship and paid him a visit in 1996, on my way back from my constituency for the last time. I later arranged for him to attend the Susman centenary celebrations in Livingstone and Victoria Falls as guest of honour in 1999.

*****

I was appointed a member of the commission of inquiry into the accident involving the vice-president of Zambia, Mr Mwanawasa.* From the hearings it became pretty clear that there was no conspiracy or attempt at assassination. To assist in allaying public suspicions, the commission decided to seek assistance from New Scotland Yard. The British High Commissioner was sympathetic and was ready to pass on the commission's request. (Four Scotland Yard officers came to Zambia and came to the same conclusion as the commissioners).

With my sole dissent, the commissioners decided to go to Britain and West Germany, all at great expense to government, to speak to Scotland Yard and to look at Daimler Benz and BMW cars, specially armoured for VIP protection. It was certainly tempting to go on a trip at government expense. I declined to go, but failed to convince my fellow commissioners that the trip was unnecessary. I was later able to hold my head high when MMD members of Parliament criticised the trip. Apart from the expense, which government could ill afford, I saw no point in inspecting the vehicles in person. After all we knew such vehicles were made by several manufacturers.

*****

In April 1993, President Chiluba reshuffled his cabinet and I was appointed minister of agriculture food and fisheries. I took over from Dr Guy Scott, who had successfully seen us through the '91/'92 drought by persuading the World Food Programme and individual countries to come to our aid with maize and fertilizer, and equipment to help us distribute the aid to the rural areas in need. I had not been following in great detail our agricultural policies and this appointment took me by surprise. I was certainly not prepared for it.

---

*The vice-president was severely injured when the official car he was being driven in was hit by an oncoming Land Rover driven by a police officer. The Land Rover had swerved lanes. There were suspicions that the collision was intentional.

Chapter Thirteen

INTO AGRICULTURE FOOD AND FISHERIES

On taking on the Ministry of Agriculture I was faced with a bumper maize crop and no money to buy it. The money provided in the 1993 budget was barely enough for an average maize crop. I set about protesting and blaming the IMF and even used an occasion at the Embassy of the USA to do so publicly in a world-wide broadcast link up. The battle for more funds to be provided went on until the end of the year.

Money could have been printed, as in the past, but government had early in '92 disciplined itself by going on to a cash budget and had also turned its back on printing money. This did not inhibit pressure on me from the media to buy in the crop before the rains set in, as the peasants and small-scale farmers had no storage facilities. We could have stood by, relying on market forces, and hoping that the millers would find the money to buy in the crop in time. After all, government did not need the crop for its own use and policy was to get out of the maize marketing business! However, in response to my pressure on the Ministry of Finance, a way was found for government to step in without printing money and fuelling inflation.

The government would find the necessary money, but only in the following budget year, in February 1994! The small farmers who had not sold their maize before the November '93 rains set in, could do so to designated principal agents of government, by accepting payment in government promissory notes. These would be redeemed in mid February 1994. Not unexpectedly, this had many critics, including MMD members of Parliament, but it was the best deal I could get from the Ministry of Finance and it was the best it could offer within the financial constraints obtaining at the time. I would have liked to have included an element of interest, but this was resisted by the Treasury.

To avoid fraud the promissory notes were especially printed and then issued under strict controls to the grower after the maize was securely delivered into a government-controlled warehouse. The controls involved not only my ministry but also the Ministry of Finance. When the amount required to redeem the issued promissory notes was quantified at 17.6 billion kwacha I had assurances from Finance that the amount would be available. I then issued strict written instructions to my permanent secretary that every effort must be made to ensure that redemption of these notes should start on the due date. Despite this, there were delays in some places of several days, delays which could and should have been avoided. Understandably, the scheme was unpopular, not least because payment would take place some ten weeks after the maize was taken into depots. However, this was not the main criticism.

In late February there were claims in Parliament and the media that many of the promissory notes were not redeemed. I offered to investigate every such unredeemed promissory note. As a result, one UNIP member of Parliament walked into my office with a whole wad of notes. On investigation, however, they proved to be promissory notes of a kind, but not one of them was a promissory note issued by the Ministry of Finance. They were all receipts, issued by agents or buyers for maize received from small farmers, but not as part of this scheme. Some of the receipts were even from the previous season. Nevertheless, rumours persisted that many promissory notes were not redeemed and I later had even to correct a North American research academic when he sent me a draft of his thesis in which he repeated this calumny.

The need to use this method of delayed payment was never understood by peasant farmers. Many felt cheated. They were used to government buying their crop and paying for it on delivery. In their eyes government had an obligation to buy the maize that they had for sale. Yet we could not spend more money than that provided for maize buying in the '93 budget, without upsetting the new financial discipline that we had imposed on ourselves. I accepted the proposal of promissory notes as the only way for government to come to the rescue of the small farmer.

Having achieved something towards rescuing the small farmer, I tried to ease the lot of the commercial farmers, who were in danger of losing their farms to the commercial banks. Bank interest rates for overdrafts and seasonal loans had jumped to 180% from the 30% obtaining when farmers first took their loans in 1992. I had pleas from the Zambia National Farmers Union to intervene with the banks. With the help of the World Bank, I commissioned a study by an agricultural economist who made a critical report which concluded that what was taking place was a major transfer of resources from the agricultural sector to the banking sector, with disastrous results for the former. I pressed the governor of the Bank of Zambia to seek a way to ameliorate this. Then, when we were in Paris for a December meeting of the Consultative Group (CG) the governor and I discussed this with the IMF. Their answer was simple: 'what you are proposing would involve printing money, if you want to ameliorate the lot of the commercial farmers, you will have to find the money from increased taxes on all tax payers'. That brought our efforts to an abrupt end.

The transfer, referred to above, was not only *within* the country. Barclays and Standard Chartered showed extraordinary profits for the year and the latter declared *all* of it as a dividend and, since they have only a token *local* shareholding, almost all of these extraordinary profits left the country! Unfortunately my attempts to avoid this were unsuccessful.

Despite liberalisation, it was still the practice for government to announce the price per bag to be paid to the farmer. My predecessor had suggested a price of 5000 kwacha per 90 kg bag. I recommended that in view of inflation this be upped to 7000 kwacha, the price that was then current in cross-border trade with Zaire. I found that this was accepted only reluctantly: the president and the urban constituency within cabinet was trying to keep the price down. The vice-president went around insisting that, irrespective of government's policy of market forces to be the determining factor, the price paid to the farmer be no more than 7000 kwacha. I, on the other hand, said publicly that this applied only if government was the buyer of last resort; otherwise market forces should determine the price. I had to explain away to commercial farmers that the VP was merely assuming the role of a market force.

One of my first tasks was to encourage the coming into being of private grain merchants to buy in the maize crop from peasant and small-scale farmers for later resale to millers. My predecessor had, as part of government liberalisation policies, terminated Namboard, the state marketing conglomerate, and, as an interim measure, appointed agents to buy maize *on behalf* of government, with government funding. Grain merchants for buying maize, *on their own account*, were non-existent, because until liberalisation of maize trading in 1992, all maize grown for sale, unlike other crops, had, by law, to be sold to Namboard by the growers. My deputy minister, Hon Nkausu, and I therefore set about holding many meetings with the agents, millers and other potential grain merchants. By the middle of 1993 we had a sufficient number of merchants keen to risk buying for their own account, but *not* with their own money! Money had to be loaned to them by government and even then, none was prepared to pledge his own assets as security for the loan.

A bill to set up The Food Reserve Agency (FRA) was worked on by my predecessor, but he failed to get it through cabinet. I realised that this was due only partly to objections to its content: it was also because he had lost the sympathy of many ministers and that of the president. I therefore set up an inter-ministerial committee to review the bill and only reintroduced it to cabinet after I judged that the personality aspect was behind us. It passed cabinet without amendment and later through Parliament. The act envisaged the FRA to be a buyer of last resort.

Throughout my period as minister of agriculture food and fisheries I found myself trying to move the agriculture industry fully into the market while much of cabinet and most members of Parliament were reluctant to go in that direction. They wanted subsidies to be brought back and the maize crop to be bought by government, as was the case before liberalisation. Yet the MOF could not even disburse, *in time,* the inadequate funds allocated in the budget for buying in that part of the peasant farmer's maize crop which remained unsold by the onset of the rains!

My predecessor, on handing over to me, warned me that I would soon find that our situation was not unlike being in 'receivership, with the dominant creditor being the IMF.' I *did* soon find this, but I could not escape also knowing that the copper mine taxes had dried up as a source for such subsidies and that our budget would be donor-dependent for many years to come. I accepted that subsidies were, for the time being, not possible and would only be possible again when there was a turnaround in our copper production and world copper prices.

There was general criticism that the MMD government had moved too fast in switching maize marketing to market forces and, indeed, three years may have been too short; or the transition mechanisms, which we devised, may have been inadequate. However, I doubt whether the switch could have been painless even if made over a longer period.

Support for the introduction of a free market economy, as part of the structural adjustment programme (SAP), came from the National Farmers Union, but in April 1994, at their annual congress, the main address from the platform contained the complaint that this adjustment was being done at the expense of the farmers. (Annexe in *Abe Galaun* by Jonathan Chileshe). While I can vouch that this was not government's design or intention, there is no escaping the fact that the impact of SAP was severest on commercial farmers. Structural adjustment, and its bedfellow, market liberalisation, resulted in an astronomical jump in bank interest rates on seasonal loans, with a major impact on farmers, as discussed earlier. Of course, this high interest rate was a reflection of the rate of inflation and the money printing that had gone on towards the end of the Second Republic and under the MMD, in coping with the consequences of the drought of '91/'92.

A reduction in the price of locally-grown wheat was also suffered by some commercial farmers and blamed on SAP, but this was brought about by liberalisation of imports, as a result of Zambia signing the new WTO Agreement, rather than by SAP. The NFU speaker was of the view that before opening our market government should have given 'consideration to set up safeguards for the most important products of our economy'. However, we had a problem with the WTO rules, in that we could not use special tariffs to reduce competition from imports, except in cases where we could prove dumping. Since we were not present at the bargaining table when the rules were hammered out between the big players, we could not have 'set up safeguards'. It might be argued that we should then not have signed the WTO agreement, but that would have impacted negatively on our exports of horticultural products. This issue continues to dog us to this day, even more severely with the zero tariff system of COMESA, not only with wheat, but also with other imports, which compete with locally-grown or manufactured products that have high-cost imported inputs of raw materials and duty and where we have not the economy of scale.

To score in regional and world trade we have to rely on our comparative advantages and we are constantly reminded that we have these in agriculture: adequate land and water, good climate and good soils. Indeed, with an area of 75.3 million hectares and a population of only ten million, we have adequate land. Of this total area, some nine million hectares are suitable for crop production, with only fifteen per cent utilized. But at present we have not got enough experienced and hard working farmers and the necessary capital to make use of our comparative advantages. We have half a million emerging farmers and less than two thousand commercial farmers, using mechanized methods in production. Most of our peasant farmers rely only on the hoe. Our farmers are involved in food production for only half of the year unless they are lucky enough to have some irrigation.

Land with potential for irrigation has been estimated at 410,000 hectares, and our total water resources available would be adequate for this, but the distribution of these resources is lop-sided. The northern half of the country has most of our water but not the best soils: these are in the central and southern parts of Zambia. To develop our agricultural potential to the full we need to transfer some of the surplus water from the north to the south. For a start we could transfer some of the water from the Luapula River to the Kafue River and this could be done at reasonable cost. I proposed this publicly in 1994 and, at my behest, discussions were started with the then Mobutu government of Zaire (now Congo). Agreement with the Congo would be necessary, since it is an interested party in the Luapula River and because the proposal involved a pipeline through the Pedicle - the tongue of Congo-owned land that juts into Zambia between the Copperbelt and the Luapula Province. (Negative effects downstream in the Luapula River would be insignificant.)

Other water transfer proposals from the north to the south, completely within our own borders, would involve longer pipelines and pumping across a higher watershed. The scheme which was discussed in the Zaire-Zambia Joint Co-operative Council would require a pipeline over only some sixty-five kilometres and pumping to a height differential of about 220 metres. Once across the watershed, which is also the international border, the water would be discharged into the North Mutundu River, a tributary of the Kafue River. From there it would flow, at no cost, to the good soils of the area around Mazabuka, where the water at present available from the Kafue is already fully allocated to hydro-electricity and sugar production. As a sweetener, it was put to the Zaire delegation that this would enable Zambia to increase its maize and wheat surplus for export to Zaire. At Zaire's request, I initiated a feasibility study with in-house MAFF personnel, and using my civil engineering knowledge. These discussions could be resumed when stability returns to the Congo.

I spent much of my time in the Ministry working towards integrating donor support for the agriculture sector, into the programme known as ASIP (Agriculture Sector Investment Programme) and I managed to launch this before I was moved to the Ministry of Works and Supply towards the end of 1995.

Before launching ASIP I had undergone, in Cape Town, an operation for the removal of part of my colon to deal with a cancerous polyp. I had rushed down to Cape Town just as I was about to involve myself in a land matter not connected with agriculture, but close to my heart, University of Zambia land! During my chairmanship of the university's building committee over some twenty-five years, I had managed to fend off many demands for Unza's undeveloped plots and now found that the MMD minister of lands had taken one for himself, had given two to the vice-president and several to a trust, the trustees of which were deputy ministers from the Luapula Province. In fact, the trust was deemed to be connected with President Chiluba. All the transfers were without any payment and based on the Kaunda legislation that defined undeveloped land as having no value. I took the matter up with the president when he came to see me at my house on my return from Cape Town after my operation. Eventually the plots were transferred back to the university, with the exception of one, which had already been sold by the vice-president.

With my encouragement the private sector millers and traders had bought the whole 1994 and 1995 maize crops, without any direct buying by government taking place and this was seen as a success by donors, World Bank and IMF. However, my liberalisation of maize marketing was not popular with MMD members of Parliament or with President Chiluba because peasant farmers in remote areas were receiving prices for their maize below cost of production. My ministry instituted a system for disseminating market information to rural areas to overcome this, but peasant farmers proved too weak in bargaining against the few buyers who were prepared to brave the bad roads to reach them. The Food Reserve Agency was established in 1996 and one of its tasks was to buy maize in remote areas at a fair price, subsidising transport costs, but it got off to a dubious start by trading in grain bags instead. In July 1996, I was moved to the Ministry of Works from the Ministry of Agriculture, ostensibly because of the need for a younger man who would get around more to the rural areas.

Chapter Fourteen
RESIGNATION

I took over as minister of works and supply from Andrew Kashita and found that compared with the Ministry of Agriculture it was a relatively stress-free post and not as interesting. Roads were a main concern and so was housing. There was widespread pressure for proposals to start selling government houses to civil servants. Some of the houses in Lusaka were in a state of repair that would make them fit only for demolition, although many of them were on valuable plots.

On housing, I submitted to cabinet proposals for sale of some houses on the basis of professional valuations and these were later acted on and, once privatised, the houses were quickly redeveloped. On roads, I regret that I was a party to a ministerial decision to proceed with the reconstruction of the Choma-Namwala road by borrowing funds from the National Roads Board. These funds were from the fuel levy and should have been used for road maintenance and not for capital works. The funds, regrettably, were never repaid to the NRB.

In 1996, the tunnels built by Kaunda for escape from State House were about to be shown by President Chiluba to the press and I was called in by Sate House assistants to give my opinion as to the wisdom of doing so. I advised against such a course of action in view of their possible usefulness in the event of an attempted coup. I quoted the case of President Makarios in Cyprus who escaped through a tunnel from State House in Nicosia at the time of the Colonels' take over in Greece. My advice fell on deaf ears and was met with surprise by Mr Richard Sakala, who exclaimed: 'A coup is unthinkable: we have such a strong mandate'. The mandate had been wearing thin during the five years since 1991. Mandate or not, and despite Chiluba's re-election in 1996, there was an attempted coup by soldiers under a Captain Solo within days of the 1997 independence anniversary!

My predecessor had revived the scheme on which I had worked as a consultant in 1965, to build a road bridge across the Zambezi at Katimo Mulilo/Sesheke and it seemed that this could be realisable. German government finance was being offered for it to Zambia and Namibia since it would link both countries. I flew to meet with my Namibian counterpart at the project site and we agreed to formalise our joint request for financing to the German government. Before this could be effected, a political storm blew up in Zambia, which would affect donor financing, not only for this bridge but for many other road projects and even for donor balance of payment support. It would also affect my position as a member of government.

In an attempt to prevent Kenneth Kaunda from contesting the presidency in 1996, the MMD made representations to the Mwanakatwe Commission, which was reviewing the Zambian Constitution, to provide not only for presidential candidates to have been born in Zambia, but for *both* parents of the candidate also to have been born in Zambia. (Kaunda's father came from Malawi.)

When the Mwanakatwe Commission recommended in accordance with the MMD submission, I was asked by a reporter of *The Times of Zambia* for my reaction and I said I would support Kaunda's right to stand. (*Times of Zambia*, October 1995). I was soon reprimanded by President Chiluba for taking a stand on this *before* one was taken by cabinet. Later, when the debate was in full blast and some demanded that a constituent assembly be convened to settle the constitution, I made my position clear at several levels: privately to the president, but also in public. On one occasion, when officiating at a function of the Zambia-Bangladesh Friendship Association I said: 'For me, the basic question.... is not *where* the constitution is to be settled, but *how*; not a question of in Parliament or in a constituent assembly. Parliament is the ideal place, but there we, the MMD, must use, not power of numbers, but power of persuasion: we must carry the opposition with us'. This, when reported in the press, earned me a public rebuke from the then minister of legal affairs, Remy Mushota, who thought that if I differed with my ministerial colleagues, I should know 'the honourable thing to do'. Yet no decision by cabinet or the MMD parliamentary caucus had been taken to *bulldoze* the matter through Parliament, without attempting to carry the opposition. I came to the conclusion that there was a cabal in the MMD hierarchy to use power of numbers, not power of persuasion in Parliament and so it proved. I was against the proposed parentage clause, but even more so against the enactment of an important constitutional amendment on a partisan basis.

I opposed the parentage clause for the following reasons:

1) The effect of the clause would be to discriminate between citizens and this goes against the national motto introduced at independence: 'One Zambia: one nation'.
2) It is against the spirit of our Bill of Rights: instead of all citizens being equal in status, we would have an Orwellian situation: all citizens are equal, but some are more equal than others. The MMD government was reluctant to test public opinion in a referendum and avoided legislating for desirable amendments, recommended by the Mwanakatwe Commission, which would have directly impinged on the Bill of Rights. government felt it could slip in this one without the need for a referendum.
3) In an inland country like ours, with artificially imposed borders, often splitting tribes, hundreds of thousands of our citizens cannot claim both parents as having been born within our borders. In my own constituency of Sikongo on the Angolan border this applies and I knew it held true for all the other border regions.
4) Many of our outstanding citizens are from families where the father went to work or study abroad and married there before returning home. These citizens have had useful international exposure and are able to contribute to our affairs all the better for that.
5) The clause is a piece of bad legislation, in that the real aim behind it was to preclude a specific person from standing for president in the coming election. Despite vehement denials, it was aimed at the former president, Kenneth Kaunda and was proposed to the Mwanakatwe Commission with that specific purpose, because the MMD did not feel confident enough of defeating him.
6) The clause would, needlessly, limit the choice of our people for their president.

When the recommendations of the Mwanakatwe Commission were being discussed in cabinet, Dipak Patel and I tried, unsuccessfully, to argue against the parentage clause. After the meeting, the two of us discussed the situation and felt we had no option but to resign our ministerial posts. He did so almost immediately by letter to the president and I somewhat later, after visiting my constituency and informing MMD officials there of my intentions at a meeting in Kalabo.

On Dipak's suggestion, I decided to resign, for greater impact *in the House* during the acrimonious debate. Before doing so I thought it wise to inform the speaker. This was a mistake. I went to see him privately and he insisted I had to resign *directly* to the appointing authority, the president. Although I accepted his ruling, he apparently did not trust my intentions and would not call on me to speak from the front bench during the debate. I therefore left the House and sent my resignation to the president and announced it to the press, but the resignation was not accepted until after the debate was over. This delay prevented me from full participation in the debate from the backbench, as well as the front bench. Nevertheless, I made an interjection which caught the press headlines. When Kaunda was being vilified by the main MMD spokesman to the effect that he was not a Zambian, I interjected that he 'was a Zambian and a worthy one at that.'

Many MMD members of Parliament took the trouble to explain to me that the clause was not aimed at me. At the same time there were some letters to the papers alleging that my opposition was because I felt blocked by the clause. However, my personal aspirations were not remotely involved. I felt it was high time that my fellow Zambians should learn that one can take a stand on principle, irrespective of personal considerations! After all, in 1951, personal considerations should have kept me from confrontation with the colonial authority!

I remained a member of Parliament until the House was dissolved a short while later, and then I retired from active politics until early 2001, when Chiluba's attempt at an illegal third term brought me back. I wrote to Chiluba, urging him to abandon his third term project, since it was divisive and I travelled overseas to canvass international support for the Oasis Forum campaign against it.

While I was overseas MMD members of Parliament signed a motion to impeach Chiluba and twenty-two of them were denied access to the MMD Convention and, because of their objection to the third term, expelled from the MMD.

On my return in May I found moves afoot to form a new party, with the expelled MMD members as its core. At the inaugural meeting I was asked to become interim chairman of the newly-formed Forum for Democracy and Development and guide it until its convention.

During my interim chairmanship I ensured that the party's constitution balanced the powers pf party president and chairman so as to avoid a repeat of the MMD history of presidential dominance. I selected the membership of the party's interim committees and ensured that the convention was run on thoroughly democratic and peaceful lines. It was widely recognised as setting a new standard for Zambian political parties. My work appeared to be appreciated by all factions as I was elected chairman of the party without challenge.

Chapter Fifteen
EPILOGUE

As I look back over the fifty-five years of my political thinking, writing and activities, I have no regrets about my involvement in the struggle for emancipation of the Southern African region from colonialism: internal in the case of South Africa and both internal and external in the case of the other territories. Cynthia also does not regret her role, which includes considerable financial assistance to various aid funds and individuals, not least to the Solomon Mahlangu Freedom College, the ANC's school in Tanzania. In fact, we are proud of our contributions.

I feel that our various public activities, before and since Zambia's independence, have assisted in achieving a situation where racism is generally absent and even frowned upon. The only time that I was subjected to a racial attack was in a by-election campaign in Lusaka in 2001, when a leading political opponent used our race against me and my Indian colleague, Dipak Patel. It received no support and was counterproductive for our opponent and his ruling party: they lost the by-election and our candidate won!

Zambia has been in economic difficulties since the drop in copper prices and the rise in oil prices in 1973. After independence we had succeeded only in minor diversification of our mono-economy, which was based on copper mining. Zambia is now an impoverished country, relative to its economic status from independence to the early seventies. Some of the impoverishment can be ascribed to our active support for ending white supremacy in Southern Africa and much to putting a major share of the economy under government control: 'nationalisation'.

The sanctions against Rhodesia during UDI, which involved the diversion of our import and export routes, impacted adversely on our economy. We suffered destruction of many bridges and had to spend on defence much that should have been spent on development. However, despite UDI and civil war, Zimbabwe had, until the nineteen-nineties, a vibrant, diversified economy with a well-maintained infrastructure. It might therefore be argued that had Federation been given a chance, our economy would have benefited from it.

Indeed, I never rejected the *economic* case for Federation with Southern Rhodesia and even stated so publicly. Nevertheless, we were right to oppose and terminate Federation on *political* grounds and I am proud of the leading role I played in this. Not only did we shorten the period of white dominance in the region, but we also avoided major ethnic complications. The current regional grouping through SADC and COMESA should now be available to do some of the good to the economy that integration through Federation might have done.

While removal of import tariffs within COMESA and reduction of them within SADC may assist Zambia's growth in the long term, at present it is closing down the few secondary industries that developed as a result of past policies of import substitution. This problem has to be addressed or the number of jobless will grow in the urban sector. Globalisation, as such, is not a threat to these industries or to our agriculture in terms of competition. The threat is from within the Southern African region and recently this has been intensified by a chaotic monetary situation in Zimbabwe, where a major discrepancy has developed between the official and black-market rate for foreign exchange. What is a threat from overseas is not globalisation, but the current farm subsidies obtaining in both the EU and the USA. These make it difficult for Zambian farmers to export profitably.

We tend to plead that the West is paying us immorally low prices not only for our agricultural produce, but also for our copper, and this has resulted in mines becoming unprofitable and even some closures. Yet no amount of pleading will make buyers of copper pay more that supply/demand dictates. High production costs could have been brought down by investment, but years of milking the copper mines by government has resulted in lack of maintenance, refurbishment and exploration. By nationalising the mines we cut ourselves off from the equity markets and had to rely on costly short-term loans. Now we have to seek new investment in the mining sector to reduce the cost of production, to extend our reserves and develop new mines. We might have done better to have kept captive the old owners.

I was initially supportive of nationalisation, but I became disillusioned with it as I saw it in practice. Nationalisation of industrial, commercial and mining enterprises was of social and political, but not economic value. It did accelerate the growth of an indigenous middle class and provided training in business management and other skills to many Zambians. Above all, it gave widespread patronage to the head of state in making appointments to state enterprises and thus assisted for a decade or so in keeping the elite supportive of the one-party system. It resulted, however, in much inefficiency, corruption and misdirection of public resources, often into purely party political channels. By the late seventies I did not need IMF persuasion to support privatisation of the various state conglomerates, including agricultural marketing, electricity distribution and telecommunications.

Agricultural development and growth will be too slow to fill the gap in our economy left by the depleted mining sector, and to keep pace with population growth, unless we attract outside investment and skills: and we should not be afraid to do so. The Tazara Corridor in the Northern Province has great potential for a massive agricultural initiative. Our stock of good farmers with capital is far too low for the required rapid development of our agricultural resources. We should be prepared to borrow from the World Bank to develop irrigation, effect large-scale water transfer from the north to the south and provide electrification to farming areas with potential for irrigation like the Mkushi Block. We should accelerate the construction of the road and bridge from Mongu to the Angolan border, for which Kuwaiti loan money has already been secured, so as to take advantage of peace in Angola and our comparative advantage in supplying their eastern areas. This would boost agricultural production not only in the Kaoma small-scale commercial farming area, only some three hundred kilometres from the border, but also amongst the similar farmers in Mumbwa, a further two hundred and fifty kilometres to the east. (In early 1992, when I was a member of Parliament for Sikongo, we officially exported almost all our locally-grown rice into Angola during their short-lived peace.) Only by bold measures will agriculture replace mining as the mainstay of our economy.

As I write this epilogue, Zambia, after an heroic people's struggle to defeat a conspiracy by Chiluba to stand for a third term as president, has now also scored a major victory for transparency, with the National Assembly's lifting of Chiluba's presidential immunity. This will clear the way for an investigation of him for alleged massive corruption, involving around a hundred million dollars. This gives me great hope that we can look forward to a revival of our national self-esteem and international respect. It encourages me to look to a future where our people will be free from misrule. Given a period of decent government, we can diversify our economy and, with good leadership and hard work, our people can be led back to prosperity. While we still have to seek donor aid for a while, I hope we shall devise an aid exit strategy and come to rely on trade rather than aid.

CYNTHIA'S EPILOGUE

Simon has deliberately written this book as a political memoir, but I thought it would be in order to add a few words on a more personal note: Simon the family man.

It is not easy for someone involved in a professional working life, as well as an active political commitment, to find a balance between that and enjoyment of family life. But Simon has spent as much time as he could with us, and until our sons grew up we always managed to have a relaxed annual holiday together, as well as most weekends.

Our sons, David and Alan, have chosen very different paths in life from their father, but in many fundamental ways they have absorbed his values and attitudes. They are both caring people with a total lack of prejudice, with full respect for other cultures and other people's beliefs. David has become a Buddhist and Alan is now a farmer and very devoted family man, close to his four children. They are both happily settled. David and his wife and baby are based in London and Alan and his partner live in Lusaka. Alan is the coffee manager on our family farm, on the outskirts of Lusaka.

Politicians don't ever really retire, but when Simon finally decides to take a back seat, we look forward to spending time enjoying being with our family and seeing the grandchildren growing up.

SELECT BIBLIOGRAPHY

Alport Lord CJM, *The Sudden Assignment,* Hodder & Stoughton, 1965.
Bledisloe, *Rhodesia and Nyasaland Royal Cmd. Report,* Cmd 949, 1939.
Caplan Gerald L, *The Elites of Barotseland 1878-1969.*
Chileshe Jonathan H, *Abe Galaun,* Walpole Parke Development Ltd, 2000.
Chipungu Samuel, *Guardians in Their Time, 1890-1964,* Macmillan, 1992.
Chisala Beatwell S, *The Downfall of President Kaunda,* Co-op Printing, Zambia, 1994.
Clingham Stephen, *Bram Fischer,* Mayibuye Books, UWC, 1998.
Christie Roy, *For the President's Eyes Only,* Hugh Keartland Publishers, Johannesburg, 1971.
Davidson Basil, *In the Eye of the Storm,* Longman, 1972.
Davidson J W, *The Northern Rhodesian Legislative Council,* Faber & Faber, 1948.
Epstein A L, *Politics in an Urban African Community,* Manchester University Press, 1958.
Foa Anna, *The Jews of Europe after the Black Death,* University of California Press, 2000.
Forman Lionel, *A Trumpet from the Housetops,* UWC Mayibuye History Series, 1992.
Gann L H, *A History of Northern Rhodesia,* Chatto & Windus, 1964.
Hall Richard, *Zambia,* Pall Mall Press, 1965.
Hochschild A, *King Leopold's Ghost,* Macmillan, 1998.
Horvitch I O, *Report on Physical Development,* University of Zambia, 1971.
International Conference on Structural Failure (ICSF 87-Singapore) Vols. 2.
Kaunda Kenneth D, *Zambia Shall be Free,* Heinemann, 1962.
Kissinger Henry, *Years of Renewal,* Weidenfeld & Nicolson, 1999.
Lamb Christina, *Africa House,* Viking, 1999.
Lessing Doris, *Going Home,* Alfred Knopf, 1988.
Luyt R E, *Trade Unionism in African Colonies,* South African Institute of Race Relations.
Macpherson Fergus, *Kenneth Kaunda of Zambia,* Oxford University Press, 1974.
Makasa Kapasa, *March to Political Freedom,* Heinemann Educational Books,

1981.

Mamdani Mahmoud, *Politics and Class Formation in Uganda,* Heinemann, 1976.

Mandela Nelson, *Long Walk to Freedom,* Macdonald Purnell, 1994.

Martin Anthony, *Minding their own Business,* Hutchinson of London, 1972.

Mebelo Henry S, *African Proletarians and Colonial Capitalism,* Kenneth Kaunda Foundation, 1986.

Mulford David C, *Zambia, The Politics of Independence,* Oxford University Press, 1967.

Mwanakatwe John M, *End of Kaunda Era,* Multi Media Publications, 1994.

Mwangilwa G B, *The Kapwepwe Diaries,* Multi Media Publications, 1986.

Mwendapole M R, *A History of the Trade Union Movement in Zambia up to 1968,* UNZA, 1977.

Pakenham Thomas, *Scramble for Africa,* Jonathan Ball Publishers, 1991.

Podbrey Pauline, *White Girl in Search of a Party,* Hodeda Books, Pietermaritzburg, 1993.

Report of the Commission Appointed to Inquire into the Disturbances on the Copperbelt, Northern Rhodesia, July-September 1935, Lusaka.

What Will Federation Mean?, Rhodesia Study Club, Cape Town 1949. See National Archives, Lusaka.

Russell Bertrand, *The Autobiography* 1944-1967 (vol. III), George Allen & Unwin, 1969.

Rotberg Robert I, *The Rise of Nationalism in Central Africa,* Harvard University Press, 1967.

Sikalumbi Wittington, *Before UNIP,* Neczam, Lusaka, 1977.

Simons H J, *Struggles in Southern Africa,* Macmillan, 1997.

Tembo Nephas, *The Lillian Burton Killing,* Apple Books, Lusaka, 1986.

Tordoff William, *Politics in Zambia,* Manchester University Press, 1974.

Turok Ben, *Development in Zambia: A Reader,* Zed Press, London, 1979.

Welensky Sir Roy, *Welensky's 4000 Days,* Collins, London, 1964.

INDEX

AFAC (see Anti-Federation Action Committee)
ANC (see African National Congress of South Africa)
ANC (see Northern Rhodesian African National Congress)
Abyssinia; 19
Achiume, Jason; 42
Ackutt, Keith; 111
Addis Ababa; 28, 29
Aden; 64
African Affairs Board (of Federal Government); 76
African Mineworkers Union; 15, 56, 59, 70, 75, 77, 87, 109
African National Congress of South Africa; 40, 95, 96, 99, 102, 103, 104, 107, 137, 147, 148, 203
African Railway Workers Union; 66
African Representative Council; 48, 75
African Shop Assistants Trade Union; 40
Africans; and Jellico Town Plan, 126; and land issues, 111; and political movements, 41, 45-6, 55; and self government, 112, 114-15, 118; and skilled work, 22, 90; and tobacco growing, 57; and trade unions, 40, 42-3, 79, 110-11; as house servants, 10-11, 14; children, 15; impact on of World War II, 30; in Belgian Congo, 21; in East Africa, 26; opposition to Federation, 38, 47, 49, 51-4, 56, 58-66, 75-9, 81-2, 96, 97, 100, 109-10, 112-13, 116-18; support for Simon Zukas, 87, 91; status in Southern Rhodesia, 18; (see also African Mineworkers Union; African Railway Workers Union; African Representative Council; African Shop Assistants Trade Union; Anti Federation Action Committee; Cha, Cha, Cha; Kitwe African Society;

Movement for Multi-Party Democracy; Northern Rhodesia African National Congress; United National Independence Party; Zambian African National Congress)
Afrikaner Nationalists; 36
Afrikaners; 10, 13, 15, 21, 35, 74, 91, 181
agriculture; 155, 175, 189, 190-7, 204, 205 (see also Chunga Irrigation Scheme; maize; wheat)
Agriculture, Food and Fisheries, Ministry of; 189, 190-7, 198
Agriculture Sector Investment Programme (ASIP); 196
Albertville; 21, 22
All African Peoples Conference; 114
Alport Lord CJM; 116, 117
amalgamation; 34, 46, 47, 48, 117
Amery, Julian; 62
Anderson, Clyde; 175
Andrews, Bill; 35, 39
Anglin, Dr Douglas; 162
Anglo American Corporation; 32
Angola; 132, 140, 143, 144, 145, 147, 148, 153, 180, 181, 183, 205
Anti-Apartheid Movement; 101, 104, 105, 107
Anti-Federation Action Committee; 53, 54, 59, 62, 64-5, 68-70, 71-2, 74-6, 77, 83, 110
Anti-Semitism; 5, 6, 16, 17, 73
Anti-Slavery Society; 100
Antwerp; 8
apartheid; 35, 68, 90, 102, 104, 108, 136, 138, 153, 155, 176
Association of Engineering and Shipbuilding Draughtsmen; 105
Atlantic Charter; 26, 28
Atlee, Clement; 97

Baganda; 26, 28 (see also Buganda)

Baldwin, Archie; 62
Balmoral Farm; 175
Banda, Dingiswayo; 130
Banda, Hastings; 94, 95, 112, 122, 138
Banda, Rupiah; 145
Bandung; 103
Bank of Zambia; 152, 167, 192
Baron, Max; 9
Barotseland; 41, 42, 56, 57, 78, 132, 135 (see also Western Province)
Baskin, Myra; 33
Bataka Association; 27
Beckett, Geoffrey Bernard; 48
Before UNIP; 50; 63
Beitar (Zionist Youth Movement); 6
Belgian Congo; 21, 22
Benn, Tony; 100
Berlin; 8
Bevin, Ernest; 29
Billing, W; 64, 66, 69, 70
Boer War; 10
Boonzaier, Gregoire; 35
Botswana; 132
Boy Scouts; 6, 17
Britain; 1, 9, 13, 14, 15, 29, 36, 41, 46, 48, 55, 56, 90, 135, 138, 139, 140, 141, 142, 143, 148, 158, 174, 175, 182; Conservative government in; 61, 76, 77, 80, 83, 84, 112, 114;Labour government in, 26, 27, 30-1, 40, 42, 43, 72, 80, 83, 112, 114-17; and Federation, 39, 58, 62, 70, 71, 75, 78, 79, 84, 94, 124; Zukas appeal, 91, 92; Zukas exile in; 93-108, 119-121, 126 (See also Colonial Office)
British East Africa; 30
British Empire; 8, 19
British Somaliland; 28, 29
British South Africa Company (BSAC); 8
Brockway, Fenner; 100, 110
Broken Hill; 20, 66, 94, 97, 110 (see also Kabwe)
Brummer, John; 149
Bucharest; 96, 98
Budapest; 103
Buganda; 24, 25, 26, 27, 28

Bulawayo; 9, 17, 18, 37, 100
Bunting, Brian; 35, 99
Burma; 24, 26
Burton, Lilian; 114
Busoga; 25
Butler, Fred; 55, 56, 58
Butler, R.A; 116
Bwana Mkubwa Mine; 15, 69

Cairo; 121
Callaghan, James; 100
Campbell, Lord Jock; 142
Cape Town; 9, 21, 28, 30, 33, 34, 35, 36, 38, 39, 50, 60, 70, 86, 91, 93, 98, 99, 102, 103, 105, 107, 114, 131, 147, 196
Caprivi Strip; 132, 134, 165
Carneson, Fred; 35
Case Against Federation; 50
Castle, Barbara; 100
Catchpole, Len; 67
Cattle Cordon Line; 183
Central African Federation (see Federation)
Central African Mail; 73
Central African Post; 61
Central African Power Corporation; 172
Ceylon; 26
Cha Cha Cha; 111, 115, 122, 123
Chalabesa, Emmanuel; 39
Chandler, Fred; 88
Changufu, Lewis; 147, 151
Chapoloko, Jamieson; 87, 97, 98, 139
Chibwe, E; 177
Chigaga, Gibson; 176
Chikamoneka, Mama Julia; 126
Chikerema, Robert; 36, 38, 127, 137
Chileshe, Jonathan; 194
Chileshe, Safeli; 63
Chiluba, Frederick; 23, 177, 179, 182, 184, 185, 186, 188, 189, 196, 198, 199, 201, 205
Chilubi Island; 111
Chimba, Justin; 44, 45, 48, 49, 53, 54, 59, 60, 74, 76, 77, 81, 121, 139, 140, 141, 164
Chimowitz, Harry; 35, 36, 37, 127, 128, 134, 137, 140, 146, 155, 170, 174

Chimowitz, Marjorie; 35, 36, 37, 99, 140, 146, 155
China; 82, 102, 173, 178
Chingola; 11, 66, 75
Chinsali; 66, 77, 155
Chipata; 64, 66
Chipenda, Daniel; 144, 145
Chisala, BS; 143, 147
Chitty, Anthony; 158
Chipimo, Elias; 150, 151, 168, 179
Chivunga, Jonathan; 44, 54, 69, 81, 82, 96
Choma; 8, 10, 135, 175, 198
Chona, Mainza; 101, 113, 120, 125, 129, 130, 136, 173
Chona, Mark; 139, 142, 149
Chiluwe, Robert; 166
Chuula, Fitzpatric; 174
Chunga Irrigation Scheme; 170-1, 175
City Radio Ltd.; 169
Closer Association of the Rhodesias and Nyasaland (cmd 8233); 48
Cohen, Sir Andrew; 44, 116
Cold War; 34, 72, 106
Coldrick, William; 62
Cole, David; 55
Collins, Canon John; 142
Colonial Office; 8, 25, 40, 44, 46, 47, 54, 57, 60, 71, 72, 75, 93, 109, 115, 116, 118
colonialism; 46, 65, 100, 155, 203
Colour Bar in the Copperbelt; 84
Coloured community; 35
COMESA; 194, 204
Commonwealth; 23, 105, 109, 116, 117, 150
Commission for Technical Education; 152, 157
Communism; 34, 72, 103, 104
Communist Party (of South Africa); 32, 33, 34, 35, 39, 83, 102, 103, 104, 148
Congo, The; 21, 67, 94, 123, 124, 195, 196 (see also Zaire)
Congress (see African National Congress of South Africa and Northern Rhodesian African National Congress)
Connell, John; 27

Conservative Party (of Britain); 62
Conservative government (see Britain)
Constitution Amendment Act, 1957; 112
Co-operative Party; 62
Cope, Jack; 34, 35
Copperbelt; 8, 9, 11, 20, 37, 41, 42, 43, 46, 48, 50, 65, 66, 67, 71, 73, 74, 78, 79, 80, 84, 85, 87, 88, 91, 92, 103, 109, 110, 111, 122, 136, 154, 162, 179, 195
coup; attempt in Tanganyika, 123; and Zambia, 149-54, 176, 177, 198
Creech Jones, Arthur; 25, 43, 57
Cyprus; 100, 198

Daily Mail; 150, 178
Dalgleish Commission; 105
Dar es Salaam; 27, 101, 121, 122, 124, 147, 164, 168, 174
Davidson, Basil; 56, 94, 134, 140, 142
de Beer, Zach; 32
Defiance Campaign; 107
Demo Estates; 8
Denton, Eileen; 93
Denton, Percy; 33
Desai, TL; 13
Development and Planning Commission; 131, 132
Development in Zambia; 167
Directorate of Manpower; 20
Dobkins, Moss; 11
Doe, Sargeant; 150
Dominion Status; 109, 112, 114
Dover; 8
Downfall of President Kaunda; 143, 147
Driberg, Tom; 50
Dumont, René; 171
Duplessis, Dannie; 39
Durban; 46

East Africa; 21, 26, 67, 168
East African Engineers; 21, 22
Eastern Province; 56, 57, 69, 111, 114, 180, 184
Economist, The; 123, 124
Edmunds, Douglas; 103
Education, Department of; 15

211

Egypt; 25, 27, 170
Electrical Trade Union (UK); 55
Elizabethville; 21
Elliot, Julian; 158, 159, 160
Elwell Affair; 40, 42, 56
Elwell, Archibald; 42, 43, 44, 45, 46, 83
Ethiopia; 28, 29, 30, 73
Europe; 6, 7, 14, 96, 103, 104, 146
Europeans; alleged incitement of Africans against, 83; and Federation of the Rhodesias and Nyasaland, 39, 44, 47, 52-6, 72, 80, 88, 94, 109, 116; and political power, 48; and segregation, 68; and support for African politics, 43, 45, 46, 62, 66; and Rhodesia, 100, 137; attitude to Africans, 67; attitude to Zukas, 73; in South Africa, 63; in the East African forces, 22
Evans, Stanley; 62
Exeter; 57
Export Board of Zambia (EBZ); 157, 172

Fabian Society; 68, 70
Fabianism; 29
fascism; 19, 24, 31
Federal Parliament; 52, 112
Federal Party; 115
Federation of the Rhodesias and Nyasaland; and African opposition to it, 38, 44-6, 48, 49-55, 59-72, 74-9, 81-2, 84, 85, 92, 94, 97, 100, 109-16, 126; and British opinion, 34, 95, 99, 123, 124; and European opposition, 55, 56-7, 73, 88, 95, 204; and European support for it, 39, 44, 47, 72, 73, 80, 88; and Rhodesia Study Club, 37-8; and the Conservative government, 83; and Mwanawina III, 135, *Closer Association of the Rhodesias and Nyasaland,* 48; costs of to Northern Rhodesia, 116, 117; dissolution of, 116; establishment of, 109; economic advantages of, 203; government of; 152
Federation of Welfare Societies; 41
Federation Working Committee; 64, 68

Fighting Talk; 102
Finance, Ministry of; 131, 185, 188, 190, 191
First Republic; 173
First, Ruth; 39, 102, 153
First World War (1914-1918); 2, 5, 56, 88, 94, 149
Fischer, Bram; 83, 90, 96
Fischer, Molly; 90
Fischer, Stanley; 18
Food Reserve Agency (FRA); 193, 196
Ford, President Gerald; 144
Forman, Lionel; 33, 39, 96, 98
Fort Jamieson; 64, 67, 70 (see also Chipata)
Fortes, Dr Meyer; 36
Forum for Democracy and Development (FDD); 201
Fox-Pitt, Commander Thomas; 42, 43, 56, 57, 58, 62, 68, 70, 71, 72, 73, 75, 77, 78, 79, 83, 87, 88, 95, 100, 101, 113, 120, 134, 135
Fraenkel, Peter; 17, 18, 135
Fram, Minnie; 9
Freedom Newsletter; 45, 74, 76, 79
Friends of the Soviet Union; 14, 15
Frog, Adam; 71
Front-line State; 153
Furmanovski, Joe; 10

Gad, Dr; 170
Garden House Hotel Conference; 23, 177
Garvey, Marcus; 65
general strike; 75, 77, 79, 81, 87, 96
George VI, King; 41
Germans; 2
Germany; 8, 119, 165, 189; government of, 199
Gersh, Maurice; 61, 62
Ginwala, Frennie; 99, 122
Golson, Harvey; 169
Goma, Professor Lameck; 162
Gore-Browne, Angela; 23
Gore-Brown, Lady Lorna; 23
Gore-Browne, Miss Lorna; 23, 39, 73
Gore-Browne, Sir Stewart; 23, 38, 45, 47, 73, 122

Grahamstown University; 27
Grayling, John; 60, 84, 85, 90
Groundnut Scheme; 94, 96
Guardian, The; 34, 35, 36, 60, 72
Gwelo; 17
Gwembe Valley; 111

Haile Selassie; 28
Hall, Richard; 116
Hammond, Brigadier General FD, CBE; 89
Hanchalutz-Hazoir-Dror (Zionist-Socialist Youth Movement); 6, 15, 34
Harar; 29
Hargeisa; 28, 29, 30
Harvey, Major John; 73, 122
Hess, Ian; 55, 56, 58, 73, 83
Hicks, Superintendant; 82
Hitler, Adolf; 19
Hodgson, Jack; 71
Hopkinson, Henry (Lord Colyton); 116
Horner, John; 100
Horvitch, Ike; 35, 160, 161, 162, 174
Hudson, Roland; 72
Huggins, Sir Godfrey (Lord Malvern); 27, 38, 44, 47, 60, 61, 76, 100
humanism; 173

Ilute Yeta; 182, 188
INDECO; 157, 164, 165, 166, 167, 168
Independence (of Zambia); 13, 40, 61, 63, 65, 70, 77, 79, 82, 95, 98, 101, 103, 108, 112, 113, 117, 123, 125, 126, 127, 129, 131, 135, 141, 149, 151, 152, 154, 157, 163, 168, 177, 198, 200, 203
India; 8, 26, 41, 50, 62, 103
Indian community (on the Copperbelt); 34, 50
Institute of Race Relations (SA); 84
International Conference on Structural Failure; 106
International Monetary Fund (IMF); 18, 153, 167, 176, 190, 192, 193, 196, 205
Israel; 2, 33, 146
Italy; 28, 29, 36

Japanese; 23, 24
Jewish Workers' Club (Johannesburg); 9
Jews; 2, 4, 6, 7, 8, 9, 20, 73, 99
Jigjiga; 28, 29, 30
Jinja; 25, 27
Johannesburg; 7, 9, 10, 20, 33, 36, 39, 50, 83, 84, 90, 96, 99
Jolly, Richard; 157, 161

Kabompo; 113
Kabulonga; 163, 174
Kabwe; 20, 39, 94, 97, 129, 131, 164 (see also Broken Hill)
Kafue River; 195
Kafunda, Alick; 44, 45, 54, 59, 60, 61, 71
Kahn, Sam; 35, 83
Kalabo; 132, 181, 182, 184, 200
Kalichini, Paul; 113
Kalima, John; 63, 82
Kalonga, Induna; 79
Kaluwa, George; 77, 94, 100
Kaluwa, Simon; 59, 60, 70, 87
Kamalondo, Chico; 113, 120
Kamanga, Reuben; 44, 54, 59, 82, 86, 91, 121, 126, 130, 131
Kambona, Oscar; 123
Kampala; 27
Kamwala; 156
Kaoma; 135, 179, 180, 205
Kapiri Mposhi; 122, 164
Kapwepwe, Simon; 41, 108, 112, 113, 121, 125, 130, 131, 136, 139, 140, 141, 142, 149, 154, 155, 169
Kariba; 111, 172
Kariba North Bank Company; 157, 172
Kashita, Andrew; 151, 198
Kasomo, Israel; 49
Kasonde, Emanuel; 151
Katanga; 15, 67, 123, 124, 152, 153
Katenga, Bridger; 44, 49, 54, 127
Katilungu, Lawrence; 41, 59, 70, 77, 78, 79, 81, 83, 87, 92, 109, 110, 116, 117
Katima Mulilo; 132, 134, 135
Kaunas; 2, 3, 5, 7, 8
Kaunda, Francis; 187
Kaunda, Kenneth Dr; 23, 61, 98, 101,

103, 121, 135-6, 177, 185-6, 187, 188, 198; opposition to Federation, 77-8; and ZANC, 112-3; UNIP and self government, 113-5; Tanganyika independence, 121-3; and the *Economist,* 124; and UNIP government of 1964, 125, 129, 130-1; and one party state, 139-47; and attempted coups, 149-55, 177; and UNZA, 162-3; and INDECO, 164-5; and ZNBS, 169; and Chunga Irrigation Scheme, 170; and UNIP HQ, 173; and economic decline, 176, 181; and formation of MMD, 178; and 1991 elections, 183; and 1996 presidential elections, 199-201
Kaunda, Waza; 172
Kawawa, Rashid; 123
Kazunga, Abrier; 49, 54
Kazungula; 132, 134
Keller, Jackie; 89
Kenya; 21, 23, 24, 25, 26, 28, 95, 100, 122, 123
Kenyatta, Jomo; 94, 95
Kings African Rifles (KAR); 23, 24-6, 28-30, 67, 73, 78
Kissinger, Henry; 143, 144
Kitwe; 12, 40, 42, 43, 45, 56, 59, 60, 61, 66, 73, 75, 79, 81, 82, 83, 84
Kitwe African Society (KAS); 42, 43, 44, 46
Kivukoni; 122
Kodesh, Wulfie; 36
Kofie, Best; 40, 42, 44, 45, 48, 54, 77, 92
Koinange, Mbiyu; 95
Konkola, Dixon; 66, 78, 96, 97, 105, 113
Kotane, Moses; 103
Krikler, Bernard; 18, 33
Kuwani, Bitwell; 120
Kynoch, Mrs; 13, 14, 15

Labour government (UK) (see Britain)
Labour Party; 20, 62, 95, 99, 105
Lake Bangweulu; 111
Langa; 35, 91, 98
Lealui; 41, 135, 188
Lechwe Trust; 156

Lee-Tattersall, Major; 43, 45, 46
Legco (see Northern Rhodesia Legislative Council)
Legum, Colin; 78
Lessing, Doris; 101
Lewanika, Akashambwata Mbikusita; 178, 187, 188
Lewanika, Godwin Mbikusita; 40, 41, 42, 43, 44, 45, 59, 60, 77, 78, 84, 86
Lewanika, King; 41
Lewey, Justice; 85, 86
Lewin, Professor Julius; 50, 84, 91
Leys, Dr Colin; 122
liberals; 13, 43, 56, 62, 72, 73, 76, 97
liberalism; 47
Liberia; 150
Limulunga; 188
Lipalile, LM; 75
Liso, Edward Mungoni; 75, 81, 87, 110
Lithuania; 1-8, 9, 10, 13, 15, 20, 34
Litunga; 78, 79, 135, 187, 188
Livingstone Mail; 61, 85
Livingstone; 8, 9, 10, 20, 30, 38, 42, 60, 61, 63, 83, 84, 85, 86, 88, 91, 92, 109, 132, 148, 149, 156, 189
London; 2, 9, 18, 26, 28, 43, 44, 46, 47, 48, 51, 56, 69, 72, 88, 90, 92, 93-108, 110, 113, 115, 116, 119-121, 123, 124, 126, 127, 128, 130, 136, 138, 149, 154, 160, 174, 175, 177, 206
Lorenz, Erhard; 146, 148, 160
Luanda; 143, 144, 145, 146
Luanshya Co-operative Store; 15
Luanshya; 11-16, 17, 20, 30, 36, 37, 38, 39, 40, 41, 66, 73, 74, 83
Luapula; 111, 122, 124, 195, 196
Luapula River; 195
Lubumbashi; 21, 152
Luchembe, Mumba; 177
Lukulu; 179, 180
Lumina, Joshua; 172
Lungwebungu River; 179
Lusaka Flying Club; 150
Lusaka; 10, 20, 21, 23, 28, 30, 37, 38, 49, 50, 52, 55, 59, 60, 61, 62, 66, 69, 72, 76, 77, 98, 103, 109, 110, 115, 124, 125, 126, 127, 128, 129, 130, 134, 135, 136, 137, 138, 140, 143, 144,

146, 147, 149, 150, 152, 154, 156, 163, 164, 165, 170, 174, 175, 178, 181, 182, 184, 186, 188, 198, 203, 206
Luvale people; 180, 181
Luyt, RE; 40
Lyttelton, Oliver (Lord Chardos); 76

MPLA; 140, 143, 144, 145, 146
Maamba Colliery; 131
Macmillan, Harold; 105, 114
Magasiner, Sacha; 119, 127, 131, 174
maize; 184, 189, 190, 191, 192, 193, 195, 196
Makasa, Robert; 108, 113, 121, 124
Makerere College, Kampala; 27
Makulu, Henry; 157
Malan, Dr Daniel; 33
Malawi Congress Party; 100, 112, 138
Malaya; 78, 79
Malenga, Henry; 40
Manchester Guardian; 93
Manda, Foch; 81, 82
Mandela, Nelson; 36, 83, 105
Mangango; 179
Maputo; 102, 122, 153
Marianhill College; 36, 39
Marxism; 6, 15, 34, 123
Marxists; 15, 72, 143, 144
Mkushi; 111, 205
Mafekeng, Elizabeth; 102
Masheke, General Malimba; 182, 183, 188
Matero; 126
Mau Mau; 95
Maudling, Reginald; 115, 123, 124
Maybank, Frank; 15, 70, 71
Mazabuka; 18, 109, 195
Mbala; 49, 135
Mbeya; 121, 122
Mbundu; 180
Mcleod, Ian; 72
Middle-East; 19
Miller, Alice; 9
Miller, Peter; 173
Milton School; 16, 17, 18
Mines African Staff Association (MASA); 110

Mineworkers Union (see African Mineworkers Union)
mineworkers; 16, 20, 40, 41, 43, 63, 70, 71, 79, 80, 88, 110, 117, 135
Mitchell, Dr Clyde; 44, 45
Mbikusita Lewanika, Godwin; 40, 41, 42, 45, 77, 84
Mobutu; 152, 195
Modern World Society; 32, 98
Modern Youth Society; 98, 107
Moffat, John; 45, 62, 75, 76, 113
Moffat, Robert; 43
Mogadishu; 28, 30
Molotov; 29
Molteno, Robert; 143
Mombasa; 27
Monckton, Lord; 114
Mongu; 42, 113, 131, 134, 135, 180, 181, 184, 187, 205
Morgan, 'Foxy'; 18
Movement for Colonial Freedom (MCF); 100, 101, 110
Movement for Multi-Party Democracy (MMD); 23, 147, 172, 178, 179, 180, 181, 182, 183, 184, 185, 186, 187, 188, 189, 190, 193, 194, 196, 199, 200, 201
Moshi; 23
Mow, Leon; 73
Mozambique; 122, 153
Mpapa Gallery; 156
Mpezeni, Chief; 94, 100
Mtete; 179, 180
Mtine, Tom; 69
Mudenda, Elijah; 145
Mufulira; 38, 66, 75, 139
Mugala, Amonson; 44, 54
Mukwaya, Moses; 105
Mulemba, Humphrey; 177
Mulford, David; 98
Mulobezi; 132, 134, 135, 165
Multi-party democracy; 178
Mulungushi Rock; 129, 130, 172
Mumbuna, Mufaya; 179
Munali School; 75, 114, 115
Mungule Tribal Reserve; 170
Murray, Professor; 34
Murray-Hughes, R; 8

Murumbi, Joe; 100
Musakanya, Flavia; 152, 169
Musakanya, Valentine; 124, 130, 151, 152, 154, 167, 176
Museums Board; 149, 156
Mushota, Remy; 199
Musokotwane, Kebby; 152, 163, 169
Musumburwa, Gabriel; 74, 114
Mutti, Jethro; 145
Muuka, Lishoma; 168
Mwanakatwe Commission; 199, 200
Mwanakatwe, John; 151, 157
Mwanamwambwa, Amusa; 184
Mwanawasa, Levy; 189
Mwanawina III King; 135
Mwanga, Vernon; 145
Mwanza, Dr Jacob; 162, 163
Mwanza, Mr; 45, 53
Mwanza; 22
Mwata Kazembe; 124
Mwendapole, Mathew; 75, 87
Mzingeli, Charles; 105

Naidoo, HA; 35, 103
Naidoo, Pauline; 103
Nairobi; 22, 28, 30, 41, 81
Nakatindi, Wina, Princess; 188
Nakuru; 22
Namboard; 192
Namibia; 134, 147, 153, 199
Namitengo; 60, 70
Namwala; 63, 84, 113, 198
Nanyuki; 22, 23, 24, 28, 31
National Arts Council of Zambia; 156
National Council for Scientific Research (NCSR); 157, 169, 170
National Economic Reform Programme (NERP); 177
National Executive Council (NEC); 179
National Roads Board; 198
National Union of South African Students (NUSAS); 33
nationalism, African; 28, 34, 139
Nationalist Government (of South Africa); 32, 33, 35, 39
Nawakwi, Edith; 185
Nazis; 2, 4, 8
Nazism; 31

Ndola; 9-12, 15, 17, 21, 30, 37, 40, 44, 45, 47-8, 60, 61, 63, 67, 73, 77, 82, 83, 84, 86, 87, 91, 92, 98, 110, 114, 125, 126, 127, 147, 155, 164, 165, 168, 183, 184
Ndola Anti-Federation Action Committee (see Anti-Federation Action Committee)
Ndola Federal Proposals Examination Group; 48-55, 71
Ndola Urban African Advisory Council; 44
Nega-Nega Brickworks; 167
Nehru Pandit; 50
Neto, Dr Augustino; 140, 144, 145
New Statesman and Nation; 56, 74
Ngwewela, Rev. Johnson; 35
Ngonye Falls; 132
Nicholson, Marjory; 68, 70
Nkana; 12, 41, 81, 87
Nkausu, Gibson; 192
Nkhoma, Francis; 151
Nkoloma, Matthew; 110
Nkomo, Joshua; 100, 122
Nkumbula, Harry; 62, 63, 66, 76, 77, 78, 79, 81, 84, 85, 91, 94, 96, 101, 103, 110, 112, 113, 115, 124
Nkrumah, Kwame; 50
Nokwe, Duma; 96
North Mutundu River; 195
North Western Province; 145
Northern News; 38, 55, 96, 97
Northern Province; 111, 154, 205
Northern Rhodesia Legislative Council; 20, 37, 38, 46, 47, 52, 57, 64, 66, 78
Northern Rhodesia News Survey; 120
Northern Rhodesia Regiment; 23
Northern Rhodesian African National Congress; 33, 40, 41, 43, 44, 45, 48, 50, 59-60, 62-3, 65, 66, 69, 75, 76, 77, 78, 81, 84, 85, 87, 93-4, 96, 101, 112, 113, 115
Northern Rhodesian government; 33, 37, 41, 61, 72, 110
Northern Rhodesian Journal; 8
Northern Rhodesian Labour Party; 20
Northern Star; 36, 38
Ntambaningwe, Simpson; 137

Nyandoro; 137
Nyasaland; 38, 44, 48, 52, 55, 97, 109, 112, 114, 123
Nyaywa, Joseph; 142, 143, 172
Nyeleti, Peter; 66

Oasis Forum; 201
Observer, The; 78, 110
Ogaden; 28, 29
one party participatory democracy; 23, 140, 150, 173, 178
Organisation of African Unity (OAU); 145
Oxford; 40

Palestine; 6
Pant, Aba; 41
Papworth, John; 139, 171
parastatals; 166, 167, 169, 186
Parker, Kenny; 91
Parliament; 13, 33, 35, 39, 52, 55, 61, 63, 78, 91, 97, 99, 112, 131, 139, 162, 177, 178, 184, 187, 189, 190, 191, 193, 196, 199, 201, 205
Patel, Dipak; 200, 203
Pathfinders; 11
Pillay, Vella; 99, 102
Pivonia; 2, 4
Plummer, Sir Leslie; 91, 94, 96
Poland; 3, 7
Poliso, Zwai; 123
Pope Square; 178
Portugal; 143
Portuguese; 140, 141, 143
Pritt, DN QC; 84, 90, 91, 94, 123
Privy Council; 91, 93, 94, 95
promissory notes; 190, 191
Punabantu, Milimo; 187
Purvis, Jack; 16
Puta, Robinson; 70, 75, 105, 136

Rabb, Maurice; 88
Raganathan, Mr; 187
railway workers; 20, 40, 66, 78, 88, 89
Rennie, Gilbert; 57, 64, 70, 78
Rhodes Livingstone Institute; 30
Rhodesia Railways; 10, 20, 22, 88, 89
Rhodesia Study Club; 36-8, 67

Rhodesia Territorial Parliament; 61
Rhodesian African Rifles; 19
Rhodesian Air Force; 19
Roan Mine; 17
Robertson, Bob; 14, 15, 41, 43, 56, 58, 70, 83, 84
Robertson, Peter; 15
Robinson, Cynthia; 98
Robinson, Julius; 99
Ross, Alick; 93
Routh, Dr Guy; 91
Rowland, Tiny; 143, 145
Royal Air Force; 19
Russell, Lord Bertrand; 94, 136
Russia; 5, 7, 14, 104

Sachs, Albie; 153
Sakala, Richard; 198
Salisbury; 160
Sambona, Noah; 63, 86
Sardanis, Andrew; 164, 167
Savimbi, Jonas; 143, 144, 146, 180
Scott, Dr Alexander; 73, 85, 113
Scott, Dr Guy; 189
Second Republic; 75, 140, 149, 173, 177, 186, 194
Second World War (1939-45); 2, 15, 16, 19, 20-4, 26, 27, 28, 31, 36, 40, 48, 54, 55, 56, 71, 84, 90, 122
Segal, Joshua; 5, 9
self-government; 25, 26, 27, 28, 39, 46, 65, 69, 70, 112, 114, 115, 118
Senanga; 131, 132, 134
Sesheke; 131, 132, 198
Seychelles; 79, 91
Shamwana, Edward; 149, 151, 169, 176
Shamwana, Stella; 151
Shangombo; 179
Sharpeville; 105
Shoniwa, Cyril; 36, 38
Siann, Julian; 131
Siavonga; 111
Sihole; 181
Sikalumbi, Witlington; 50, 63, 113
Sikasula, Rankin; 122, 147, 153
Sikatana, Mundia; 153
Sikongo; 181, 182, 184, 200, 205
Sikongo, Joe; 182

Silitoe, Sir Percy; 33
Silundika; 137
Silungwe, Annel; 187
Simon Zukas and Partners; 127, 174
Simons, Professor Jack; 32, 34, 36, 38, 50, 91, 101, 136, 142, 143
Simons, Ray; 91, 98, 101, 102, 136
Sinclair, Mrs; 15, 16, 74
Singapore; 106
Sinjambela; 179
Sioma; 132
Sipalu, Munu; 41, 103, 112, 120, 135
Sisulu, Walter; 96
Skinner, James; 130, 131, 140, 141, 142
Smith, Ian; 18, 137, 143, 145, 149, 172, 176
Smuts, Jan; 33
socialism; 14, 33, 72, 153
Sokota, Pascale; 64, 66, 75, 100
Solo, Captain; 198
Solwezi; 113, 162, 165
Somaliland; 23, 28, 29
Songolo, Josaiah; 166
South Africa; 4-5, 6, 7, 9, 13, 15, 17, 27, 32-8, 40, 55, 68, 72, 74, 90, 91, 95, 96, 98, 99, 100, 101, 102-5, 108, 119, 128, 129, 132, 136, 137, 138, 144, 148, 149, 152, 153, 165, 176, 186, 203
South African Congress of Democrats; 102
South African Freedom Association; 105
South African Student Association; 99
Southampton; 9
Southern Province; 48, 112
Southern Rhodesia; 15, 16, 17, 18, 19, 20, 27, 36, 38, 39, 46, 47, 49, 53, 58, 62, 69, 81, 84, 89, 99, 100, 109, 110, 114, 115, 116, 127, 160, 171, 176, 204
Soviet Union; 14, 15, 29, 34, 153
Spanish Civil War; 6
Spearhead, The; 122
Stalin, Joseph; 6, 34, 104, 153
Stalinists; 6, 32
Standard Bank of Zambia; 150
Standard Chartered Bank; 192

State House; 131, 139, 140, 142, 149, 154, 162, 164, 166, 185, 187, 188, 198
state of emergency; 109, 110, 112
Structural Adjustment Programme (SAP); 194
Student Socialist Party (SSP); 32, 33
Students Liberal Association; 32
Subulwa, Leonard; 187
Sudan; 29, 64
Sudden Assignment, The; 116
Supreme Action Council; 77, 78, 79, 81, 87
Susman Brothers and Wulfsohn Ltd; 166
Swift, Cecil; 136, 137
Symba, Deogratias; 152
Szur, Dr Leon; 100

Tafuna, Chief; 49
Tambo, Oliver; 137, 147
Tanganyika; 21, 23, 25, 94, 96, 101, 121, 123
Tembo, General Christon; 177
Tembo, Nephas; 55, 68, 70, 74, 86, 98, 107, 113
Temple, Rev. Mervyn; 114
third term (for President Chiluba); 23, 201, 205
Times of Zambia; 150, 171, 199
Times, The; 69, 97, 101
Tireman, Mr; 124
Tory government (see Conservative government)
Tory Party (see Conservative Party)
Trade Union Congress (TUC) of the United Kingdom; 40, 109, 179
Trade Union Congress of Zambia; 77, 109, 179
trade unions; 40, 42, 43, 46, 48, 72, 79, 123
trade unionism; 43
Train Apartheid Resistance Committee (TARC); 35
Tredgold, Justice Robert; 91
Trevaskis, Kennedy; 64, 69
Trotskyists; 32, 34
Tshombe, Moise; 67, 123, 124

Turok, Ben; 167
Uganda; 24, 25, 26, 27, 28, 123
Ukmerge; 1, 2, 3, 5
Ukraine; 5
Unilateral Declaration of Independence (UDI); 18, 143, 149, 165, 172, 173, 203
Union of Democratic Control (UDC); 94, 95
UNITA; 143, 145
United Kingdom (UK) (see Britain)
United National Congress Party; 113
United National Independence Party (UNIP); 13, 50, 63, 79, 101, 103, 108, 113, 114, 115, 116, 117, 120, 121, 122, 124, 125, 126, 128, 129, 130, 139, 143, 144, 147, 150, 151, 154, 155, 156, 157, 164, 168, 169, 172, 173, 176, 177, 178, 179, 180, 182, 184, 186, 187, 188, 191
United Nations (UN); 67, 97, 180
United Party; 33
United Progressive Party (UPP); 139
United States of America (USA); 4, 5, 105, 120, 184, 190, 204
Unity Movement; 34, 35
University of Cape Town; 21, 28, 34, 36, 40, 98, 107
University of Grahamstown; 27, 55
University of Zambia (UNZA); 157, 162, 167, 169, 196
Unsworth, Edgar; 78
Urban Advisory Council; 41, 49, 64, 68, 71

Veritas Trust; 169
Versfeld, Dr Martin; 34
Verwoerd, Hendrik; 104
Victoria Falls; 10, 116, 189
Victoria Falls Conference; 37, 38, 75, 76
Vilnius; 2, 7, 20
Voice of UNIP; 120

Wajir; 28
Walubita, Kelly; 179
Washington; 144
Waterfield, Hugh; 36
Webber, Dr Harry; 136

Webber, Noreen; 98
Weeks, Sir Hugh; 96
Welensky, Roy; 20, 37, 38, 44, 47, 48, 51, 55, 56, 60, 67, 71, 72, 74, 76, 80, 88, 99, 112, 114, 115, 117, 123, 124
Welensky's 4000 Days; 116, 117
welfare societies; 41, 43
Western Province; 135, 179, 180, 181
What will Federation mean; 37
wheat; 194, 195
white settlers; 6, 8, 14, 24, 30, 47, 65, 70, 76, 79, 83, 95, 100, 116, 126 (see also Europeans)
Whitehead, Edgar; 101, 122
Williams, AT; 97
Wilson, Harold; 149
Wina, Arthur; 120, 151, 172, 178, 179, 182, 184, 187
Wolpe, Harold; 39, 96
Wood, David; 69, 93
Works and Supply, Ministry of; 196
World Bank; 154, 172, 191, 196, 205
World Peace Council; 96
World Trade Organisation (WTO); 194
Wulfsohn, Edwin; 166, 175
Wusakile; 87

Yamba, Dauti; 64, 66, 69, 75, 94, 100
Years of Renewal; 143, 144
Yeta III, King; 41
Yorkshire Post, The; 55
Young, Commander Edgar; 94
Young, Jimmy; 105
Young, Lindsay; 159

Zaire; 192; 195
Zaire-Zambia Joint Co-operative Council; 195
Zambezi Sawmills; 165
Zambezi Ranching and Cropping; 175
Zambezi, River; 111, 131, 132, 134, 179, 180, 184, 198
Zambezi River Transport; 134
Zambia National Building Society (ZNBS); 157, 167, 168, 169
Zambia National Farmers Union (ZNFU); 191
Zambia Privatisation Agency (ZPA); 187

Zambia Steel and Building Supplies; 166, 167
Zambian African National Congress (ZANC); 103, 112, 113, 114
ZANU; 137
ZAPU; 101, 137
Zaza, Victor; 121
ZCCM; 187
Zimba, Richard; 113, 120
Zimbabwe; 18, 36, 153, 172, 173, 203, 204
Zimbabweans; 150
ZIMCO; 168
Zionism; 33
Zionist-socialist youth movement; 6, 15, 34
Zionist-socialists; 32, 33
Zukas, Abraham; 8
Zukas, Chaim Wulf; 1, 4, 5, 6, 7, 8, 9, 10, 11, 12, 20, 92, 146
Zukas, David; 2, 3, 4, 104, 128, 139, 155, 206
Zukas, Jake; 12, 17, 37, 58, 59, 73, 82, 84, 91, 98, 122, 125, 146, 147, 155
Zukas, Libe; 4, 5, 6, 7, 8, 9, 17, 83, 91, 146
Zukas, Samuel; 3, 7
Zukas Papers; 38, 50, 52, 56, 135, 147
Zukas and Magasiner Consulting Engineers; 119, 127, 174
Zulu, Dr Justin; 152, 167
Zulu, Grey; 141, 169, 187